REGULATING SOCIAL EUROPE

Regulating Social Europe

*Reality and Myth of Collective Bargaining
In the EC Legal Order*

ANTONIO LO FARO

with translation by
RITA INSTON

·H A R T·
PUBLISHING

OXFORD – PORTLAND OREGON
2000

Hart Publishing
Oxford and Portland, Oregon

Published in North America (US and Canada) by
Hart Publishing c/o
International Specialized Book Services
5804 NE Hassalo Street
Portland, Oregon
97213-3644
USA

Distributed in the Netherlands, Belgium and Luxembourg by
Intersentia, Churchillaan 108
B2900 Schoten
Antwerpen
Belgium

Hart Publishing Ltd is a specialist legal publisher based in Oxford, England.
To order further copies of this book or to request a list of other
publications please write to:

Hart Publishing Ltd, Salter's Boatyard,
Folly Bridge, Abingdon Road, Oxford OX1 4LB
Telephone: +44 (0)1865 245533 or Fax: +44 (0)1865 794882
e-mail: mail@hartpub.co.uk
www.hartpub.co.uk

British Library Cataloguing in Publication Data
Data Available
ISBN 1 901362–90–6 (cloth)

Typeset in 10pt Sabon
by Hope Services (Abingdon) Ltd.
Printed in Great Britain
by Biddles Ltd.,
Guildford and King's Lynn

Contents

Acknowledgements

On reaching the completion of a research study that was begun some time ago,* I feel bound to express my thanks to all those who during the years concerned have accompanied me along paths rich in opportunities for academic and personal development.

Special mention is due to Brian Bercusson and Gunther Teubner, under whose guidance I commenced my researches in the Department of Law of the European University Institute, Florence, and also to Antoine Lyon-Caen and Spiros Simitis, with whom I had the great pleasure and privilege of discussing the initial results of the study.

With Silvana Sciarra, whom I had the good fortune to meet at the Pontignano Seminar, I have shared a specialised interest in many of the topics examined in the course of this work. Our numerous conversations at Fiesole have always provided me with highly prized debate and support.

My debt of gratitude to Bruno Caruso extends beyond the bounds of the present book. The direction of my studies and the thrust of research itself within the University would not be the same without the influence of his intellectual stimulation and the example of his own cultural curiosity.

I am infinitely grateful to Rita Inston, whose meticulous and competent translation has contributed enormously to making this book accessible to a readership wider than the Italian-speaking audience.

Finally, no words could be adequate to express the thanks I owe to Massimo D'Antona, who was the original source of inspiration for the entire work and also read through the final manuscript. This book is dedicated to his memory.

A.L.F.
Catania, October 1999

* The drafting of this volume was completed during a period of research spent at the British Library of Political and Economic Science (London School of Economics) under the auspices of the *European Union Programme on the Training and Mobility of Researchers* (EUSSIRF).

Introduction: Subject and Scenario—Defining the Framework of the Study

It is often no easy matter to define the precise boundaries of a research study, and this is particularly true of a study relating to law and, above all, labour law. Since the various topics which go to make up its subject can never be entirely isolated from their surrounding scenario, there is a danger, unless they are properly contextualised, of their being wrongly perceived as suspended in the vacuum of a spurious completeness.

The subject of the present study (a legal analysis of European collective bargaining) is no exception, dealing as it does with an area for which any notion of exhaustive treatment based on the few formal provisions that constitute its positive legal framework would be purely artificial. A survey of European collective bargaining confined to an examination of the specific provisions on the matter would not only be methodologically questionable but, even more importantly, would also ignore elements of information and evaluation which, when taken into consideration, overturn what might initially seem predictable conclusions.

The study described here represents an endeavour to retrieve the "visibility" of the many different factors—legal, institutional, political and industrial-relations oriented—which converge on the conceptual area occupied by European collective bargaining and hence play a part in defining and qualifying its outlines. Consequently, my treatment of it is the result of an attempt at reconstruction marked by a continual tension between the demands of an analytical examination and the requirements of a general evaluation; between a focused approach which risks masking the context and an overall view in which the clear lines are in danger of disappearing, and between the conditioning of a training in labour law geared to the "industrial relations system" dimension and the need to bear in mind the complex institutional fabric which, in a "plural" system like that of the Community, affects any form of legal regulation. In short, a continual tension between the specific subject of the study and the entire scenario within which it is sited.

More than forty years after the Treaty establishing the European Economic Community was signed, a period which has witnessed a lengthy series of political developments, institutional changes, case law innovations and theoretical analyses, the conceptual enigma which since the start has made the Community a political and legal entity *sui generis* remains unresolved. Today, a long way from embodying a federal state model and by now too highly evolved to lend continued credence to determinist incrementalism of the functionalist type, the integration process is caught between numerous doubts and few certainties. Nevertheless, the difficulties of the process of political integration, both economic and structural, cannot blind lawyers to the undeniable reality of the creation of a Community legal order which is distinct from the national legal orders of individual Member States but bound to interact with them.

The research presented here is based on the initial presumption of the existence of a self-contained legal system—the Community legal order—in which from the very outset greater efforts have been devoted to strengthening the *instruments* of effectiveness, as progressively refined by the Court of Justice, than to enhancing the qualitative depth of the *rights* guaranteed: an overemphasis on instruments relative to paucity of content which can plausibly be said to apply in the case of what is now conventionally called "European social law".

This terminology is not without ambiguity.

Although it is now generally accepted that when we talk of "European social law" we are referring to a kind of surrogate of "European Community labour law", the same conceptual clarity does not apply to the expression "European social rights", which can assume meanings potentially involving more general issues within whose scope labour law and social security law were formerly conceived as founding elements of the economic constitutions adopted by socially evolved models of State and democracy. In this sense, the concept of social rights has also frequently been called into play by the labour law literature in dealing with the institutional and systematic implications associated with the "European social dimension". This has never, however, been accompanied by consideration of the corresponding debate which, in relation to the same issues, has unfolded more vigorously in other scholarly communities (sociologists, legal philosophers and political philosophers) than among positivist lawyers (Giddens, 1982; Walzer, 1983; Barbalet, 1988; Habermas, 1992; Bobbio, 1990).

It will not be possible to do justice in what follows to the theoretical richness of these analyses, all of which are to some extent related to the mainstream of studies on citizenship inaugurated by the celebrated scholar Thomas Humphrey Marshall (Marshall, 1950). It must suffice to emphasise, as concerns our present purpose, their heuristic usefulness to the attempt made here to ascertain the degree of relevance of the social rights forming the subject of the theoretical studies mentioned above to the much proclaimed "European social dimension", and whether collective bargaining processes have any significance within that dimension.

Up till now, attempts to classify the concept of social rights have failed to provide either unambiguous or sufficiently well-defined points of reference. Although numerous general definitions of social rights exist, their abundance is due to the very fact of their generality. Many of the rights (education, health, housing, sex equality, environment, employment, social security) featuring in instruments of international law (Eide, Krause and Rosas (eds), 1995) and in the "lengthy constitutions" of the years following the Second World War (Rodotà, 1994) derived from the concepts of social law and/or social citizenship. It should, however, be noted that, since the very inception of this notion of social rights, collective bargaining has been conceived as an integral part of an industrial, and therefore social, citizenship system (Marshall, 1964), an approach reformulated more recently in the context of a taxonomy of social citizenship rights in which "trade union and industrial rights" are also included (Zolo, 1994). This has to be borne in mind at a time when a clearer definition is emerging of relations between the economic constitution and processes of European integration (Joerges, 1994, 1997; Poiares Maduro, 1998) and, more directly relevant here, between social rights and supranationalism; that is, at a time when the concern is to define the *an* of a "social dimension" of the European integration process which evidences its significance and function in the light of a heritage firmly rooted in the historical, political, legal and constitutional traditions of the Member States.

It must always be remembered, however, that the Community is not a politically and legally homogeneous entity. It is therefore not enough to identify the *nature* of the function assigned to the social dimension in the integration process. Given the complexity of the system, we must pause to consider another aspect, namely the *extent* to which the Community authorities are called upon to take direct action in developing and implementing a European model of social and, more immediately relevant here, labour law regulation.

The question is in itself neither a new nor an unusual one. It involves issues which have traditionally formed part of developments over the years regarding the definition and/or extension of Community competences. The terms in which it is couched are somewhat different, however, in referring specifically to as strongly "constitutionalised" an area as that of labour law and trade union law.

In these circumstances (and given the increasingly unitary nature of the European economic and financial context), the question of the *quantum* of Community intervention assumes a relevance impinging directly on the fundamental rights and principles prevailing in the systems of individual Member States. Consequently, it would seem more appropriate to approach it from a special perspective in which the criterion for defining the extent of Community social action must be neither an unfettered inclination to enlarge its scope nor an excessively "efficiency-driven" search for cases where "the objectives of the proposed action cannot be sufficiently achieved by the Member States and can therefore . . . be better achieved by the Community" (Article 5 TEC).

In the particular case of labour law we have to remember that the gulf between the differing origins of national labour law systems and Community social law, and between the differing functions respectively allocated to them, constitutes one of the more striking examples of divergence between domestic legal orders and the supranational legal order. There is therefore a very real danger of labour law and trade union law losing, in the process of transition from national models of social regulation to a European model, their principal "dowry" of constitutionalised principles of protection (Jeammaud, 1991). The question is obviously one that needs to be examined in the wide-ranging terms posed by the complex relationship between European integration and fundamental principles within the Member States (Cartabia, 1995).

Alongside the case law and positive law aspects, therefore, the question of the *quantum* of Community social intervention—as viewed from the perspective of relations between "constitutional" systems—also has resonances at a more narrowly theoretical and institutional level, with regard to the entire configuration of the model that has progressively emerged in the course of the European integration process (Joerges, 1997). It clearly involves arguments which, although this has sometimes been questioned, are also of demonstrably direct relevance to sectoral legal analyses.

THE SUBJECT: THE *QUOMODO* OF COMMUNITY SOCIAL LAW

The conceptual parameters set out above are the ones within which I shall analyse the particular subject of this study, namely European collective bargaining or, more precisely, its function in the context of the Community legal order in which it has to operate.

The general scenario surrounding studies on the role of social and labour legislation in the integration process (*an*) and its extent (*quantum*), aspects which will be dealt with only marginally, therefore also encompasses analysis of the regulatory techniques used by the Community institutions in shaping, in conjunction with other sources (national and supranational, voluntary and normative), all aspects of labour law within the European Union. These considerations may be referred to collectively under the heading of a third conventional formula—the *quomodo* of Community labour law—which neatly completes the logic path in which the aspects described above as the *an* and the *quantum* represent the first two segments.

The question of the *quomodo* of Community labour law clearly falls within the context of the broader doctrinal and institutional debate prompted by recognition of the crisis in the Community regulatory system (Dehousse, Joerges, Majone and Snyder, 1992; Snyder, 1993a and 1993b). The now widely discussed impasse affecting the "harmonisation by directive" model in the face of the problems posed by the complexity of the matters to be regulated and the number of different systems to be subjected to regulation (Dehousse, 1994) also applies, with particular features of its own, in the field of labour law.

These problems are analysed in the first part of the study. Chapter 1 outlines the Community institutional arrangements within which collective bargaining has to operate (sections 1 and 2) and presents some deliberations on the choice of methodological approaches which this situation allows (section 3).

Chapter 2 examines what some legal scholars have dubbed the Community "regulatory deficit". The possible presumptions for such a deficit are identified, first theoretical (sections 1, 1.1 and 1.2) and then legal and institutional (section 2), and this is followed by a review of some recent developments which would appear to confirm the diagnosis (section 2.1).

The outcome of the widespread and ongoing debate among experts in Community law has in some cases pointed to other "resources" which warrant consideration as potential alternatives to the Community harmonisation model. The diversification of regulatory sources proposed from several quarters as a potential antidote to the ineffectiveness of the traditional model of harmonisation by directive (sections 2.2 and 3) echoes the pluralistic structure which has from the outset characterised labour law as an autonomous discipline, and incorporates some interesting elements of comparison (section 2.4). In the Community context, the traditional polycentricity of labour regulation has yet further dimensions which entail a somewhat innovative approach to any study of the multiple-source system of labour law sources (Sciarra, 1995a). However, this new scenario amounts to more than the mere addition of a Community level to the bargaining hitherto carried on by the social partners at national level. In the overall context of a general redefinition of Community regulatory techniques, European collective bargaining is just one of the possible means by which the Community hopes to overcome the regulatory dilemmas with which it is confronted.

It is from this perspective that European bargaining is examined here, avoiding the methodological mistake of applying to its analysis the same conceptual categories as those used with reference to national bargaining systems (Chapter 3, section 1). The legitimation "from above" which Community bargaining enjoys unquestionably represents a break in continuity from the historical genesis of national bargaining systems (section 2) and forces us to question whether information and reasoning based on previous experience of bargaining in national contexts retain any validity as hermeneutic tools in the Community context (section 3).

The method used to demonstrate the functional difference posited here between the two "bargaining phenomena", i.e. national and Community bargaining, is based on a process of reasoning *a contrario* and consists in an attempt to review the latter from the perspective of a number of traditional categories and tools evolved with reference to the former: employee representation through union "agency" (Chapter 4, section 1), collective autonomy (Chapter 4, sections 2, 2.1), pluralism (Chapter 4, sections 3, 3.1) and neo-corporatism (Chapter 6, section 1).

Closer analysis of the provisions contained in the new social chapter of the Amsterdam Treaty shows that a distinction can be made between two separate types of European collective bargaining, both of them difficult, for different reasons, to equate with the notion of collective autonomy. More specifically, an outline is given of the technical features which make one type "inconsequential" (Chapter 5, section 1), principally because of the non-existence in the Community legal order of a constitutional principle of freedom of association (section 1.1), and characterise the second type as "tied" collective bargaining (section 2). This provides the context for an examination of the events surrounding the adoption of Directive 96/34/EC on parental leave, Directive 97/81/EC on part-time work and Directive 99/70/EC on fixed-time work, the first directives to be adopted on the basis of a prior European collective agreement in accordance with the mechanism created by the Maastricht Agreement on Social Policy and now incorporated within the new Treaty (section 3).

The closing sections of the study represent its *pars construens*. Given that European collective agreements cannot, as argued here, be considered true products of collective autonomy, an interpretative hypothesis is formulated regarding the real function that can be attributed to collective bargaining within the Community legal order: as a regulatory resource (Chapter 6, section 2.1) and a legitimacy resource (section 2.2).

In establishing a functional connection between European collective bargaining and regulatory techniques, such a conclusion must necessarily include consideration of the broad lines of a long-standing debate between legal scholars and economists on the identification of normative techniques which are capable of ensuring economically "efficient" regulation. This is a debate in which there is a dangerous tendency for its conclusions to elevate economic efficiency to the status of a normative principle, with obvious repercussions on the constitutional facet of regulatory sources in the field of labour law. In so far as neither current Community provisions nor the present-day practical circumstances of industrial relations allow it to be described otherwise, collective bargaining constitutes, at the moment, a regulatory technique within the Community legal order. As such, it is in danger of becoming a mere adjunct to the latter's objectives and policies, unless it is given the backing of "constitutionalised" recognition that will allow it to become the subject of, and at the same time a vehicle for, an effective Community social dimension (Chapter 6, section 3).

1

A "Community Based on the Rule of Law"

1 FROM THE WHITE PAPER ON COMPLETING THE INTERNAL MARKET TO TODAY:
APOGEE AND DECLINE OF THE COMMUNITY HARMONISATION MODEL

I N THE NOW wearisome conflict of views on social Europe which has for years divided euro-optimists and euro-pessimists, something seems to be missing.

Apart from certain obvious exceptions, the debate has been focused on, so to speak, the *static* dimension of Community law-making in the matter of social policy, thereby confining itself to what is danger of amounting to no more than anticipating and/or keeping a tally of increasingly awaited "new social directives". Equating progress of the social integration process in this way with the adoption of new Community measures of a legislative nature does not, however, seem wholly feasible, or at least not in such linearly automatic terms. It fails to take account of the *dynamic* dimension of Community rule-making, in neglecting to examine a variety of questions which, in social policy as in other areas, can jeopardise the reality and the effectiveness of the Community's regulatory aspirations.

In maintaining the validity of the equation "more harmonizing directives = further development of social Europe", the academic and institutional debate surrounding social law is in danger of swimming against the tide of a number of developments, both institutional and doctrinal, which clearly indicate the existence of a crisis in the "harmonization by directive" model traditionally adopted by the Community with a view to establishing and completing the internal market.

These issues, which are dwelt on at some length below, have general connotations and do not relate solely to Community rule-making in the field of labour law. It is undeniable that the quest for regulatory techniques better suited to fulfilling the Community's needs is already today more important (and will become more so in the future) than the bare substance and content of Community norms: "Less action, but more effective action" the Commission admonishes,[1] thus bearing witness to the very real relevance of problems

---

[1] *Report on Implementation of the Commission's Work Programme in 1995* (COM(95) 513, 13.10.1995).

associated with regulation that were pointed out some time ago by leading experts in Community law (Snyder, 1993a).

The crisis exhibited by the harmonisation model represents a turn of events which could not be more out of tune with expectations that were alive until quite recently. Only a decade ago, the hopes and attitudes displayed by the Community institutions were still indicative of an almost total confidence in the capacity and efficacy of the traditional model of "legislative" harmonisation by way of directives. This seems the only possible interpretation to be placed on two of the major measures adopted in the Community context during the 1980s in conjunction with each other: the 1985 White Paper on Completing the Internal Market and the 1987 Single European Act (Pipkorn, 1990). It is worth pausing at this point to consider the significance of these events in the development of the Community approach to regulation, if only to identify the main features of a process whose outcome forms the starting-point for the observations that will be made here regarding the *quomodo* of Community social regulation.

The link of complementarity existing between the two initiatives, although not stated explicitly,[2] seems fairly clear and perhaps even taken for granted. Given its ambitious objective of abolishing existing barriers of every type—physical, technical or fiscal—likely to stand in the way of the realisation of a fully unified internal market, the Commission had drawn up an equally ambitious action programme which committed the Community institutions to carrying through an extensive body of legislation, mainly in the form of harmonising directives.

However, the Commission's trust in the effectiveness of the chosen method of regulation was not limitless: even the White Paper itself contained some signs of a lack of confidence in the complete reliability of the "harmonisation by directive" model.[3] But these uncertainties concerned not so much the structural *adequacy* of the directive instrument as such (the aspect which interests us here) as the sheer *possibility* of achieving the adoption of a large enough number of directives while the requirement for unanimity in Council decisions was still in force (in 1985).

In short, the major concerns regarding the success of the action programme set out in the White Paper were concentrated—to use the well-known terminology proposed by Joseph Weiler—on the *decisional* dimension of supranationalism, that is, on the possibility of overcoming the resistance shown by certain

---

[2] The SEA's function as a complement to the programme previously outlined by the White Paper is, however, explained in a number of subsequent documents. See, for example, the *Third Report of the Commission to the Council and the Eurpean Parliament on the Implementation of the Commission's White Paper on Completing the Internal Market* (Com(88) 134 final, 21.03.1988), where it is stated that "the entry into force on 1 July 1987 of the Single Act . . . has given added strength both to the objective and to the comprehensiveness of the programme set out in the Commission's White Paper". The complementarity between the two initiatives is demonstrated by Bieber, Dehousse, Pinder and Weiler, 1988 at p. 13. See also Van Empel, 1992 at p. 6.

[3] "A strategy based entirely on the harmonisation method would be over-regulatory" (para. 64 of the White Paper).

Member States to Community sources of regulation.[4] The *normative* dimension of supranationalism, that is, the appropriateness and effectiveness of the chosen regulatory techniques with respect to the stated objectives, prompted fewer uncertainties:[5] the assumption was that, in so far as the requirement for unanimity in Council decisions allowed, the directives specified by the White Paper would produce in full measure the harmonising effect expected of them. Consequently, replacement of the unanimity requirement in favour of the extended use of qualified majority voting was seen as the key factor in enabling the stated objectives to be fully realised.

Given this diagnosis, it is not surprising that subsequent remedies also progressed along the same lines. The institutional measures introduced in the years that followed—above all, the Single European Act (SEA)—were confined to the area of decisional supranationalism,[6] and did not touch on the still open questions of normative supranationalism and the effectiveness in general of Community law, probably because of a sense of "satisfactory" progress recorded in this area backed up by the stance on the effect of directives adopted at that time by the Court of Justice.

However, events subsequent to the White Paper and the Single European Act showed that—in the area of social policy as elsewhere—the problem of the effectiveness of Community regulation neither ends with nor can be resolved by the question of qualified majorities for decision-making within the Council, but comes up against issues associated with the structural regulatory capacity of the instruments available to the Community.[7]

If there was an error of judgement in the Community strategies of the 1980s, it therefore lay in the illusion that overcoming the principle of unanimity and thereby limiting the scope of the national veto constituted the panacea for all problems associated with the effectiveness of Community rule-making. The institutions' view of matters remained oblivious to the very different question of the real "regulatory capacity" of the preferred instruments, and in particular directives.

To avoid any misunderstanding, it must be said that the regulatory ambitions expressed in the 1985 White Paper have to a large extent been realised (a good many of the planned directives have in fact been adopted), mainly owing to the

---

[4] According to the well-known definition provided by Weiler, 1981, "normative supranationalism is concerned with the relationship and hierarchy which exist between Community policies and legal measures on the one hand and competing policies and legal measures of the Member States on the other. Decisional supranationalism relates to the institutional framework and decision-making processes by which Community policies and measures are, in the first place, initiated, debated and formulated, then promulgated and finally executed".

[5] As remarked by Easson, 1989 at p. 101: "it is surely of some significance that the Commission's White Paper *Completing the Internal Market* devotes only eight short paragraphs, out of a total of two hundred and twenty-two, to the 'Application of Community Law' ".

[6] Typically, Article 100a TEC.

[7] On this point see also Ladeur, 1997 at p. 52, according to whom "the focus is more upon the complexity of regulation, the reconstruction of which can in a second step be related to institutions and decisional problems".

institutional innovations which the White Paper itself foresaw (Article 100a TEC). This is not why it is mentioned here, however. The only reason for recalling the event is to identify it as the high point of the confidence which until some time ago was placed in the virtues of the "harmonisation by directive" model (Dashwood, 1981; Waelbroeck (ed.), 1976); a confidence which remained unshaken until the emergence of certain symptoms of a crisis in the harmonisation model already amply demonstrated by legal scholars (Dehousse, 1997; Harding, 1997) and also explicitly acknowledged—with respect to social policy matters—by the Community institutions themselves: "Outright harmonisation of social policies is not a Community objective".[8]

Aside from the success or failure of the programme of legislative harmonisation outlined in 1985, the point to be emphasised here is therefore that the White Paper can be viewed as a paradigm, in being a manifestation of a widespread consensus which, at a certain stage in the Community's journey, grew up around the feasibility of a particular way of looking at the procedure of legal integration and the corresponding regulatory techniques. That model, at one time predominant, is nowadays in decline, or at least no longer perceived as having absolute primacy, much less as the only one possible.

Today, given that a whole series of factors have been singled out which prompt us to conclude that the traditional harmonisation model built around the predominance of the directive is in crisis (Dehousse, 1994), there is manifestly a need to subject the problem of regulatory techniques in the Community system to critical scrutiny, albeit one which is still mainly "negative" in slant: for the time being, the assorted hypotheses, trends, analyses, proposals and expectations which crowd the agenda of the legal and institutional debate at Community level are all classified under the generic heading of "alternatives to legislative regulation in the Community system",[9] lacking as yet any systematic constructions which unify the many different motives and influences characteristic of this particularly "fluid" phase in the growth of the Community legal order.

These developments, both doctrinal and institutional, are examined below mainly in order to ascertain their relevance to the more specific subject of the present study. Clearly, the question of the *quomodo* of Community labour law, which is our primary interest here, cannot be examined in isolation from the broader context of the changes currently affecting the system of sources of Community law. European collective bargaining, like any other legal institution, has to be seen as *part of an institutional whole*. Only in terms of its place within that whole can its significance and function be defined.

---

[8] Communication from the Commission to the European Parliament and the Council, *The Impact and Effectiveness of the Single Market* (COM(96) 520 final, 30.10.1996).

[9] For an introduction to the issues involved, see Dehousse, Joerges, Majone and Snyder, 1992.

2 THE ROLE OF LAW IN THE EUROPEAN INTEGRATION PROCESS

The symbolic importance of the White Paper on *Completing the Internal Market* and the Single European Act as expressions of the confidence placed by the Community institutions in regulatory techniques based on legislative harmonisation has already been mentioned. It therefore comes as no surprise that during the same period, around the middle of the 1980s, other events of various kinds lent systematic rationality to a model of Community legal regulation which appeared to be attended by a high—or at any rate growing—degree of effectiveness, in the added light, in particular, of the "federalist" position (Mancini, 1989; D'Antona, 1994) increasingly adopted by the European Court of Justice. During those years the progressive affirmation of a self-contained Community legal order and, more directly relevant here, an *effective system of law-making* brought about a situation where legal integration, which advanced in forced stages, was pulling along behind it the more difficult process of political integration. Once again, the division into two facets formulated by Weiler (1981 and 1982) provides an effective representation of this dual situation. The successes of normative supranationalism, as an expression of legal integration, obscured the uncertainties of decisional supranationalism, prompting the European Court of Justice to emphasise—"dans une proposition dont la concision n'affecte pas l'importance" (Kovar, 1987a at p. 318)—that the European Economic Community is essentially a "Community based on the rule of law".[10]

Given that we attribute to the expression used by the Court on that occasion both of the meanings inherent in the general conception of a "State governed by the rule of law", this signifies, first, a Community whose acts are subject to law and, second (the aspect more directly relevant here), a Community which can be defined as such in so far as it acts and legitimises its own existence through law.[11]

It is therefore not irrelevant to stress—albeit incidentally, given the limits of the present study—the comprehensive importance, extending beyond the purely legal, wielded in the context of the broader process of European political integration by the increasing degree of regulatory effectiveness which the legislative harmonisation model seemed, for a certain period, capable of guaranteeing. Consequently, the importance of law in the course of the European integration process was (according to widespread opinion) "self-evident[:]Law is not simply *an* instrument, but is *the* instrument through which integration is achieved" (Easson, 1989 at pp. 115–116).[12]

The leading role which the substantiality progressively acquired by the Community legal system (Dehousse and Weiler, 1990) occupied in the process

---

[10] Case 294/83 *Parti écologiste Les Verts v European Parliament* [1986] ECR 1339, ECJ.
[11] Taxonomy borrowed from La Torre, 1994.   [12] Emphasis in original.

of construction of the Community political entity is well portrayed and encapsulated in a phrase used as the title of what is considered by some (Easson, 1989 at p. 116; Baldwin, 1992 at p. 237) to be one of the most impressive studies of European legal integration, a highly evocative phrase which, like the expression used in the Court of Justice judgment cited above, accurately depicts European integration around the middle of the 1980s. The authors concerned (Cappelletti, Seccombe and Weiler (eds),1986) used the phrase *Integration Through Law* to express the essence of a process of European integration structurally based on law and of a legal regulation technique based on the "harmonisation by directive" model.[13]

All these apparently diverse events are linked by an undeniable proximity in time which suggests that they should be "understood" in common. The relationship of complementarity that can readily be identified between the 1985 White Paper on *Completing the Internal Market* and the 1987 Single European Act has been mentioned. The Court of Justice's description of the European Economic Community as a "Community based on the rule of law" occurred between these two events, in 1986. And in the case of the doctrinal debate, the theorisation of the essentially normative nature of Community supranationalism dates back to 1981–1982,[14] while the thorough multi-sectoral study leading to the use of the phrase "integration through law" to symbolise the European integration process dates from 1986. In short, this coincidence in time reveals a widespread attitude on the part of institutions and commentators which predisposed them to regard the regulatory instruments and techniques peculiar to Community law as highly appropriate and functional with respect to the declared objectives.

It is notable, from the history of the decade following these events, that European integration has in point of fact advanced along a route which may perhaps be called *judicial* rather than *legal*.[15] Within the process of the formation of the Community legal order, we cannot help but distinguish at least two integration profiles: integration on the positive law plane and on the judicial plane. Up until now, the latter has helped to obscure the limitations of the former by establishing both principles intended to improve the effectiveness of Community legislation[16] and remedies which, conversely, presume its structural

[13] This instrumental view of law as a means of pursuing the goal of European integration has recently been challenged by Armstrong (1998a at p. 158), according to whom "allied to these instrumentalist images of law is an assumption of law's ability to deliver integration both in terms of the integration of the national and Community legal orders and in respect of law's ability to deliver social, political and economic integration".

[14] The first formulations (see Weiler, 1981 and 1982) were followed a few years later by the publication of Weiler's text in Italy (see Weiler, 1985).

[15] The role of the Court of Justice in the European integration process has been analysed by various scholarly communities, not exclusively by legal writers (Weiler, 1991; Mancini and Keeling, 1994). Among the most recent contributions written in the field of *integration studies* with special reference to the dialogue between the Court and national courts, see Burley and Mattli, 1993; Alter, 1996; Golub 1996; Stone Sweet and Brunell, 1998.

[16] Principles of the supremacy and the horizontal direct effect of Community law, on which see De Búrca, 1992; Emmert and Pereira de Azevedo, 1995; Eleftheriadis, 1997; Craig, 1997.

regulatory inadequacy.[17] In both cases, however, the activity of the Court of Justice, while undeniably of the utmost importance, has left the structure and techniques of the Community rule-making system entirely untouched (and could not have done otherwise). Consequently, these still constitute the presumptions of and at the same time the limits on the Court's "constitutional" decisions.

In other words, the wide-ranging scope of intervention by the judges in Luxembourg over the years both presumes and reveals a *pathology* of the Community model of legislative harmonisation. It must also be pointed out that the judicial remedies developed in order to provide appropriate solutions in a context of regulatory deficit have proved so valid and effective that they have brought about a paradoxical situation where the most "effective" directives end up being those which have not been transposed. This view is also shared by the former ECJ judge Pierre Pescatore, who, in an article on the dynamics of the interaction between Community legislation and case law, pointed out that "la carence du législateur a entraîné, par contre-coup, une extraordinaire mise en valeur [jurisprudentielle, *author's note*] des éléments de système inhérents au droit communautaire, au niveau tant des règles générales de droit matériel que des principes de structure". In view of the outcome, the shortcomings of Community legislation and the consequent rationalising activity of the Court can therefore be referred to as a "*felix culpa*" (Pescatore, 1983a at pp. 577 and 580).

It is, however, clear that in this context the question of the relationship between legal orders has proved to be one that is pursued less and less in terms of the interaction between systems of norms (as was the original intention) and more and more as synonymous with dialogue between courts.[18] Given the absolute institutional centrality of the Court of Justice, it is therefore hardly surprising that, on the academic front as well, debates focused on the judicial dynamics of integration have overshadowed analyses concerned with evaluating the particular system of Community rule-making and its limitations.

This has happened both in the case of studies of Community public law and in the more specific context of labour law.

In the past, public law doctrine certainly concerned itself with the intractable contradictions of the Community rule-making system. Even at a time when all seemed well, it demonstrated the anomalies of a system lacking the instruments which national governments have at their disposal in order to ensure the implementation of positive norms: in sum, the lack of a Community administration.[19]

---

[17] Principle of damages against the state for its failure to fulfil its Community obligations, as widely discussed by legal scholars. See, by way of example, Van Gerven, 1994a; Goffin, 1997: Wathelet and Van Raepenbusch, 1997; Harlow, 1997; Barav, 1997; Steiner, 1998.

[18] On the dialogue between the European Court of Justice and the Italian labour courts, see Ballestrero, 1998 and Lo Faro, 1998 in the special issue of *Lavoro e diritto* (3–4/1998) dedicated to a comparative overview of the judicial dialogues between the ECJ and national courts in the field of labour law.

[19] The subject is one of those most widely debated. See Schwarze, Becker and Pollak, 1994. The effects of the lack of an administrative apparatus on the form of the Community rule-making model

However, analyses adopting this approach remained in the minority and, as already stated, were supplanted by subsequent developments in Community doctrine, which became increasingly "taken over" by analysis of developments in the constitutional case law of the European Court of Justice. It is only recently, therefore, that a number of innovative reconstructions have been presented which are directed at questioning, for the purposes of integration, the adequacy—or at least the monopoly—of legislative harmonisation models (Snyder, 1993b; Ladeur, 1995a).

Labour law doctrine has followed a path which is in some ways similar. Recognising the centrality to the effectiveness of Community law of instruments of a judicial nature, it has turned its attention to evaluating the leading role played in this field by the ECJ judges (Watson, 1994; Simitis, 1996; Davies, 1996; Roccella, 1997) rather than to the system of positive sources of Community social law.

For the time being, therefore, the traditional attention always paid by labour lawyers to the evolutionary processes of regulatory dynamics is not being echoed in the Community context, or at least not in the form of the inrush it has resembled in the past in various historical and political contexts,[20] where it has given birth to theoretical reconstructions breaking, in various ways, the state monopoly of law-making.

That said, it is nevertheless possible to cite evidence of the renewed interest with which labour lawyers have, relatively recently, resumed pondering on the problems connected with Community regulatory procedures in the field of social law (Sciarra, 1995a; Simitis and Lyon-Caen, 1996). The reasons for this renewed attention are easily identifiable in the provisions introduced by the Agreement on Social Policy annexed to the Maastricht Treaty, and in particular those dealing with European collective agreements. Made even more "intriguing", from the point of view of a systematic reconstruction of Community rule-making, by the uncertain institutional framework within which they were originally contained,[21] these provisions—now incorporated into the new

---

are also emphasised by Joerges, 1996 at p. 6. On the need to ensure co-operation between national administrations in the implementation of Community law see the Commission's Report on *Cooperation between Administrations for Enforcement of Internal Market Law—A Progress Report* (COM(96)20 final, 29.01.1996), and its earlier Communication on the *Development of Administrative Cooperation in the Implementation and Enforcement of Community Legislation in the Internal Market* (COM(94)29 final, 16.02.1994). The duties of national administrations under EC law have recently been discussed by Temple Lang, 1998 and Knill, 1998.

[20] An obvious example is the German legal sociology of the early decades of the twentieth century and the Weimar experiment, one of the first laboratories in which the consideration of extra-normative factors assumed direct relevance in the context of legal analysis. For a labour law insight into the period of the Weimar Republic, see Lewis and Clark (eds), 1981; Arrigo and Vardaro (eds), 1981; Kettler, 1987.

[21] After a few initial skirmishes, the thesis which finally prevailed in doctrine was that recognising the Community status of the Protocol on Social Policy and its associated Agreement (Mancini, 1995; Sciarra, 1995b and 1996a; Aparicio Tovar, 1996b; Bercusson, 1996), partly in the light of the explicit position on the matter taken by the Commission (COM(93)600 final, 14.12.1993). All discussion on the matter was, however, ended with the incorporation of the ASP as provided for by the Amsterdam Treaty.

Amsterdam Treaty—quickly proved such as to turn the spotlight once again onto issues relating to the structure of the system of Community sources of law, putting back on the labour law agenda the question of the regulatory techniques best suited to accomplishing or assisting the processes of integration.

What has been said so far regarding the relations between (the respective roles of) Community legislation and case law perhaps needs some further qualification. The comments made are in no way intended to express value judgements,[22] but merely to demonstrate what appear to be the facts of the matter: the function of "guarantor of the effectiveness" of Community law taken on by the Court of Justice in the face of the structural inadequacy of the legislative harmonisation method hitherto given preference in the Community system; and the corresponding focus placed by legal scholars both in the field of labour law and elsewhere on the judicial aspects of integration.

The magnitude of the contribution made by the Court in affirming and refining the principles which govern the process of European legal integration is too obvious and indisputable to bear repetition here. Suffice it to say that the "1992 Project" has advanced more through the efforts of the Court than through those of the Commission or the Council, in so far as its progress has been due more to the effects of the so-called *Cassis de Dijon* case law[23] than to the adoption and effective implementation of the more than 300 legislative measures specified by the White Paper (Dehousse and Weiler, 1990 at p. 247).

All this helps to explain why the solution of the problems associated with Community regulation has so far not been perceived as a particularly urgent institutional task. Given that the Court, acting on the basis of what has been described as "purposeful opportunism" (Wincott, 1995), has proved itself capable of "defusing" the problem of the effectiveness of Community law, it has, as it were, "appropriated" the problem and removed it from its original and natural sphere of reference in the Community system of positive regulatory techniques.

Some commentators have gone still farther, maintaining that the Court's successes have not only had the effect of delaying a possibly timely revision of

[22] There is, by contrast, a high and strongly critical value-judgement element in the remarks recently made by a scholar who, in an open polemic against the "judicial legislation" role assumed by the Court, levelled against the latter the outright accusation that it "interprets provisions of the Treaty contrary to the natural meaning of the words used" (Hartley, 1996 at p. 95). This strong attack on the Court's case law as being excessively "federalist" represents one of the first breaches in the wall of the general acceptance with which the activity of the ECJ judges has so far been greeted, and has not failed to generate immediate responses. For a no less vigorous reply "in defence" of the Court and its role in the integration process, see Arnull, 1996 at p. 411, who accuses Hartley of having adopted a viewpoint which "oversimplifies" the Court's activity to the point of "caricature", and of having deliberately "neglected cases which are inconsistent with his overall thesis".

[23] Starting with the judgment in Case 120/78 *Rewe—Zentrale v Bundesmonopolverwaltung für Branntwein* [1979] ECR 649. The importance of the judgment in question even prompted an intervention on the part of the Commission (a rare event, although it has recently occurred again in regard to the equally significant *Kalanke* judgment) in the form of the *Communication from the Commission concerning the Consequences of the Judgment Given by the Court of Justice on 20 February 1979 in Case 120/78 ("Cassis de Dijon")* (OJ C 256/2, 3.10.1980).

Community regulatory models but have to some extent also hindered potential developments: in short, that the more the Court "reinforced" directives, the more "fear" the latter aroused in the Member States, making them less and less inclined to support any strengthening of Community decision-making processes. In other words, that the weakness of Council decision-making recorded from the 1980s onwards was the "price to be paid" (Joerges, 1994 at p. 41) for the work done by the Court of Justice in strengthening the instruments of the effectiveness of Community law.[24]

We are led to ask ourselves, however, whether the breadth of the role (not assigned as such) "won" for itself by the Court—both in terms of constitutional dynamics and in the arena of legal theory—should not be seen as a confirmation of the "weak" nature of Community legislation, centred as it is on an instrument (the directive) which is a complete anomaly on the national and international institutional scene,[25] so weak that even the doctrine of direct effect, which is no more than a natural corollary of any legal norm, was nevertheless greeted, understandably, as a real triumph. In this connection we can but endorse the happy turn of phrase used by someone who was in a position to regard the doctrine of direct effect as an "infant disease of Community law" (Pescatore, 1983b) and therefore destined to become no more than a memory once the supranational legal order reaches "adulthood".

With the function performed by integration of a legal nature thus set in its context—a function which another member of the Court did not hesitate to describe as "instrumental" to the purposes of integration (Koopmans, 1986 at p. 927)—we are also led to ask ourselves whether all this is enough. Some observers have pointed out that experience gained in other "integrated market" systems (the USA) suggests that, in the Community context, such heavy reliance on the ECJ's virtues in fostering integration may well not be an adequate solution (Sunstein, 1988 at p. 141).

From a different viewpoint, even an author like Mancini, who certainly cannot be accused of lacking sensitivity when it comes to the Court's role, identifies the reason for the transition from "activism to self-restraint" discernible in the latter's judgments as lying in a kind of acquired awareness, on the part of the Luxembourg judges, that it would be inappropriate (both constitutionally and in terms of legal process) to continue the "instrumental"[26] phase of Community case law which was exercised successfully during the 1970s and 1980s: after giving of its best in that phase, the Court must "pass on the baton" to others with institutional responsibility for finding regulatory instruments and techniques

---

[24] See also, along the same lines, the comments of Berlin, 1992 at p. 21.

[25] Prechal (1995, at p. 1) talks of the impossibility of "capturing" the nature of directives, given that they have no equivalent in international law or national legal systems. Other factors which characterise the directive as a special normative act which cannot be compared to others are discussed in Kovar, 1987b at p. 359.

[26] The term "instrumental" is expressly used in the "worthy" sense meant by Koopmans, 1986 , above.

which are self-sufficient, i.e. capable of operating effectively without the added assistance of the Court's activism (Mancini, 1990).

3 LABOUR LAW AND THE INSTITUTIONAL CONTEXT: A METHODOLOGICAL NOTE

The statements made in the preceding section are intended to evidence a separation of the present phase of European legal integration from institutional practices and the consequent systematic reconstructions which until some time ago seemed firmly entrenched.

In the observations which follow, an attempt will be made to contextualise those institutional presuppositions within a more specifically labour law framework; that is, to place them in a context which, as one historically affected by developments in regulatory techniques, constitutes an ideal area in which to examine and evaluate the legal and institutional developments currently attending the redefinition of Community regulatory procedures.

First, however, a brief but necessary digression must be allowed in order to give at least some idea of the justification for the methodological approach adopted here and explain its essential characteristics.

There is an obvious departure, in some ways, from the canons of orthodox labour law. Far from constituting an expression of wild imaginings, however, this departure is to some extent imposed by the very subject under study. As is widely recognised, Community labour law (unlike national systems of labour law) does not constitute an ordered and systematic corpus of norms endowed with its own particular overall rationality. Nor does Community labour law share with national systems the largely unitary nature of the sources of positive regulation and associated instruments of implementation and jurisdiction; on the contrary, it represents the composite outcome of norms which are heterogeneous in their origin, nature and degree of binding effect and which above all are supported, as has been affirmed time and time again, by different *rationes* and objectives.[27]

A study of Community social law which confined itself to the few social provisions contained in the Treaty and the secondary law would therefore be adopting a methodologically mistaken viewpoint which would not succeed in resolving problems that it would not, in fact, even be capable of envisaging. This misunderstanding can be highlighted by using a form of wording which portrays effectively the different ways of framing the analysis of Community social law: talking of labour law *in the* European Community rather than the labour law *of*

---

[27] For a clear example of such overlapping, see Lyon-Caen, G., 1992 and Davies, 1995. "Indirect effects" of European integration on labour law issues are discussed by D'Antona, 1996. On the relationship between competition law, convergence criteria and labour law, see Wedderburn, 1995b at pp. 375–379, who also goes on to consider the potential negative effects on minimum standards of employee protection of another corpus of Community norms which has so far received little attention from labour lawyers, namely *public procurement law*.

the European Community, emphasises that the interaction of labour law norms with the institutional context in which they are sited creates a structural legal space within which actual labour law norms (the labour law of the Community) constitute only a part which cannot be equated with a whole (labour law in the Community) whose content is bounded by co-ordinates that must also be sought outside Community social law. Restricting an analysis of the sources of Community labour law exclusively to the directly relevant norms would amount to losing sight of a dimension which perhaps remains part of the back-drop but, like all scenery, constitutes a substantial element of the legal frame-work in which Community labour law operates.[28]

Consequently, although those who (obviously referring to what is here called the labour law *of the* European Community) maintain that the latter simply does not exist, is instrumental to the Community's economic objectives, is an unwanted descendant of the original Treaties or is not comparable to national labour law systems are expressing opinions which are undeniably well-founded, feasible and certainly shared, the very act of stating such truths necessarily implies, at the same time, the need to broach the analysis of Community labour law in radically different terms. It is precisely because it cannot be compared to national systems of labour law that it must be placed within, and examined as a part of, an institutional context which contains it and outside which it would amount to no more than a collection of haphazard and in many cases relatively meaningless regulations and directives.

Besides, the notion that the study of labour law (and other phenomena) must be supported by an examination of contexts which are, so to speak, "external" to it is an established methodological assumption (Collins, 1997). The only thing is that, in moving from the national to the Community level, there is a change in the nature of the context within which the labour law system is analysed and with which it is confronted:[29] no longer (most optimists would say not yet) the industrial relations system, but rather the institutional context formed by the structured legal space within which labour law *in the* Union has to operate and which conditions its function, its formulation and its implementation.

It has been said that "if labour law is the seismic zone of every legal order, the sources of its production are its epicentre" (Romagnoli, 1990 at p. 11). That is why, rather than with reference to its few provisions, Community labour law needs to be examined from the aspect of its regulatory techniques; an aspect which can be regarded as a *locus* in which the various problems indicated above converge:

---

[28] For comments on the need to frame the study of social law within a more comprehensive context which avoids the danger of a "hyperspécialisation . . . condamnée à la myopie", while at the same time abjuring a theoretical approach which is "trop souvent presbyte", see Supiot, 1996 at p. 120.

[29] See Collins, 1997 at p. 308, who concludes his analysis of labour law discourses by stressing that "the subject remains contextual, but discussions proceed by engaging with insights supplied by diverse interpretations of context". The same author welcomes a methodological approach which resists "any settled attachment to any particular interpretation of context".

(a) the regulatory difficulties of a normative system which quite early on revealed its own regulatory weakness, only partly compensated by the Court of Justice's activism;

(b) the impossibility of regarding the labour law of the European Community as a self-contained and homogeneous system of norms endowed with an autonomous rationality of its own, as much as, rather, one sector of a legal order which is influenced, often indirectly, by decisions, choices and contradictions developed in the context of other sectors apparently extraneous to that of labour law; and

(c) the knowledge that all of the provisions adopted by the Community (both those which affect the field of labour directly and those which do so only indirectly) combine to form a labour-related legal system in the European Union which perhaps requires, precisely because of its complexity, forms of Community intervention other than the traditional instruments of the directive and the regulation.

The methodological approach indicated thus forms part of (or at least aspires to do so) a theoretical debate which witnesses lawyers, political experts and economists engaged in re-examining regulatory procedures, in the Community context as well as in the national and international context. Consequently, whilst agreeing with an author who warns that it is "generally inadvisable to transplant into the legal field analytical models developed within the context of other disciplines, [in so far as] their transposition into a different environment, unsupervised by an adequate critical awareness, creates the risk of apologetic or culturally subordinate attitudes" (Mariucci, 1985 at p. 442), in what follows I shall necessarily consider a number of reconstructive profiles "belonging", so to speak, to disciplines other than labour law or even law *tout court*.[30]

Furthermore, the separateness of labour law discourse, as of all other disciplinary "discourses", is not something incontrovertible *a priori* but a historically contingent product of the methodological options exercised within a given discipline. As epistemology has shown, the practices of discourse do not consist in the mere reconstruction of pre-existing objects of knowledge; on the contrary, they define and shape the object of their cognitive activity (Foucault, 1969).

---

[30] An exhortation to eschew a "purely legal interpretation" of European collective bargaining is issued in a very "Proustian" article of some years ago by Lyon-Caen, G., 1973–74 at p. 587.

2

Social Complexity and Regulatory Dilemmas in the Community System

1 REGULATORY DEFICIT AND ALTERNATIVES TO LEGISLATION: THE POST-POSITIVIST LABOUR LAW TRADITION

T HE EMERGENCE OF regulatory problems in modern-day societies is certainly not an unknown fact, nor have the prominence and interest progressively acquired by the associated issues in the academic world remained marginal. After being widely studied by legal philosophers and sociologists,[1] the phenomenon in question also went on to be contextualised with particular regard to labour law, the sources of its production and conflict resolution techniques.[2]

It is, however, notable that even legal theorists who are not labour lawyers have frequently made reference to labour law in their reconstructions, in its dual guise of an example of a branch of the legal order affected by these developments in regulatory dynamics and an academic discipline of primary interest for the purposes of a critical evaluation of the theoretical postulates concerned. The fact that labour law is nowadays the subject of theoretical suggestions directed at a re-examination of regulatory sources and techniques is therefore hardly surprising, and indeed is merely a repetition of what has already happened on other occasions.

For this is not the first time in the history of modern-day legal thinking that the particular normative status of labour law, which has historically taken shape as a typically and even paradigmatically polycentric branch of the legal order (D'Antona, 1990 at p. 212), has been the locus of doctrines and theories characterised by an innovative approach to the problems of regulation. It happened in the very early years of the twentieth century, with German sociology

---

[1] The literature on the subject is very extensive. See Teubner, 1983, (ed.) 1986, 1987a, 1989, 1991, 1992; Wiethölter, 1986 and 1989; In't Veld and Schaap (eds), 1991; Teubner and Febbrajo (eds), 1992. For partly different assessments, see Febbrajo, 1986; Reich, 1983; Arbòs, 1991; for a critical position, see Rottleuthner, 1989; Montanari, 1990. For a more strictly sociological approach to the analysis of the dialectic between autonomous and heteronomous regulation of social systems, see Reynaud, 1989.

[2] See Rogowski and Wilthagen (eds), 1994; Maestro Buelga, 1996; Wilthagen (ed.), 1998. The interest which the subject of the legal regulation of complex societies aroused among labour lawyers at a certain stage (Vardaro, 1984; Giugni, 1987; Clark and Wedderburn, 1987; Simitis, 1987; Sciarra, 1987; Mengoni, 1988; Caruso, 1990a; D'Antona, 1990; and Lo Faro, 1993a) seems to have lessened somewhat in the past few years.

of law and its theorisations of *lebendes Recht* (living law) (Ehrlich, 1913), direct ancestors of the first systematic reconstructions of the then emerging experiences of collective bargaining, in its turn the premise of the *kollektive Autonomie* which went on to be conceptualised in detail by the Weimar jurists.[3] It happened with the first formulations of institutionalist theories (Hauriou, 1925) and social law (Gurvitch, 1946) which were developed by French jurists in the period between the two world wars; also with the diverse theories of the *ordre juridique* which so strongly inspired the methodological turning-point that characterised the labour law of the 1960s; subsequently with the theorists of legal pluralism, especially those belonging to the Oxford School (Flanders, 1968; Fox and Flanders, 1969; Fox, 1973; Clegg, 1975); and then with responsive law (Selznick, 1969) and, lastly, with reflexive law (Teubner, 1983) and (perhaps to a lesser extent) autopoietic law (Teubner, 1987a and 1993a). Labour law also features in some manifestations of a move towards the affirmation of a procedural rationality of contemporary law (Lenoble, 1994; Habermas, 1992; Ladeur, 1995a), as will be discussed more fully later.

All these schools of legal thought therefore share a particular and explicit regard for the issues associated with the sources of labour law production, something which would in itself be worth reflecting on. However, it is even more relevant to point out that, in addition to this common feature (which, although significant, is "external" to the structure of the theories in question), they are linked fundamentally by another lowest common denominator, in this case one which is "internal" and transversal to them: theoretical positions which may be described, even if only conventionally and in a negative sense, as "post-positivist" (D'Antona, 1990; Montanari, 1994 at p. 86) in that they exclude the unequivocal and inescapable equation between "legal" and "of the state" (La Torre, 1994 at p. 656). To capture the origins of this thinking, we cannot do better than to return to the spare syntax of the description of the situation given in a still unsurpassed historical legal analysis of collective labour law: "Sinzheimer threw open to discussion the basic presupposition of the legal formalism reigning at the time: perfect coincidence between state and society, and between written statute law and law" (Vardaro, 1984 at p. 4).

The logical connection between the two common denominators of the various theories named above—one "external" and the other "internal"—is straightforward and almost syllogistic in its linearity: a quantitatively and qualitatively significant proportion of the theoretical proposals developed in the course of almost a century of legal thinking have expressly featured labour law as an example or confirmation of their respective postulates; all these theories, although inevitably disagreeing in certain respects, can with an acceptable

---

[3] The strong link of direct complementarity between the works of a scholar who is regarded as the founder of collective labour law, namely Hugo Sinzheimer, and the earlier theorisations of "living law" developed by German sociology of law is established by Vardaro, 1984 at p. 2. See also Rottleuthner, 1988 and, on the role of *kollektive Autonomie* in the shaping of the Weimar constitutional order, Kettler, 1987 at para. 4.

degree of approximation be classed in a single *genus*, namely legal post-positivism; therefore there is an obvious historical relationship between labour law and post-positivism (D'Antona, 1990) which justifies and even imposes, on the methodological plane, a "contextual" approach to the study of the sources of labour law in which the "context" is not so much the sheer socially relevant facts as, rather, the fresh thinking on those facts offered by sociology of law and the general theory of law. It amounts to what could perhaps be boldly described as a meta-context which any analysis of the system of Community labour law sources cannot and must not ignore if it is to be properly in perspective.

The highly theoretical element attending the subject of the present study therefore introduces a second category of considerations which play a part in further determining the outlines of the methodological approach followed. Thus, the non-unitary nature and particular structure of the Community rule-making system mean that the issues concerned cannot be viewed in isolation and that due importance must be attached to the institutional and constitutional dimension (Chapter 1, section 3 above); and the polycentricity which has traditionally characterised rule-making in the labour law field means that the "post-positivist" postulates which can be deduced from an examination of the theoretical positions to which reference has and will be made must be taken into account.[4]

1.1 At the root of the regulatory illusion: loss of the epistemic authority of law

There is no doubt that the current debates on identifying the possible causes of the regulatory crisis and seeking hypotheses for its solution originate, chronologically at least but also in other ways, from the intense doctrinal deliberation which since the 1980s has surrounded the notion of juridification (Habermas, 1984)[5] and in which much of the focus—in the writings both of Habermas and of later authors—has been on "social law" in the sense of the accumulated set of norms of which the reduction of working hours, freedom of organisation and bargaining autonomy, protection against dismissal, social security, etc. are classic examples (Habermas, 1984).

There seems no need to dwell on the meaning of this "ugly word" (Teubner, 1987b), if for no other reason than that lively doctrinal debate on the subject has already yielded a number of results at least some of which are by now fairly widely recognised: following their analysis by legal theorists, sociologists and philosophers, the problems of juridification were also taken up by labour lawyers, giving rise to the well-known conflicts of views between those who

---

[4] For a collection of articles on the concept of legal polycentricity, see Petersen and Zahle, 1995.
[5] The date given refers to the first English translation of the book, which was originally published in 1981.

detected tendencies towards juridification in labour law itself and those who remained wholly unconvinced that such tendencies really existed.[6]

The comments made below are confined to what seems directly relevant to the purposes of the present study, the question to be answered being defined, in essence, as follows: can the theoretical debate on juridification, and its resonances, be used to help us better to understand the evolutionary dynamics of collective bargaining as a form of social self-regulation? To anticipate the conclusions that will be reached, it seems likely even at this stage that the answer will be a cautious "yes".

There are two doctrinal developments which can be traced back directly to the theoretical richness of the Frankfurt philosopher's writings and in particular to the notion of juridification.

(a) In a first perspective, which we shall conventionally call a "critical sociology perspective", the stigmatisation of trends towards juridification falls within the framework of a critical theory of society and democracy which borders on the plane of political value-judgements *sensu lato*: "the juridification of life's worlds exacts a heavy price in the form of encroachments on the worlds of those possessing rights" (Habermas, 1984).

(b) In a second and more circumscribed perspective, which we shall conventionally call "juridical", the postulates inherent in the critical theory of Habermas have, by contrast, provoked a debate in which the protagonists have been legal theorists and philosophers and which is more directly relevant to what concerns us here. That is because it is possible to extract from the debate a different category of uncertainties, this time related not merely (as in the first perspective) to the *advisability* of juridification as much as to its actual *feasibility*.

In this second category of doctrinal developments deriving from the original notion of juridification it is possible to identify *in essence* the terms of the problem which we are examining here: the waning of the myth of the universal rationality of the legal system and, ultimately, of the state monopoly of law-making,[7] respectively cause and effect of the regulatory crisis of the contemporary state. Hence, the need to define the limits of the effective regulatory capacity of law in complex societies. From this point of view, the subsequent developments have been strongly directed towards the quest for alternatives to legislation, a quest

[6] See, for example, the divergent appraisals given by Simitis, 1987, Clark and Wedderburn, 1987 and Giugni, 1987; also the observations made from the sidelines of the debate by Vardaro, who also identified a kind of underlying terminological confusion due to the fact that the word juridification has a "multiplicity of meanings" as a result of, among other things, the "lack in English of a linguistic distinction between law as a general concept and written statute law" (Vardaro, 1987 at p. 602). For a review article on juridification in industrial relations, see Clark, 1985.

[7] The crisis of the rule-making system represented by the traditional bodies possessing legislative power is described by Wilhelmsson, 1995b at p. 133 as the "disintegration of legislators". With particular reference to the European integration process, see also Ladeur, 1997 at p. 43, according to whom "it may be necessary simply to abandon the concept of the state as a central institution which controls society in accordance with an equilibrium model".

which is made urgent by what has been called the "regulatory trilemma": a gloomy perspective according to which the effects of legal regulation cannot help but be one of three possibilities:

(a) an incongruence of law and society, with the result that legal regulation remains "ineffective because it creates no change in behaviour";
(b) an "over-legalisation" of society, synonymous with the Habermas concept of colonisation; or
(c) an "over-socialisation" of law, in which law is instrumentalised by policy or by the sectors being regulated (Teubner, 1986 at p. 311).[8]

Rather than being synonymous with juridification, therefore, the regulatory trilemma is an inevitable consequence of juridification in the sense of a quantitative increase in legislation. As a result, the only way of avoiding the trilemma is to change the associated presuppositions by identifying other rationalities of legal action, post-material rationalities which involve forms of post-positivist regulation.

The distinction inherent in the writings of Habermas between (a) juridification as a factor in the "colonisation of life's worlds" and (b) juridification as a term denoting a range of issues relating to legal regulation techniques, therefore enables us to avoid some of the ambiguities which occur when the two aspects are superimposed and value-based considerations regarding the "political" advisability of a greater or lesser degree of heteronomous regulatory intervention consequently impinge on the second aspect. Lumping the two aspects together in that way alters the nature of things, reducing to the banal political level a debate which has been more fruitfully developed on the basis of entirely theoretical and epistemological principles. According to a convincing theoretical interpretation, it is problems of an essentially epistemological nature which threaten the rationality of the legal system as a predominantly cognitive system, a system whose very capacity to grasp and recognise social complexities in order to regulate them effectively is, however, denied from a viewpoint of radical gnosiological scepticism (Teubner, 1989; Ladeur, 1995b).

For the purposes of the present study, we can disregard the sophisticated hinterland of these theoretical positions[9] and confine ourselves to their fundamental methodological presuppositions in the attempt to identify their essential implications as regards the problems of legal regulation under examination.

The basic assumption of the approach followed here derives from two circumstances of a differing nature, one empirical and the other linked to a systematic reconstruction of social evolution, which are not readily compatible: on the one hand, Weber's materialisation of law in the post-liberal state, with its growing regulatory ambitions; and on the other, the functional differentiation

---

[8] For further refinement of the non-deterministic mechanisms which govern relations between the legal system and the social systems which are the object of regulation, see Teubner, 1991.
[9] Although for a more in-depth treatment, see Lo Faro, 1993a at pp. 143–147.

of society (Luhmann, 1982 and 1990a) into a plurality of subsystems which in the most radical version are regarded as mutually inaccessible,[10] since each of these systems acts on the basis of differing codes and rationalities through which the surrounding reality is interpreted by the system concerned and metabolised as an element of its own internal functioning.

Viewed from this angle, the limitations of legislative strategies inspired by the material rationality characteristic of rule-making in the *welfare state* are obvious. Like any other social system, in its access to knowledge of reality the legal system is confronted by the cognitive problems deriving from the functional differentiation which has just been mentioned. Even more than the question of the effectiveness of legal control of the subsystems to which it is addressed, therefore, for law the cognitive problem is systemic complexity, given that "law is also imagination, representation and description of reality" (De Sousa Santos, 1987 at p. 281).

The adoption of this approach highlights governing factors which can be traced back to theories of knowledge with a constructivist and post-ontological slant.[11] The main contribution of systemic theory as regards these conclusions can be largely identified in a process of the extension to social systems, viewed as new objects of knowledge, of the cognitive relativism theorised by constructivist epistemology with respect to individuals (Habermas, 1988). The "personification" (Papaefthymiou, 1990) of the legal system as an object of knowledge, and the application to it of a cognitive relativism on the basis of which reality is characterised not as a pre-existing entity but rather as the product of cognitive activity, therefore imposes the theorisation of a kind of legal inaccessibility to social reality which renders legislation structurally (rather than merely incidentally) inappropriate for the effective regulation of complex societies.[12] In the context of this post-ontological epistemology, no social system (including the legal system) is capable of universalising its own rationality or of comprehending, let alone changing, the rationality of other systems (Teubner, 1996). The break with the epistemological bases of modern law could not be cleaner, if one only agrees with the assumption whereby the legal system produces rules with reference to its own internal representation of the surrounding social reality, but those rules actually influence the latter only partially because of a specular phenomenon whereby the systems being addressed develop their own representation of legal control, reinterpreting it in the light of their own internal code.

---

[10] In this approach, the differentiation of society into functional subsystems is the fourth phase in a process of social evolution whose first three phases are, respectively, segmentation, differentiation between the centre and periphery and hierarchical differentiation between systems (Luhmann and De Giorgi, 1992 at ch. IV).

[11] The application of constructivist epistemological principles to the relationships through which each of the social subsystems "understands" external reality is examined critically by Belardinelli, 1993.

[12] The same topics are dealt with from a different and more specifically sociological viewpoint by Crozier, 1991.

On the basis of this representation, any idea of direct and deterministic causality between legal norm and effect has to be rejected, and relations between the legal system and the social systems that are the object of its regulation pictured, rather, as an indirect and often indeterminate external "stimulation" or "perturbation" of social autonomy (Willke, 1992), with results which can also differ from those predicted (Ladeur, 1995a at p. 43).

Functional complexity and the multiplication of social "grammars" revealed by systemic differentiation theorists therefore make it necessary for the legal system to solve problems of a primarily cognitive nature. The cognitive relativism of constructivist epistemology, flanked by the growth in social complexity, finds expression—in relation to the legal system—in a deep regulatory scepticism which can be represented imaginatively by using the literary metaphor suggested by an author who wrote of the end of the myth of the "Etat omniscient qui, comme le romancier balzacien sait tout de ses personnages, sait tout ce qui est bon pour la société civile" (Cohen-Tanugi, 1985 at p. 118).

In the light of such a demystification of the state's omniscience and the resulting distrust of the quality of the regulatory capacities concerned, more than one conclusion can be drawn regarding the concrete options for legislative policy.

First, as was in fact envisaged in terms of an instrumentalisation of the theoretical premises recounted above, purely deregulatory hypotheses are outlined which, setting aside any evaluation of their broadly political objectives, appear to share essentially the same diagnosis of the underlying reasons for the regulatory deficit, but not the same possible remedies. In radically renouncing any form of regulation, such positions obviously presuppose the immutability of the intervention models typical of "substantive" state legislation and an inability to conceive of alternative models.[13]

Secondly, there are some who, expressing strong doubts regarding the possible perspectives of legal policy to be derived from the theoretical and epistemological presuppositions of regulatory scepticism, question whether it is in fact necessary "for a post-positive culture of the legal . . . to accept the legal viewpoint's loss of authority as unavoidable" (Montanari, 1994 at p. 96). In assuming a position which tends to relativise the postulates of constructivist epistemology as applied to the legal system, this doctrine appears only partially to accept the diagnoses of regulatory scepticism put forward by systemic legal theory; and with reference to the normative polycentricity perspective which will be examined more closely in the next section, it cautions against a "functionalist fungibility of sources" (Montanari, 1994 at p. 88) which would cancel out any distinction between public and private in the typology of sources of law production.[14]

---

[13] A neo-liberal political instrumentalisation of the legal strategies proposed by reflexive law theorists persists, despite the positions of the opposite tendency explicitly adopted by the authors who developed those theories. See Teubner, 1993a at ch. V. For a problematical view, see Black, 1996 at pp. 47–51 and Arthurs, 1998.

[14] For a re-examination of the public/private distinction in a situation of increasingly numerous spheres of self-regulation (rules governing sports associations, trade, financial markets and stock exchange transactions), with particular reference to the UK system, see the interesting comments

Lastly, there are others (many of them labour lawyers) who prefer, instead, to formulate assessments of their own which, although heterogeneous, appear to share the same underlying hypothesis that deregulation is nothing other than "a redistribution of normative power" (Romagnoli, 1990 at p. 10), otherwise described as a "dissemination of normative power" (Cohen-Tanugi, 1985) or a "structural dispersion of law" (De Sousa Santos, 1990). This presupposition seems to justify treating together in a single category the varied and distinct forms of non-legislative regulation which were placed on the agenda of legal debate (mainly in the Community context) some time ago, although there is no alternative but to conclude by agreeing with an author who states that "la crise de la régulation étatique est évidente, mais l'alternative globale n'arrive pas à se dessiner assez nettement" (Arbòs, 1991 at p. 142).

1.2 An evergreen paradigm: legal pluralism

Without question, however, beyond the degree of conviction with which the theoretical assumptions underlying the perspective just indicated (sometimes marked by a certain assertiveness) are accepted, the tenor of the statements encountered in an analysis of the doctrine mentioned above directly and inevitably evokes the broad, very general and as yet undifferentiated "family" of legal pluralism: "the increasing legal pluralism . . . is primarily a result of the increasing social and functional differentiation taking place in society" (Sand, 1995 at p. 90).

It has been said that "postmodern jurists love legal pluralism" (Teubner, 1992) or are "fascinated" by it (Wilhelmsson, 1995a at p. 13). Such statements are hardly surprising, bearing in mind that, on the basis of the main postulates of the systemic theories applied to law, the hierarchical relationship between the legal system and other social systems is replaced by a non-hierarchical or heter-archical network of autonomous systems which constitutes the presupposition of what has elsewhere been called legal pluralism "revisited" (Lo Faro, 1993a). "Revisited", in that in contrast to what is postulated in "first generation" plu-ralistic theories it is not characterised solely or so much by the operation of social norms formalised in legal terms; rather, and above all, it is characterised by the "presence of specialised institutions delegated to put the legal system in communication with a multiplicity of functional subsystems" (Teubner, 1992), each endowed with its own peculiar rationality which cannot be universalised to the other systems: "Nous sommes donc confrontés à un pluralisme aussi rad-ical qui celui dont la sociologie du droit a l'habitude de parler. L'on n'entend pas simplement par là une multiplicité de droits locaux, d'ordres éthiques et religieux ou une pluralité d'institutions et d'organisations, mais une multiplicité

made by Black, 1996. The disappearance of the public/private distinction is also referred to by Sand, 1995.

de rationalités incompatibles dotées de prétentions universelles à l'intérieur d'un système juridique moderne" (Teubner, 1996).

Clearly, this perspective presupposes the disappearance or blurring of the rigid distinction between public and private[15] in the classification of sources of law (Kennedy, 1982; Ladeur, 1995b) or at least, as has reasonably been suggested, the need for the notion of what is public to be considered in non-unitary terms (Black, 1996 at p. 51). This has a bearing on two phenomena which are both contextual but mirror-image opposites: a "privatisation" of the public sphere (*Enstaatlichung*) and an incorporation of private organisations into the sphere of public competence (*Verstaatlichung*) (Teubner, 1993b at p. 569). As has been pointed out by an author who has become one of the advocates of a new conceptualisation of legal categories in the broad canvas of Community integration:[16] "In stark contrast to the once well-known forms of the stable, corporatist balancing of interests which developed under the umbrella of the social or welfare state, the new phenomenon of 'micro-pluralism', or the creation of public-private networks, is characterised by heterogeneous regulatory concerns . . ." (Ladeur, 1997 at p. 34).

Therefore, the multiplication of the centres of law production gives rise not so much to an elimination of the "public" element as to a need to break down its monolithic authority by accepting a perspective—dubbed polycorporatist (Teubner, 1993b) or polycentric (Petersen and Zahle (eds), 1995)—in which the public sphere disappears as a result of becoming diffused or becomes diffused as a result of disappearing. Starting-points along these lines are also discernible in a number of analyses carried out by an author who, along with others, has examined in particularly meticulous detail the issues associated with the neo-corporatist tendencies of national industrial relations systems. In an article published some years ago on the possibility of defining a neo-corporatist theory of the state, Philippe Schmitter wrote: "If citizens were to have to choose between a neo-liberal dismantlement of state functions and a neo-socialist distention of them, they might prefer and be prepared to justify a neo-corporatist dispersion of them" (Schmitter, 1984 at p. 38).

In more recent theoretical contributions this idea of a "dispersion" of the state, and hence of the centres of law production, becomes more radical and generalised, with the statement that "instead of being the collective personification of a centralised governmental hierarchy, the state is now being transformed into the self-description of a loose network of private and public actors. In such

[15] On the different but associated question of the incorporation of labour law into the public or the private sphere, see Klare, 1982; Lyon-Caen, G., 1997; and, in more detail, Chapter 6, section 1 below.

[16] "The EU should be regarded as an avant-garde body which, through its experiments with self-organised and flexible public-private decision-making networks, might function as a testing ground for the much needed modernisation of the 'state' in the light of rapidly changing social and economic conditions. Seen in this light, the incomplete and flexible nature of the EU's institutions may prove actively advantageous as they are not trapped within the traditional state model" (Ladeur, 1997 at p. 35).

a network, governmental bureaucracies, political parties and autonomous social organisations form a loosely joined cooperative configuration which replaces the hierarchical unity of old state government" (Teubner, 1993b at pp. 569–570).

In this sense the last frontier of pluralism, or at least that which seems the most promising, is what we shall call network legal pluralism (De Sousa Santos, 1987 and 1990); it is no accident that this concept is featured both by autopoietic law theorists when making the "transition" from theoretical formulations to the illustration of possible working strategies (Teubner, 1992 and 1993a at chs V–VI) and by those who have attempted, from a sociology of law viewpoint, to outline possible hermeneutic categories for the new European legal scenario (Arnaud, 1991 at p. 235; Ladeur, 1997). These positions take the postulates of traditional legal pluralism and make them their own, combining them, in an original construction, with what appears to be the greatest and tangible contribution made by autopoietic law: the revelation and identification of the causes of the loss of state law's epistemic authority.

As we shall see, these approaches seem to offer an effective representation of the complex "interlegal" dynamics encountered in the "doubly" complex area (section 2 below) of the Community legal system, and this line is followed by a number of recent proposals directed at a radical redefinition of the role of Community-level regulation in terms of proceduralisation (Ladeur, 1995a, 1995b and 1997).

If it is true, as the next section attempts to demonstrate, that legal supranationalism should be perceived not simply in terms of a hierarchy between systems but rather as the creation of a new legal space in which the various regulatory systems involved have to coexist, Community regulatory techniques cannot be conceived and construed as if it were (merely) a question of regulating lower-ranking systems from a hierarchically superior position, but must reflect an attempt to find a way of enabling rules to operate in conjunction with each other: "A description of these relationships simply as an influence between EC legislation and the national implementation legislation would be a very rough oversimplification" (Wilhelmsson, 1995a at p. 5).

2 THE PECULIAR NATURE OF THE COMMUNITY LEGAL ORDER:
LEGAL SOVEREIGNTY LOST "TWICE OVER"

What has just been said regarding theoretical presuppositions which are capable of clarifying the regulatory difficulties of traditional legislative instruments must now be referred to the particular context of the Community legal order.

There is no questioning the fact that the most significant contributions relating to sources theory remain, to this day, yoked to legal realities confined within a predominantly national dimension. Nevertheless, that does not prevent us from making use of some of the hermeneutic instruments developed with reference to national legal systems in order to ascertain their functionality in a supra-national context as well.

Many commentators are in agreement in pointing out that up until now the attention devoted by both the general theory of law and the philosophy of law to the legal profiles of European integration has been scant (Bengoetxea, 1991 and 1994;[17] Ward, 1993; Joerges, 1994; Wilhelmsson, 1995b), as has in fact also been the case in the field of sociology of law, giving rise to what has been called a "betrayal" of the discipline's historical origins (Ferrari, 1993 at p. 29).

However, starting from the bald but none the less valid statement that "a federal system is a form of legal pluralism" (Friedman, 1993 at p. 41), it seems perfectly possible to propose a reconstructive hypothesis which uses the pluralist paradigm as the interpretative key to the processes of "unification and restructuring" of law (Ferrari, 1993 at p. 29) currently in progress in the Community context:[18] "We speak about pluralism when dealing with the coexistence of a plurality of different legal orders with links between them. Indeed, this is precisely what happens in the building of Europe" (Arnaud, 1995 at p. 150). If that is so, it can feasibly be commented that it is "precisely with reference to a phenomenon of political unification such as that in Western Europe, which from the outset leads us to expect monist rather than pluralist outcomes in the evolvement of modern law" (Ferrari, 1993 at p. 27), that legal theories in any way traceable to the "hard core" of legal pluralism are illustrated.

But before considering what forms the pluralist idea is susceptible of assuming in Community law, and more particularly in Community labour law, we may usefully pause to appraise the presuppositions which lead to the allusion, in these contexts, to a now inescapable fragmentation of the formerly familiar scenario: a scenario, once prevailing, "in which the concepts of law and legal system have with almost inevitablity got themselves rather hooked on to state law and particularly the law of the sovereign state" (MacCormick, 1993 at p. 15). Obviously, that type of scenario, with its entrenched certainties on which more than one lofty general theory of legal thought has been developed, is as far removed as it is possible to get from the reality of the Community legal system, which is marked not only by the absence of a sovereign state, if not of a state *tout court*,[19] but also by instruments of intervention different from those which have historically characterised action by national governments.

Furthermore, the Community institutions themselves have demonstrated their awareness of these scenarios of fragmentation, at least on the still embryonic and prospective plane of fact-finding and research activities. In an interesting report drawn up by a group of experts on behalf of the European

---

[17] It is this author who has attempted to extend to the relationship between national laws and Community law the theory of institutions developed by MacCormick and Weinberger, 1990.

[18] Garapon (1995 at p. 503) regards the multiplication of centres of law production as an effect of European integration and globalisation. On the appropriateness of adopting a pluralist-type approach to the study of Community legal integration, see also Wilhelmsson, 1995a and 1995b.

[19] On support for, or opposition to, "statehood" of the EU, see the recent interesting debate between Mancini, 1998 and Weiler, 1998.

Commission, the problem of the overall redefinition of forms of Community legal action was finally plucked from the fragmentary and intermittent context of short-term solutions and rightly placed on the plane of more systematic reflection, in being tackled from the viewpoint of the general theory of law.[20] According to the Research Report concerned, "among the most obvious developments are decentralised regulation and the disengagement of the state associated with the increased use of independent administrative agencies,[21] decentralisation and delegation of responsibilities to replace previous hierarchical and centralised command structures . . . As mechanisms for associating actors, both public and private, they represent pragmatic responses to social problems and new modes of governance or of co-ordination of collective action". These observations, initially attuned to the regulatory developments in progress in national legal systems, are then also turned directly towards the context of Community regulation: "The Commission is by no means on the periphery of these developments . . . if the Commission wishes to improve the effectiveness and accountability of its action and its capacity of anticipation, then it needs to consider its approach to certain aspects of governance. All of these have implications for its general ability to achieve a contextualisation of the process of the production and application of norms and ultimately they all point to the need for the Commission to consider its ability to operate as a body which can *animate collective action or networks of actors*. Significant among these is its engagement in such processes as *consultation* with and the *participation* of stakeholders".[22]

This category of problems, relevant from the point of view of regulation theory, is compounded by another problem even more directly linked to the specific non-state characteristics of the Community legal order as a system lacking the typical attributes of a national sovereign state. Although there is no need to recount in detail here the terms of the widespread doctrinal debate conducted among political historians, economists and scientists on the subject of the presumed erosion of national sovereignty resulting from the advancement of the European integration process,[23] this process—still a long way from being unanimously recognised as complete (Moravcsik, 1993)—can nevertheless be broken down into separate facets and the extent to which the alleged relinquishment of sovereign powers corresponds to reality assessed separately for each: whereas *economic* sovereignty is probably no more than a memory and *political* sovereignty is a myth which shows no sign of waning, the partial disappearance of *legal* sovereignty allows a number of conclusions to be drawn for the purposes of what concerns us here; not so much purely with regard to the supremacy of

----

[20] The Research Report (*Governance Progress Report* (CdP(96)2216), European Commission, Forward Studies Unit, December 1996) was co-ordinated by two academic institutions: the Centre for the Philosophy of Law of the University of Louvain, and the European Institute for Public Administration, Maastricht.

[21] See section 2.3 below.   [22] Emphasis in the original.

[23] For a political history approach, see Milward and Sørensen, 1993.

Community law over national law (which in itself embodies a direct loss of sovereignty) as, rather, in relation to the decline of a certain form of normative intervention which is an attribute indissolubly linked with the existence of a sovereign state.

For it is readily discernible that, if the ultimate reasons for the regulatory dilemmas mentioned earlier lie in the complexity of the systems to be regulated and the cognitive difficulties of the subjects of regulation (section 1 above), these presuppositions are simply multiplied in the Community system.[24] First, as regards the object of regulation, it is clear that the *systemic* complexity which already constitutes an obstacle for national systems of legislation is compounded by an additional dimension of *geopolitical* complexity making it even more difficult for regulation to gain access to the composite legal, economic and social reality which is the object of that regulation. However, the impact of this added dimension of complexity is not confined to the structure of the sources of *law-making* at Community level. It also exerts an effect from a second point of view, namely, the subjects and instruments of the *application* of supranational law, where the distinctive features of the Community legal system as compared with the corresponding national models are obvious (Schwarze, Becker and Pollak, 1994) and such as to jeopardise the functionality of Community norms in terms of their implementation or, to use a word which is more general but for that very reason more appropriate,[25] their *effectiveness*.

Consequently, relativisation of the notion of sovereignty, in the sense just described, constitutes another factor to be considered when analysing the new procedures of legal action at Community level. And it is not enough to argue that when sovereignty is transferred from one level to another this amounts to no more than adapting to a higher level the same normative instruments through which sovereignty was formerly manifested at a lower level. We have to agree with an author who points out that "we must not envisage sovereignty as the object of some kind of zero sum game, such that the moment X loses it Y necessarily has it" (MacCormick, 1993 at p. 16). It is therefore not enough merely to observe that sovereignty has shifted, because in shifting it has not simply moved from one level to another but has also changed its own particular forms and its own particular manifestations, including the legal one.

Attempting to establish at this stage a logical connection between the arguments developed so far, it could be said that the disintegration of national sovereignty corresponds, on the political and institutional plane, to the loss of law's epistemic authority on the theoretical and philosophical plane. In regard to Community law, therefore, the traditional sovereignty of state law is violated

[24] According to Ladeur, 1995a at p. 22, "what, with justice, is known as Eurosclerosis is a consequence of complexity which is no longer manageable".

[25] This is because the word implementation denotes a specific mechanism of incorporating into national law a specific source of Community law, namely the directive. However, the effectiveness of Community law depends on far more than the smoothness of the processes of national implementation of directives. For some interesting comments on the subject with special reference to the UK legal system, see Daintith, 1995.

twice over, as "law" and as being "of the state", with a consequent breakup of the traditional "Aristotelian unity" between government, market and law at national level which throws open to question the entire heuristic apparatus provided by legal dogma and knowledge on the basis of the observation of totally different scenarios. The "new" sovereignty—no longer national and not yet Community—requires, instead, new instruments of action, more appropriate to the ambitions in view, which are capable of surmounting the twofold territorial and systemic fragmentation mentioned earlier. As one of the few legal sociologists to have examined the matter said sensibly, to continue trying to contain the process of Community legal integration within the positivist paradigm and without cutting into the structure of national sovereignty would be a "superhuman effort" (Arnaud, 1991 at p. 227).

To conclude, it is hardly necessary to point out that, as in all federal, quasi-federal or otherwise non-unitary systems, likewise in the Community system the problem of the techniques and levels of regulation is linked inseparably to the problem of legitimacy and therefore, in the final analysis, to the idea of democracy (Dahl, 1989). This, of course, is one of the topics most widely debated in the literature on Community law, but is often related (or to put it perhaps more accurately, reduced) to the role which the European Parliament should play in the process of Community rule-making (Raworth, 1994). In reality, the Parliament's "centrality" in guaranteeing democratic control of the Community institutions constitutes an undoubtedly important but probably not exclusive aspect, since it in fact largely consists in the inertial residue of an excessively mechanical transposition to Community level of problems debated at national level and of an inability to envisage a perspective in which democracy can also develop along paths different from those particular to national governments:[26] a perspective of "postnational democracy" (Curtin, 1997) which an ardent supporter of Community statehood such as Judge Federico Mancini described as a desirable—although in his view as yet unlikely—"stateless democracy" (Mancini, 1998).

Setting aside, then, the extent of the role attributed to the European Parliament, the questions raised by issues associated with the democratic legitimacy of the Community[27] are in fact located on a plane which is rather more comprehensive and at the same time differentiated, if for no other reason because of the need to maintain a separation between at least two different profiles of it—a bivalence which has been conceptualised by referring to the two separate notions of *federal democracy* (as relating to the Member States) and *popular democracy* (as relating to citizens) (Cappelletti, Seccombe and Weiler,

---

[26] In the European Commission's *Governance* Research Report (see n. 20 above), the traditional model of representative democracy is deemed "restrictive" in the face of the challenges presented by contemporary society in terms of complexity, diversity and interdependence.

[27] On the democratic legitimacy of the Community, see Weiler, 1993 and, with particular (and critical) reference to the decision of the German Constitutional Court (*Bundesverfassungsgericht*) on the Maastricht Treaty, the "Karlsruhe judgment", Weiler, 1995 and 1998.

1986 at p. 27). From this second perspective, it can be said that the recognition of a change in the important notion of the "state" and the increasingly multiple-source structure of the system for the production of binding norms, with an extension of normative powers to private or quasi-private subjects or subjects in some other way extraneous to the ordinary circuit of rule-making laid down by the Treaties, reveal very clearly the two-way connection between the redefinition of regulatory techniques and the question of the democracy of the Community system.

2.1 Some symptoms of the Community harmonisation model's regulatory deficit

In what has been said so far it has been maintained that the legislative harmonisation model based on directives is beginning to be perceived, by the Community institutions themselves, as a model which, if not actually in crisis, is certainly imperfect and therefore not adequate, on its own, for achieving the objectives pursued.

There is no lack of concrete evidence to this effect, as is shown by the profusion of documents issued by various Community institutions in recent years in an attempt to provide a first response to emerging regulatory problems. These documents, although apparently heterogeneous in type, purpose and area of intervention, all actually share the common feature of representing critical comment on the inadequacy of the traditional regulatory techniques hitherto preferred.

At the end of 1992 it was already possible, reading between the lines of several Commission documents concerning the arrival of the momentous date of 31 December 1992,[28] to find statements revealing an awareness of the primary importance which this situation was assuming. When undertaking to publish regular progress reports on the harmonisation programme set out in the 1985 White Paper, the Commission expressed its intention to monitor "not only aspects relating to the decision-making process [*the number of directives adopted*], but also problems relating to the transposition and implementation [*their effectiveness*]"[29] of the measures envisaged by the White Paper.

Furthermore, the inadequacy of the legislative harmonisation method was already made clear in the second half of the 1980s in regard to the harmonisation of technical norms[30] (Goerke and Holler, 1998; Burns, 1998), when in the

[28] Communication of the Commission to the Council and the Parliament, *The Operation of the Community Internal Market after 1992. Follow-up to the Sutherland Report* (SEC(92) 2277, 2.12.1992).

[29] Wording in emphasis added.

[30] See the *Green Paper on the Development of European Standardisation: Action for Further Technological Integration in Europe* (COM(90)456, 8.10.1990) and the subsequent Communication of the Commission on *Standardisation in the European Economy. Follow-up to the Commission Green Paper of October 1990* (COM(91)521, 16.12.1991). The last publication on the subject was the Communication of the Commission *On the Broader Use of Standardisation in Community Policy* (COM(95)412(final), 30.12.1995).

context of the intensive legislative programme adopted with a view to 1992 there were emerging signs of recourse to the "delegation of regulatory powers" to private standards-making bodies other than those institutionally responsible for Community rule-making, such as CEN and CENELEC in the field of electricity and ETSI in the field of telecommunications. These were clear symptoms of the crisis of the legislative harmonisation model (it was not by chance that the ECJ's doctrine of mutual recognition also became established during the same period), recognised and noted as such by especially alert observers of Community affairs (Dehousse, 1989 at p. 125; Joerges, 1990; Joerges (ed.) 1991; Everson, 1998).

In the more recent Research Report on *Governance* already cited,[31] developments in technical harmonisation are also traced back to pre-existing and underlying regulatory problems: "The diversity of jurisdictions in which rules must be applied and the lack of a strong executive capacity on the part of the Commission . . . have led it already to develop methods which can better deal with this gap and to some extent this has led to a transformation of the ways in which rules are formulated and implemented. It is possible to see in the new approach to technical harmonisation, to however limited an extent, some attempt to contextualise the formulation and implementation of rules".

The Commission Communication on the implementation of its work programme in 1995[32] follows the same line and confirms what by now seems a fact difficult to deny: the "playing-down" of the tendency towards legislation in the Community system and the quest for instruments capable of guaranteeing the effectiveness of existing rules.[33] The Commission itself appears anxious to draw attention to a quantitative decrease in its legislative activity, declaring that this is not by chance but the result of a deliberate choice made on the basis of the principle that what counts is not the quantity of legislation, but its quality, although by this last word the Commission means not so much a major change to the regulatory models used (Bieber and Salome, 1996) as an improvement in the quality of drafting (Timmermans, 1997) and a *consolidation* of existing legislative texts.[34]

More recently, this effort to reduce the weight of Community legislation has also been pursued through the SLIM programme (Simpler Legislation for the

---

[31] See n. 20 above.

[32] See Ch. I n. 1 above.

[33] Similar considerations, although perhaps directed towards objectives which are more overtly and straightforwardly deregulatory, underlie the Molitor Group's *Report of the Group of Independent Experts on Legislative and Administrative Simplification* (COM(95)288, 21.06.1995), a special section of which is devoted to Community regulation in the field of *Employment and Social Policy*. In the document, the techniques, scope and actual function of Community legislative intervention in social matters are criticised as a potential obstacle to the competitiveness of European undertakings.

[34] This word, used by the Sutherland Report, signifies the non-innovative rationalisation of existing Community rules in particular areas, which are often scattered over a multiplicity of successively adopted sources. See *Follow-up to the Sutherland Report. Legislative Consolidation to Enhance the Transparency of Community Law in the Area of the Internal Market* (COM(93)361, 16.12.1993).

Internal Market),[35] under which a simplification of pre-existing legislation has been carried out in some areas of Community law.

Moving on to topics more closely related to social law, it is possible to identify from a Council Resolution[36] the concerns with which the Community institutions are most preoccupied: concerns regarding not the adoption of new legislation, but rather an "effective implementation and enforcement of Community legislation in the area of social affairs [, in which] there is already a significant body of Community legislation, notably in the area of health and safety at work".

In this particular connection, one last document should be mentioned[37] by virtue of the fact that it concerns an initiative in one of the areas of Community social law which, until recently, was most affected by an approach to regulation of the paradigmatically "harmonising" type: safety protection in the workplace (Aparicio Tovar, 1996a), an area of Community social action which has always been marked by a large number of harmonising directives.[38] Second only to the massive corpus of legislation progressively accumulated on the subject of freedom of movement, Community intervention in the area of health and safety at work—encouraged by the existence of provisions such as the former Article 118a TEC[39]—can be cited as a prototypical manifestation of the classic model of harmonisation in the field of Community social law. It is therefore all the more startling to find the Commission adopting, in a field in which its action has previously been very much in accordance with the typically "legislative" model, a document which expressly sets out to extol the virtues of an action programme based on "non-legislative" measures: "in the past, Community strategy has been legislative in nature, [but in the future] the Commission intends to adopt an approach of a non-legislative nature".[40]

The Commission's resolve to change its attitude to regulation in the field of safety at work is also all the more significant when this action programme (the fourth on the subject) is compared with the previous programme of 1988, which

[35] COM(96)559, 6.11.1996.

[36] Council Resolution of 27 March 1995 on the Transposition and Application of Community Social Legislation (OJ C 168, 4.07.1995).

[37] *Proposal for a Council Decision Adopting a Programme of Non-Legislative Measures to Improve Health and Safety at Work.* The document forms part of the Commission's fourth programme on safety in the workplace for the years 1996–2000 (COM(95)282, 12.07.1995).

[38] "Harmonisation has been the main vector of Community intervention in areas ranging from environmental protection to health and safety at work" (Dehousse, 1997 at p. 247).

[39] On the significance of this provision in the context of the whole of Community social policy, see, as an example, Banks, 1993.

[40] COM(95)282 (see n. 37 above) at p. 4. The document mentions: development of information; control of implementation [*author's note*: obviously through methods other than the institutional procedures under Articles 226 and 227 TEC]; more intensive use of technical and scientific expertise in the production and application of rules; publication of information booklets, guidance notes, etc.; involvement of the social partners; observance of the principle of subsidiarity; study of the socioeconomic effects of existing legislation; adoption of a cost-benefit approach; and ensuring that Community action in this field is consistent with and complements measures and policies applied in other fields. Each of these alternatives actually entails a detailed doctrinal debate which could not be examined in the proposal itself.

was, by contrast, visibly driven by an essentially and typically legislative logic. If we recall what was said earlier in Chapter 1 regarding the importance assumed by the SEA in shaping the lines followed by Community law-making, the circumstance just mentioned can be interpreted as confirming it. The Commission itself, in contrasting the "non-legislative" approach of the current programme with the "legislative" approach of the previous programme drawn up in 1988, mentions that the latter "coincided with the adoption of the Single European Act",[41] clearly intending to stress, in so saying, that the chronological proximity of its third programme (1988) to the adoption of the SEA (1987) reflected the climate of unconditional confidence in the "harmonisation by directive" model which the SEA had helped to instil.

Lastly, one other fact is worth mentioning. The subject of safety at work is unquestionably one of the areas that have received most of the renewed attention to regulatory issues displayed not only by labour law doctrine but also, and perhaps mainly, by experts in public law (Baldwin and McCrudden (eds), 1987; Sunstein, 1990; Baldwin, 1990 and 1992) and "specialists in regulation"[42] (Majone (ed.), 1990; Eichener, 1997; Ogus, 1994 and 1995). The advent of institutional initiatives such as those just mentioned therefore marks the creation of a kind of short circuit between doctrine and Community "legislator", in that the limitations of legislative harmonisation in the field of safety at work pointed out by some of the authors cited above have been largely taken up and acted on as its own idea by the Commission.

The documents named in this section represent only some of institutional materials which can be cited in support of the basic thesis presented here: the inadequacy of the regulatory techniques adopted in the Community context, in the face of the problems posed by the complexity of the matters to be regulated and the plurality of the systems that are the object of regulation. It represents a phenomenology which—albeit partial and necessarily synthetic—can nevertheless be regarded as testifying to the regulatory "discomfiture" which it was felt could be examined afresh in the light of the institutional and theoretical considerations described above.

2.2 "First generation" alternatives: mutual recognition, regulatory competition, standardisation

The events recounted in the preceding section cannot, of course, be regarded as conclusive for the purposes of understanding the institutional processes sparked

---

[41]   COM(95)282 at p. 4.

[42]   The expression is not a particularly elegant one, but the difficulty of classifying the studies concerned under the heading of any one of the traditional branch disciplines of law reveals an important fact, namely the emergence of a thread of research characterised by a typically interdisciplinary approach, which is giving birth to a new and autonomous discipline. For a review article on theories of regulation, see Hägg, 1997.

off by a regulatory crisis of which they represent only evidence, and certainly not an explanation.

Nevertheless, it is in the recurrence of a series of situations similar to those just mentioned that we can identify the origin of the various alternative strategies to legislative harmonisation which have been discernible in the Community system since the beginning of the 1980s. These strategies can, to a fair degree of approximation, be grouped into two chronologically successive phases, whose essential characteristics will be tentatively described here.

It is safe to say that one strategy falling within the first phase is that which even today, twenty years after its "invention", can be regarded as one of the most important tools from the point of view of an overall understanding of the process of Community integration (not just legal integration): the principle (or the technique?) of mutual recognition.[43]

(A)

The origin and purport of *mutual recognition* in the Community context are well known and need be recalled only briefly. At the end of an affair which arose in relation to the marketable product standards stipulated by a Member State for the importation of certain food products, the Court of Justice established the principle that any product lawfully produced and marketed in one Member State must be admitted to the market of any other Member State. It is also widely known that the Commission was not slow to grasp and restate the importance which such a principle was likely to have at that particular stage in history, that is, at a time when the Community's declared priority objective was the establishment of the Single Market.[44] Following similar indications by the Fontainebleau European Council of June 1984 (Schmitt von Sydow, 1988 at p. 94), the Commission proposed extending the validity of the principle of mutual recognition from the free movement of goods, for which it had originally been formulated, to the free movement of services and persons,[45] thereby taking the opportunity to appropriate a formidable instrument as an alternative to legislative harmonisation and the difficulties which the latter was progressively revealing.

That mutual recognition is a radical *alternative* to, and not merely a technical *variant* of, the harmonisation strategy is confirmed by the eloquent words of a protagonist of Community institutional life, according to whom: "Mutual recognition is not part of the new approach. It is the very opposite, because the

---

[43] For an analysis of the principle of mutual recognition as a regulatory technique in federal systems, without special reference to the Community legal order, see Majone, 1993.

[44] See the *Communication from the Commission Concerning the Consequences of the Judgment Given by the Court of Justice on 20 February 1979 in Case 120/78 ("Cassis de Dijon")* (OJ C 256/2, 3.10.1980).

[45] See the 1985 White Paper on *Completing the Internal Market*, as cited several times, in particular at para. 58. On the repercussions of the *Cassis de Dijon* jurisprudence and the subsequent regulatory strategies developed by the Commission, see Siebert, 1990 and, more recently, Alter and Meunier-Aitsahalia, 1994.

new approach defines the ways of harmonisation whereas mutual recognition is meant to avoid harmonisation" (Schmitt von Sydow, 1988 at p. 96).[46] In mutual recognition we are therefore confronted not with a new approach to harmonisation but with a non-approach, which shows its full "political" significance. It has been called the "most ingenious institutional innovation" of the neo-liberal approach to European integration (Joerges, 1994 at p. 42); others have described it as an example of how European integration can proceed through deregulation (Streeck, 1995a at p. 34): "EC 'harmonisation', which was originally intended to combine elements of a maximalist French-style industrial policy with a German-style social market economy, has been moving via regulatory mutual recognition towards a minimalist British-style competition policy" (Hayward, 1995 at p. 19).

The point regarding a potential deregulatory drift resulting from mutual recognition applied indiscriminately as a general canon of the establishment and functioning of the Single Market was also raised, in the course of the *Cassis de Dijon* case, by the German Government, according to whose observations: "In the final analysis, the rules of the least exigent Member State would be authoritative in all the others . . .; in an extreme case, a single Member State could enact legislation for the whole Community, without the collaboration or even the knowledge of the other Member States. The result would be to lower minimal requirements to the lowest level . . . The solution sought . . ., which amounts to the adoption of the lowest national minimum requirements, is further to be discounted on the basis that the provisions in question serve purposes which are legitimate in relation to the Community law and fall within the ambit of *social*, consumer or fiscal law".[47]

The "negative" view of mutual recognition briefly indicated here has, however, been countered by interpretations which are partly (but perhaps only apparently) different. It has been maintained by a member of the Commission, apparently speaking at the time in precisely that capacity, that in attributing substantial importance to the role of the principle of mutual recognition the White Paper is pursuing aims of an essentially practical and tactical kind, far removed from any option of a broadly political or ideological nature. Consequently, it would not have concerned itself with taking into account any of the collateral consequences which might have ensued and might ensue from the regulatory policy choices inherent in it (Schmitt von Sydow, 1988 at p. 96). These arguments, however, can equally well be interpreted in terms of an *excusatio non petita* which does not negate, and even confirms, the plausibility of the feared consequences in excluding, if anything, only the idea of their being deliberately intentional. Furthermore the same author, having discharged the task of a dutiful *ex officio* defence, is constrained to admit that "harmonisation is not

---

[46] For the opposite view, see Alter and Meunier-Aitsahalia, 1994, who see mutual recognition also as part of the so-called "new approach".

[47] Emphasis added. Case 120/78 *Rewe-Zentral AG v Bundesmonopolverwaltung für Branntwein* [1979] ECR 649, ECJ, at pp. 656–657.

dead" in view of the fact that, even if it is true that mutual recognition assists the achievement of the four freedoms, it is still not enough to satisfy consumers' aspirations entirely or—I would add[48]—to guarantee the achievement or perhaps even the preservation of satisfactory standards of social protection: "No simplifying rule similar to mutual recognition is likely to prove politically acceptable for social policy integration" (Pierson and Leibfried, 1995a at p. 32).

And as regards the political and ideological neutrality claimed for the regulatory techniques concerned (as for any "technique" or "science" in the field of law), we can only refer to the more than convincing arguments formulated some time ago with a view to unveiling their illusory, if not instrumental, nature (Tarello, 1972; Corsale, 1993). The problem has also been tackled with specific reference to the Community system, reaching conclusions which negate the ideologically neutral nature of the changes recorded in this context over the course of the 1980–1990 decade: "A *single European* market is . . . also a single European *market*"[49] (Weiler, 1991 at pp. 2476–2478); the principle of mutual recognition therefore represents a kind of "sophisticated version of negative integration . . . offering a way to separate market-making from state-building" (Streeck, 1995b at p. 394).

To sum up, in the face of the need to ensure the effectiveness of the Community regulatory system, the principle of mutual recognition operates like an impatient doctor who prefers to amputate the ailing limb rather than search out the forms of treatment that will restore its full functionality. Consequently, the problem of regulation, staved off but not resolved, is left with its original features untouched. Mainly as regards some areas of the legal order which are particularly exposed to the competitive internationalisation of markets (levels of social and employee protection, environmental and consumer protection), despite its apparent functionality it does not seem the best of the available solutions.

(B)

The second of the three alternatives to legislative harmonisation "trailered" in the title of this section—*regulatory competition* (Ehlermann, 1995)—can be regarded as the operative reverse face of the first: as has rightly been said, it represents nothing other than the dynamic profile of the principle of mutual recognition (Sun and Pelkmans, 1995 at p. 70).

Mutual recognition is by its very nature a static concept: on the basis of this principle a Member State must accept the rules of the Member State in which the good or service concerned is produced and marketed, but this does not necessitate any regulatory intervention. By contrast, regulatory competition (or competition

---

[48] For some deliberations on the significance likely to be assumed by the principle of mutual recognition in the field of labour law rule-making, the reader is referred to what I have said elsewhere (Lo Faro, 1993b).

[49] Emphasis in the original. The remark is also to be found in Weiler, 1993 at p. 34. For further comments regarding the presumed political neutrality of regulatory techniques, see section 2.3 and Chapter 6, section 3 below.

between national regulatory systems in a Single Market context underpinned by full establishment of the four freedoms of movement) indicates a dynamic perspective, in that the actual existence of mutual recognition prompts national authorities to alter their respective domestic rules on the basis of a calculation of the likely effects of such changes on the movement of goods and services.[50]

As argued above in the case of mutual recognition, regulatory competition likewise seems capable of producing potentially negative effects on levels of social protection. If, for example, goods produced at low cost in Member States which are less "exigent" in matters of employee protection could circulate freely throughout Union territory without there being any need to be obliged to observe standards of protection set at Community level (mutual recognition), it is quite conceivable that in all the Member States a race to the bottom would be triggered as regards standards of protection, with results that are easy to imagine[51] (regulatory competition), all the more so from the perspective of enlargement to new Member States in central Europe.

(C)

One of the areas in which the burden of regulatory difficulties has been most evident is, without doubt, that of Community rules on technical harmonisation and product quality standards.[52] it is therefore no accident that it is this field of Community action which has been the locus of one of the most important strategies developed by the Community institutions in recent years as "alternatives to regulation".[53]

The area in question is *standardisation*, a regulatory practice which, as in the two cases just described under *A*) and *B*), is depicted as "an important factor ... which ... has the capacity to be an effective, rapid, generally acceptable and easily used complement to legislation—and sometimes an effective substitute for mandatory regulation".[54]

The salient point here is not so much the merits of this or that choice made within the processes of European "standardisation"[55] as, in particular, the growing significance of these techniques in the context of the overall redefinition

[50] According to the definition provided by Sun and Pelkmans, 1995 at p. 68: "Regulatory competition is the alteration of national regulation in response to the actual or expected impact of internationally mobile goods, services or factors on national economic activity".

[51] The alleged race to the bottom brought about by an extensive application of regulatory competition has been questioned by Genschel and Plümper, 1997, who claim that "regulatory competition may at times also push the level of regulation upwards".

[52] The causes of the considerable inadequacy of the traditional approach in this field and the possible advantages offered by the "new approach" are commented on by Pelkmans, 1987.

[53] This is the official expression used as a heading by the Commission in its Communication from the Commission to the Council and the European Parliament, *On The Broader Use of Standardisation in Community Policy* (COM(95)412 final, 30.10.1995), at p. 4.

[54] This "authentic" definition is given in the Commission document cited in n. 53 above.

[55] For some recent assessments, particularly on the role of expertise in Community technical regulation procedures, see the proceedings of the Conference on Integrating Scientific Expertise into Regulatory Decision-Making, EUI Florence, 5–7 October 1995, published in Joerges, Ladeur and Vos (eds), 1997.

of the system of Community sources. From this point of view, standardisation activities (or, more relevantly, the institutional support which the Community demonstrably intends to give them) can be assigned a function which is fairly clear and in any case spelt out by the Commission documents cited: the statements they contain leave little room for interpretation as regards identifying the real motives underlying the regulatory choices which the Community institutions declare they intend to pursue. After emphasising that standardisation is "a mechanism by which interested parties (such as industry, workers and consumers, contributing through their organisations in an appropriate way) establish, on the basis of a consensus, by means of an open and transparent procedure, in the framework of recognised standards organisations, technical specifications which are adopted as standards after a public enquiry, and with which compliance is in principle voluntary", the cited Commission Report on standardisation goes on to indicate, without actually giving it the prominence it probably merits, what appears to be the ultimate reason for Community support of standardisation: the fact that it is functional in *"avoiding . . . excessive regulation"*,[56] given that "use of standardisation could, in principle, replace regulatory action with voluntary standardisation action . . . it is based on consensus and relies on acceptance of the results by those who will use them".

2.3 "Second generation" alternatives: the agency model

It seems reasonable to assume that the regulatory difficulties briefly described in the preceding sections also constitute the presuppositions of the lively theoretical and institutional debate which has developed in recent years on the possibility of developing, either alongside or in place of legislative harmonisation, new avenues of regulatory action. One of the most important of these is perhaps the notion of Community action through agencies,[57] although for the time being this is still at a purely or predominantly potential stage.[58]

---

[56] Emphasis added.

[57] The agency model is, however, not the only development "troubling" the Community administration and its regulatory role in the face of the "internal market challenge" (Everson, 1998). According to Everson, administrative law within the EU "must explicitly move away from its idealised view of legitimate administration as the technical executor of a pre-existing and unitary will . . . it must at last acknowledge that the legal oversight of administration is less a case of safeguarding the narrow execution of legislative mandates, and more one of ensuring the fair representation of a wide range of interests within ongoing political processes . . . It must, moreover, dispense with formal legal paradigms, basing its authority not upon an idealised legislative/executive/judicial divide, but upon its ability to ensure the relevance, quality and social responsibility of European administrative decision-making". From this new perspective, the author indentifies three main academic discourses focusing on the most recent developments in European administrative law: the "non-majoritarian avenue" (i.e. the agency model); the "deliberative model of market governance" (essentially, the so-called comitology debate, on which see the special issue of *European Law Journal*, Vol. 3(3), 1997; Haibach, 1997; Wessels, 1998; and Vos, 1998); and the "heterarchical theory" (on which see Ladeur, 1995a, 1995b, 1997).

[58] The activities of the new Community agencies have not yet been fully incorporated "into the system". On the new Community agencies, see Kreher, 1997.

This approach, discussed some time ago, has been evidenced fairly recently in the establishment by the council of eight new Community agencies[59] to join the two "pioneer" agencies that have been operating for some time in, as it happens, the field of employment and labour.[60]

Within the context of several European and extra-European legal orders this *agency model* of regulation has been interpreted as a kind of logical institutional fall-out of the standardisation model, since the regulatory activities carried on by standards-making bodies are the same as, or largely similar to, those now being performed by the regulatory agencies in those countries where the model has already taken concrete shape. However, given the possibility, in theory, of identifying a logical connection between the *regulatory technique* of standardisation and the *institutional form* of the agency, the facts of the matter as they transpire from the conformation of the new Community agencies and, in particular, the initial comments on the subject by doctrine (Everson, 1995 and 1998; Majone, 1996; Kreher, 1997; Shapiro, 1997) do not endorse any such conclusion.

Even a cursory assessment of the powers granted to the Community agencies makes it clear that they cannot easily be fitted into the category of the regulatory commission. The agency model as used at Community level is therefore far removed from those used in other legal systems (among which the American system serves as a leading example) where regulatory commissions are endowed with extensive rule-making powers as well as powers of administration and jurisdiction over the rules produced, thus giving rise, among other things, to the well-known criticisms advanced by those who have predicted the problematic profiles to which such a superimposition of the traditional functions of the modern constitutional state can lead. Although an exhaustive analysis of the US model of regulation through agencies lies outside the scope of the present work, it seems useful to sketch it briefly since it is so often referred to as a possible form for importation into the Community context or a source from which lessons can be drawn for the development of the Community system.

According to those authors who have studied the subject closely, the regulatory model as established in the USA in the form of independent regulatory commissions has developed in response to a series of needs and expediencies relating to the mechanisms governing the economic efficiency of markets. Regulatory intervention by agencies responds, in particular, to the need to correct so-called market failures, i.e. market-distorting situations (disruptions of competition, formation of monopolies, recurrence of negative externalities such as technological risks and environmental pollution, information deficit) in which the possibility of spontaneous achievement of the Pareto optimum becomes less. The

[59] European Environment Agency (1990); European Training Foundation (1990); European Monitoring Centre for Drugs and Drug Addiction (1993); European Agency for the Evaluation of Medicinal Products (1993); European Agency for Safety and Health at Work (1994); Office for Harmonisation in the Internal Market (1994); Community Plant Variety Office (1994); and Translation Centre for Bodies of the European Union (1994).

[60] European Centre for the Development of Vocational Training (CEDEFOP) and European Foundation for the Improvement of Living and Working Conditions, both founded in 1975.

type of public intervention in question is therefore destined to operate, at least in principle, on a plane which is structurally and functionally different from that traditionally reserved to legislation. The ambit of the powers and responsibilities of agencies does not include any instances of the redistributive fairness or macroeconomic stabilisation which respectively characterise the legislation of the welfare state and the Keynesian state (Majone, 1996 at pp. 13–15); on the contrary, the sole guiding criterion of regulatory action by agencies is (or is intended to be) microeconomic efficiency, elevated to the rank of a normative principle.

These doctrinal reconstructions, as can be seen, give countenance to the possibility of establishing a clear separation between economically efficient regulation and redistributive fairness, attributing the associated functions, respectively, to regulatory activities carried on within agencies and to legislation (Majone, 1998). From this assumption, it follows that no democratic or constitutional principle precludes vesting competences as thus delimited in institutions—such as agencies—which doctrine describes as non-majoritarian in order to indicate that they are politically neutral and, more particularly, politically non-accountable. As Martin Shapiro relates, this kind of separation between the technical-managerial rationale of the agencies and the political rationale of legislative regulation is epitomised in the well-known American saying: "There is no Republican or Democratic way to pave a street" (Shapiro, 1997 at p. 282).

However, this assumption does not seem entirely feasible. In the first place, it may be argued that, far from being a fact which is important on a purely descriptive plane, the possibility of distinguishing and separating the different functions to be performed respectively by legislation and by regulation is a *quod demonstrandum*, the absence of which would strike at the roots of the "democratic" plausibility and indeed the constitutional legitimacy of the veritable "independent governments in miniature" (Majone, 1996 at p. 42) which the regulatory agencies represent.

From this viewpoint, the identification of regulatory activities with no even indirectly redistributive effect is in fact problematical, both conceptually and in terms of concrete regulatory action. It is significant in this connection to note the conclusions reached by several authors who have recently described events in the United Kingdom, where the independent authorities set up during the 1980s in the privatised public service sectors[61] frequently diverged from the ideal model of microeconomically efficient technical regulation, coming instead to exert an influence, as was probably foreseeable and perhaps almost inevitable, "on the balance between the commercial interests of the suppliers and the social interests of the consumers" (Everson, 1995 at p. 185). "In other words, activities which in the abstract and/or most of the time are perceived as non-discretionary, managerial and technical will be reconstructed in the public perception as discretionary and political when they produce results that are significant to public

---

[61] In particular, telecommunications (1984) and the supply of gas (1986), water (1989) and electricity (1990).

policy choices or to the clash of political interests" (Shapiro, 1997 at p. 284). Paving a street too, then, could become a matter of political choice, once it is ascertained that technical "information constrains decision about which policies are or are not to be initiated and when initiated policies are to be implemented . . . the technical becomes political when it becomes policy-relevant" (Shapiro, 1997 at p. 290).

Therefore, the capacity to guarantee an efficiency and continuity of regulatory action unconstrained by the political strategies associated with the alternation of electoral cycles (Majone, 1995 at p. 103), pointed to as the principal "dowry" of the agency model, is also its inescapable Achilles' heel: the political non-accountability of the actors of supposedly "aseptic" microeconomic regulation diverges irremediably from some of the elementary postulates of the democratic principle.[62] And even if it is true that Community legislative procedures are not a model of democratic legitimacy, "the point is that curing weak democratic legitimacy by a move to technocratic (and thus obviously élite) legitimacy has a certain 'out of the frying pan into the fire' aspect" (Shapiro, 1997 at p. 284).

That said, it should be added immediately that, for the time being, in the Community context the option to delegate fully regulatory functions to non-majoritarian institutions remains a distant prospect.

In fact, as briefly indicated earlier, the path followed in establishing the Community agencies has been very cautious, perhaps partly because of the "constitutional" uncertainties just described, and also despite the fact that there was no shortage on the doctrinal scene of voices and suggestions supportive of a bold and generalised adoption in the Community context of the regulatory agency model which we may call "American". These approaches were essentially justified on the basis of a preliminary categorisation of the Community as an "*Etat régulateur*", with the redistributive functions typically performed by national governments through legislative instruments lying, by definition, outside its purview. Given that this is so, it was maintained and is still maintained today, the regulatory technique most consonant with the nature of Community objectives and competences is, in fact, regulation through agencies (Majone, 1996).

As stated earlier, exegetic analysis of the Regulations[63] establishing the new Community agencies fundamentally excludes the possibility of placing the latter in the category of independent regulatory commissions: there is no delegation at all of real normative powers, and the quality of independence also seems

---

[62] These problematic aspects are recognised, but probably underestimated, by Majone: "It is of course true that efficiency-enhancing policies, like all public policies, will normally have redistributive impacts. This is not a serious problem if the efficiency gains are large enough to compensate the losers, and if it is politically feasible to do so" (Majone, 1998 at p. 28).

[63] See OJ L 120, 11.05.1990 (Environment); OJ L 131, 23.05.1990 (Training); OJ L 36, 12.02.1993 (Drugs); OJ L 214, 24.08.1993 (Medicines); OJ L 216, 20.08.1994 (Safety and Health at Work); OJ L 11, 14.02.1994 (Office for Harmonisation); OJ L 227, 1.09.1994 (Plant Variety); and OJ L 314, 7.12.1994 (Translation Centre).

somewhat dubious, in view of their composition and, above all, the relationship of direct *functionality with respect to ordinary decision-making procedures* which seems to characterise the role assigned to them. The range of the tasks delegated to the Community agencies gives a clear indication of their function: from the collection and archiving of data to the definition of homogeneous assessment criteria to be applied in developing national policies and rules; from the promotion of more widespread exchange of technologies to the co-ordination of Community activities with those of other international organisations and institutions (Environment Agency); from collaboration with Community institutions in identifying needs and priorities to monitoring the overall effectiveness of Community policies (Training Agency); from the development of studies and research to the formulation of "non-binding" criteria and indicators (Drugs Agency); from the dissemination throughout the Member States of technical, scientific and economic information to the promotion of exchange of experience; and from providing assistance to other Community bodies in searching for information they need in order to formulate and implement effective policies to making a contribution to the development of future Community programmes (Health and Safety at Work Agency).

Even though we have to agree with an author who warns against classing all the new agencies together in a single model (Dehousse, 1997), it may still be said that the particular nature of the Community agencies is determined by their lack of normative powers and the propaedeutic nature of the cognitive activities they pursue. They are bodies (and activities) which are functional to the purposes of a hoped-for increase in the operative rationality of the machinery and procedures of Community decision-making: bodies essentially charged with "instructing" a decision-making process which is otherwise destined to be given expression in the traditional forms—still the only forms, in fact, permitted by the typology of Community acts deducible from Article 249 TEC.

Given that this is so, the Community agencies cannot be categorised as regulatory agencies, but rather—according to a taxonomy suggested some time ago (Everson, 1995)—as information-collecting agencies: an agency model, that adopted in the Community system, which for the reasons just given can therefore be described as "weak" compared with other "strong" models developed across the Atlantic. The grounds for this choice are diverse in origin: apart from objections based on the dubious compatibility of the bodies in question with the entrenched postulates of democratic theory, there are also limits, legally more cogent, which are specifically linked to the institutional structure of the Community system.

They arise from the provision in Article 7 TEC, which enumerates the Community institutions expressly[64] and specifies in its second subparagraph

---

[64] They are named as the Parliament, Council, Commission, Court of Justice and Court of Auditors plus, in an advisory capacity, the Economic and Social Council and the Committee of the Regions. It is true that the Treaty on European Union added to this list the European Central Bank and the European System of Central Banks (Article 8 TEU) as well as the European Investment Bank

that each of them "shall act within the limits of the powers conferred upon it by this Treaty". It was on the basis of a strict interpretation of this provision (to be more accurate, of the corresponding provisions in the ECSC Treaty) that the Court of Justice delimited rather rigorously the boundaries of the so-called "delegation of powers" in the Community system. In one of its first and most important judgments[65] the Court stated, in essence, that the dictum in the second subparagraph of Article 7 TEC operates both as a limit on possible "excesses of competence" of Community institutions and (the point to be noted here) as a limit on the delegation to others by those institutions of the powers conferred on them by the Treaties. In plain, non-technical language, it could be said that the obligation on the institutions is to do neither more nor less than the Treaties stipulate that they should do. According to the Community judges: "To delegate a discretionary power, by entrusting it to bodies other than those which the Treaty has established to effect and supervise the exercise of such power each within the limits of its own authority, would render that guarantee [the principle of balance of powers] ineffective".[66] Such delegation is possible only where the activities of the internal bodies which will be exercising the delegated powers "simply tend to improve the quality of Community law-making or of the enforcement of Community law" (Lenaerts, 1993 at p. 43). Which, as it happens, is the function nowadays assigned to the Community agencies being considered here.

To draw some partial conclusions, it can first of all be said that inclusion of the agency model as one of the alternatives to legislative regulation is wholly justifiable only in the case of one of the possible perceptions of an agency: the agency with real regulatory functions, which at present is not the one adopted in the Community context. The sole exception is the highly particular "agency" in the shape of the European Central Bank, which is certainly not a matter of chance: the single "agency" endowed with real regulatory powers, the only one representing a change in the Community's institutional structure in accordance with a statute, is a body charged with the task of pursuing objectives which, to this day, constitute the very *raison d'être* of the Community and the Union: the stabilisation of financial systems, currencies and prices.[67]

(Article 9 TEU); but these are new institutions which do not prejudice, and even confirm, the principle of express enumeration, in that their establishment necessitated a formal amendment of the Treaties.

[65] Case 9/56 *Meroni v High Authority* [1958] ECR 133. The *Meroni* judgment, pronounced with reference to the ECSC Treaty, establishes principles which are fully applicable to the European Community system. Certain doubts about the possibility of considering this case relevant to the new European agencies are expressed by Dehousse, 1997 at p. 257 and, more directly, by Majone, 1998 at p. 26.

[66] The Agreement on Social Policy's provisions on European collective bargaining are regarded as potentially contrary to this principle by Van Gerven, 1994b at p. 12, who wonders "whether the Community structure and institutional balance is not jeopardised by the possibility, as referred to in Article 118b EC and further elaborated in Article 4 of the Agreement on Social Policy . . . by virtue of which representatives of management and labour may enter into agreements on matters of social policy".

[67] On the problems of democratic legitimacy raised by the establishment of such an institution, see, recently, Gormley and de Haan, 1996.

This prompts a second conclusion regarding the role of agencies in the redefinition of Community regulatory procedures: only if "assisted" by objectives which are well defined and inherently unequivocal and unmistakable (as is the case with monetary and price stability in the Community context) are agencies capable of attaining the rank of regulatory instruments which are real alternatives in comparison with the other Community institutions. This would appear, firstly, totally to refute the presumed political neutrality of regulation produced by agencies, and secondly, to exclude from the sphere of sectors likely to be affected by any extension of the agency model those areas of Community policy in which such an unequivocal definition of objectives does not exist. And social law clearly has to be included in this latter category.[68]

As specifically concerns the labour law aspects which are of more direct relevance here, if may be said as a matter of general principle that any potential role of agencies lies more usefully, and perhaps exclusively, within the area characterised by intervention on the part of the public administration or public authorities; it is, on the other hand, more difficult to imagine what function it could fulfil in the regulation of relationships between individuals lying outside the purview of public intervention. When we apply this interpretative filter, Community regulation effected through agencies can be envisaged in a number of particular fields such as regulation of the labour market, vocational training, several aspects of social insurance and certain forms of industrial policy. Not, however, as regards the regulation of the employment relationship, except (as the sole exception which proves the rule) health and safety at work, which is in fact not regarded as part of the regulation of the individual employment relationship but as an area which involves manifestly public interests and in which the importance of intervention by public authorities has consequently always been recognised.

2.4 . . . And in labour law: the *quomodo* of social Europe

The evaluations made in this chapter touch on a number of different planes of analysis which are, truth to tell, somewhat heterogeneous; but they all relate to a single explanatory objective which requires treating them as a composite whole. The purpose has been to represent, essentially, a situation of Community regulatory deficiency which is undeniable, or at least well documented: the institutional developments which have been outlined (section 2 above) constitute its most obvious manifestation, and the theoretical assumptions invoked on the subject (section 1 above) help to identify its possible underlying causes. An attempt will now be made to demonstrate that any analysis of European collective bargaining must be set in the conceptual context of this regulatory deficiency.

[68] See the comments in this connection addressed by Scharpf, 1997 to Majone, one of the most active supporters of the agency model at European level.

If we briefly recall what was said earlier regarding the "institutional" perspective which an examination of the sources of Community labour law necessarily entails (Chapter 1, section 3), it need only be added, in support of the approach adopted here, that "the non-existence of a strict conceptual connection between social policy and labour law at Community level" (Grandi, 1995 at p. 142)[69] obliges legal discourses on the sources of Community labour law to penetrate beyond the limits of social policy provisions. Such discourses cannot, therefore, ignore the overall EC regulatory background and the shortcomings which its analysis reveals.

This situation will consequently need to form the backdrop to the deliberations that will be presented below in analysing the particular ways in which regulatory problems occur and are dealt with in the specifically labour law context. For there is no doubt that the scale and urgency of these problems beset labour law just as much as other areas of the Community legal order.[70] Furthermore, as will have emerged from the analysis given above, none of the alternatives to legislative harmonisation which have so far made an appearance on the scene of Community law seems appropriate to the particular nature of the system of regulation and set of principles which traditionally characterise the sources of labour law: not mutual recognition, which cannot ensure the preservation of adequate levels of protection (section 2.2); not the agency model, whose relevance is structurally limited in the sense described (section 2.3); and not even (or if at all only partly) other alternatives on the agenda of the academic debate such as soft law, which—at least in the way in which it has been used up till now—represents an influence that is somewhat indirect, although of undeniable importance.[71]

To stick to a script frequently rehearsed on national stages, labour law seems in fact to symbolise, in the Community system as well, an area of the legal order characterised by a degree of autonomy which gives it a special place within the framework of the conceptions, principles and regulatory practices common to other areas of the law. In other words, in the transition from national systems to the supranational legal order labour law seems to have retained an "originality" of its sources of production, although for the time being the foundations for this are more *presumed*, on the basis of a century-old historical tradition which recognises the singular nature of the system of labour law sources, than actually *measured* against the concrete legal, economic and social reality of the Community context. Repeated reference has been made above to the historical peculiarities of regulatory techniques in the field of labour law. It will be obvi-

---

[69] A connection which is non-existent on the collective level also, as pointed out by authors who have criticised the position of those who mistakenly "equate the social dimension with industrial relations" (Pierson and Leibfried, 1995b at p. 452). Similarly, with particular reference to the field of industrial relations, see also Bercusson, 1996 at p. 540.

[70] See the comments in this connection by Negrelli and Treu, 1994 at pp. 41–43 and Hall, 1994 at pp. 290–293.

[71] For some pointers on the possible labour law applications of the principles and techniques of soft law, see Sciarra, 1995a and Kenner, 1995.

ous, by this stage, what this alluded to: when discussing alternative models of regulation, labour lawyers are inevitably thinking of collective bargaining. And indeed, a Community context where what is being basically suggested is a need to diversify and to co-ordinate a multifarious system of regulation represents quite a home from home for collective bargaining, in that the diversification of regulatory sources aptly echoes the traditional pluralistic structure of labour law: "Labour law might be seen as the precursor of, even the template for, post-modern theorising about law . . . it is not surprising that the social relationships of production have been closely examined in recent sociological and socio-legal scholarship or that labour law frequently appears as a case-study in theoretical works on legal pluralism" (Arthurs, 1998 at p. 26). It is therefore not by chance that other authors who are not labour lawyers have also started to include col-lective bargaining in the list of alternatives to the Community regulatory gaps: "Recently, alternatives to legislation have also been explored. Examples include the agreement negotiated with European industry on environment policies, codes of conduct (like that on fiscal competition between Member States) and *forms of self-regulation by both sides of industry offered by the Maastricht Social Protocol*"[72] (Radaelli,1998).

In the new institutional scenario introduced by the Agreement on Social Policy, (European) collective bargaining therefore assumes the guise of a regu-latory instrument which is at least *nominally* not a new one but whose real cor-respondence to the constituent elements that have hitherto defined the collective bargaining we are accustomed to know at national level nevertheless has yet to be verified (Sciarra, 1996a).

For the apparent analogy between European collective bargaining and the pre-existing forms of bargaining at national level seems to have lulled observers of the phenomena in question into making not entirely justified and probably inertial assumptions, according to which the legislative support given to collec-tive bargaining by the European institutions has been interpreted as recognition of the collective autonomy of the European social partners and evidence of a Community wish to promote free European collective bargaining. However, such an interpretation seems in some cases to be too hasty. Many authors do not stop to ask themselves whether and to what extent the use of the same term for the two forms of "collective bargaining" (national and Community) justifies the automatic transposition to the latter of instruments and interpretative cat-egories developed with reference to the former. In my view, such a conceptual transposition is deceptive. In national contexts, collective bargaining has traditionally been regarded as an epiphenomenon of social and legal pluralism and, more particularly, as a manifestation of what is referred to as the collective autonomy of the actors of industrial relations. The main argument put forward here is that the role assigned to the social partners in the Community legal order should be seen in rather different terms: far from being a supranational

---

[72] Emphasis added.

realisation of the autonomy of the social partners, European collective bargaining is mainly intended—in the overall context of a general redefinition of Community regulatory strategies—as one of the Community's potential remedies to its decision-making bottlenecks and implementation problems in the field of labour law and social policy.

Chapters 3, 4 and 5 below seek to demonstrate why European collective bargaining should be viewed not as evidence of Community legal pluralism but as a normative construction of the Social Chapter. The assumption that it is not a socially typically phenomenon but, rather, a construction of Community law implies that none of the traditional interpretative categories derived from observing previous experience of bargaining in national contexts can be referred to European bargaining, and that a new and specific theoretical framework therefore has to be provided for it. Before simply proceeding to use the traditional categories, we need to ascertain whether the actors, structures, procedures, content and, above all, functions of collective bargaining at Community level still correspond to the actors, structures, procedures, content and functions of what has in the past been meant by the term "collective bargaining" at national level. That is, we need to find out—as it was worded in an article written over twenty years ago on the then early experiences of supranational bargaining—whether or not "peut-on verser ce vin nouveau dans la vieille outre" (Lyon-Caen, G., 1973–74 at p. 593).

That is what will be attempted in the chapters which follow.

3

European Collective Bargaining: Between Old Systems and New Realities

1 IN THE BEGINNING THERE WERE COLLECTIVE AUTONOMY, PLURALISM AND COLLECTIVE LAISSEZ-FAIRE . . .

" COLLECTIVE LABOUR relations presuppose the existence of autonomous and voluntary organisations on the workers' and frequently also on the employers' side; they further presuppose the willingness of both sides to enter into and to observe agreements, and they presuppose the legal freedom and the factual power to use industrial action, social sanctions for the enforcement of the bargaining process and of the standards agreed upon" (Kahn-Freund, 1972 at p. 134).

These evaluations, which embody the core of the thinking on collective bargaining developed by Sir Otto Kahn-Freund, may justifiably be regarded as part of the common heritage of concepts whose progressive creation has shaped the very birth of labour law as a distinct legal discipline.[1] Among the undeniable diversity of schools of thought which have surrounded collective labour relations, they came to constitute the subject of a true "labour law orthodoxy" (Davies and Freedland, 1983 at p. 2), accepted in more than one country[2] by whole generations of legal scholars, and not just labour lawyers.

---

[1] In Italy, the question of the asserted autonomy of labour law with respect to the general corpus of civil law has for years been a matter of heated dispute: for a negative opinion on the possibility of classing labour law as an autonomous or special branch of the legal order, see Santoro Passarelli, 1969.

By contrast, with reference to the British common law system (but drawing illuminating comparisons with the French civil law system), the autonomy of labour law is firmly vindicated by Wedderburn, 1987 now 1991. For a response to this latter article, see Howarth, 1988.

Reference to a "never-ending debate" on the autonomy of labour law is made by Supiot, 1994 at p. 196, who uses the traditional Weberian distinction between formal legal rationality and material rationality to illustrate the eccentric position taken up by labour law with respect to the general law of obligations. The question of the autonomy of labour law with respect to ordinary civil law is deemed "largely metaphysical" by Lyon-Caen, G., 1990 at p. 513, who urges us to reflect, instead, on the relations which labour law nowadays maintains with other legal areas and disciplines such as constitutional law or international law.

[2] For an analysis of Kahn-Freund's intellectual range and his contribution to the development of British labour law, see Wedderburn, 1983, Lewis, 1979 and McCarthy, 1992. For some evaluations of the Anglo-German author's influence on Italian doctrine, see Ballestrero, 1982.

The widespread and largely unqualified consensus exhibited by the international academic community towards Kahn-Freund's conceptual categories needs no confirmation, of course. It is mentioned here only because this broad and generalised acceptance of the pluralistic model as an appropriate scheme in rationalising collective bargaining phenomena allows the associated corollaries to be used as necessary elements to sketch the essential outlines of the notion of collective bargaining as it has developed historically.

That certainly does not mean outlining some illusory and artificial model which standardises collective bargaining, but merely emphasising that the different forms of collective bargaining which are identifiable synchronically and diachronically can be characterised, in all their heterogeneity, by a "common feature: the contextuality between the affirmation of a social practice (collective negotiation of terms and conditions of employment) and a political fact (recognition of the legitimacy of forms of 'self-protection' on the part of the employee)" (Mariucci, 1985 at p. 12). It therefore does not seem arbitrary to adopt the evaluations mentioned at the start as ideal reference points for analyses exploring what nature and function can be ascribed to the particular forms of collective bargaining recognised (or, more accurately, provided for) by the Community legal order: the objective is to ascertain whether and to what extent European collective bargaining too can be fitted into the established interpretative schemes which its actual name would seem to imply.

The purpose of such an operation does not consist in moving on to type-defining procedures, of dubious usefulness, to test whether European collective bargaining can be issued with a "certificate of conformity" to some non-existent ideal-type model. That is to say, the intention is not to present some "defining technique", since no ideal-type version of collective bargaining exists to which the concrete version of European collective bargaining[3] can be related. The observations presented below aim, rather, at drawing a series of conceptual co-ordinates useful to an understanding of the function which it seems possible to ascribe to collective bargaining procedures in the Community system and, *above all*, at deciphering the provisions of the EC Treaty which make reference to them.

2 . . . AND ON THE SEVENTH DAY THE MAASTRICHT SUMMIT CREATED EUROPEAN COLLECTIVE BARGAINING

The content of the various provisions introduced by the Maastricht Agreement on Social Policy (ASP) and now incorporated in Articles 137, 138, 139 TEC with regard to rules on European collective bargaining is well known by now (Fitzpatrick, 1992). Although each of these provisions will be analysed in detail

---

[3] The expressions "Community collective bargaining", "European collective bargaining" and "supranational collective bargaining" have been used freely throughout the book as synonymous, on the assumption that in this particular context there is no possibility of misunderstanding or confusion with social phenomena or legal institutions other than those meant.

in Chapter 5 below, before moving on to develop the conceptual background which is necessarily propaedeutic to that analysis it seems useful to explain in summary form the textual content of the (few) Community norms explicitly devoted to the subject of our present study.

First of all, Article 137(4) TEC recognises the possibility of implementing Community directives by way of collective agreements concluded between the social partners at national level.[4] This first typology of collective bargaining— described as "implementational" (Lo Faro, 1993b at p. 140) or "transpositional" (Ojeda Avilés, 1993 at p. 75)—lies outside the scope of the present study, since it actually constitutes a form of collective bargaining which is structurally *national*, despite the fact that in functional terms it is linked to the Community dimension (Lyon-Caen, A., 1997a):[5] the agreements concerned are essentially national ones which are subject to the same legal aspects as those affecting other national collective agreements and with respect to which the possibility of singling out a special legal regime justified on the basis of the "Community" nature of their content should be verified within each national legal system.[6] These are also the terms in which it has always been treated by the Court of Justice case law, whose position remained largely unaltered after the entry into force of the ASP.[7]

---

[4] "A Member State may entrust management and labour, at their joint request, with the implementation of directives adopted pursuant to paragraphs 2 and 3. [These paragraphs refer, respectively, to the adoption of directives by the Council in accordance with the principle of qualified majority voting and in accordance with the principle of unanimity.] In this case, it shall ensure that, no later than the date on which a directive must be transposed in accordance with Article 249, management and labour have introduced the necessary measures by agreement, the Member State concerned being required to take any necessary measure enabling it at any time to be in a position to guarantee the results imposed by that directive".

[5] For comments on the problems of a national nature which still underlie the functioning of the implementation mechanism as provided for by Article 137(4) TEC, see Sciarra, 1996a at pp. 197–198. With specific reference to the British system, Wedderburn, 1994, now 1995a at p. 299, argues that the provision in Article 137(4) cannot be regarded as satisfactory, given the possibility available to employers under that system to renegotiate individual contracts of employment at any time for the purpose of excluding any reference to collectively agreed standards. The same author returns to the subject in Wedderburn, 1995b at p. 393. See also Deakin and Morris, 1995 at p. 77.

[6] It can, however, be said that, setting aside the question of the legal status of collective agreements in individual countries, it is the structure of national industrial relations systems which plays a decisive part in the functioning of the implementation mechanism established at Maastricht: clearly, since it is generally a matter of the formulation and reception of framework rules, those national systems which are centred on confederal or cross-industry bargaining are better equipped for the purpose than those where the focus is on industry-level, territorial or company-level bargaining. For some comments in this connection, see Streeck, 1994 at p. 168.

Some predictions regarding a potentially growing role for national collective agreements in the "*mise en oeuvre*" of Community law are proffered by Lyon-Caen, A., 1997a, who singles out the possible role of national collective agreements with respect to the application of Community social *principles* and *policies*.

[7] For an analysis of pre-ASP Community case law on the implementation of directives through collective agreements, see Adinolfi, 1988. The essential judgments of reference on the matter are those in Case 91/81 *Commission v Italy* [1982] ECR 2133; Case 131/84 *Commission v Italy* [1985] ECR 3531; and Case 143/83 *Commission v Denmark* [1985] ECR 427. The Commission itself, in its Communication on the *Medium-Term Social Action Programme 1995–1997*, stated expressly that the guiding criteria of the procedure, to be set out in a later Communication, were to be based on the principles to be found in the case law of the Court of Justice (COM (95) 134, 12.04.1995).

Other provisions of the TEC social chapter, however, regulate bargaining activity carried on by the social partners at *European* level.

Article 138 TEC starts by referring to promotion of the social dialogue, assigning an active supporting role to the Commission: "The Commission shall have the task of promoting the consultation of management and labour at Community level and shall take any relevant measure to facilitate their dialogue by ensuring balanced support for the parties" (Article 138(1)). The chosen means of developing the still embryonic potential of the European social dialogue is then identified, in the form of involving the European social partners in the preparatory phase of Community decision-making: "To this end, before submitting proposals in the social policy field, the Commission shall consult management and labour on the possible direction of Community action. If, after such a consultation, the Commission considers Community action advisable, it shall consult management and labour on the content of the envisaged proposal. Management and labour shall forward to the Commission an opinion or, where appropriate, a recommendation. On the occasion of such consultation, management and labour may inform the Commission of their wish to initiate the process provided for in Article 139. The duration of the procedure shall not exceed nine months, unless the management and labour concerned and the Commission decide jointly to extend it" (Article 138(2), 138(3) and 138(4)).

Lastly, Article 139 TEC, after recognising the possibility of the social dialogue leading to the conclusion of actual collective agreements ("Should management and labour so desire, the dialogue between them at Community level may lead to contractual relations, including agreements", Article 139(1)), goes on to regulate the details of their implementation and normative effect: "Agreements concluded at Community level shall be implemented either in accordance with the procedures and practices specific to management and labour and the Member States or, in matters covered by Article 137,[8] at the joint request of the signatory parties, by a Council decision on a proposal from the Commission. The Council shall act by qualified majority, except where the agreement in question contains one or more provisions relating to one of the areas referred to in Article 137(2), in which case it shall act unanimously" (Article 139(2)).

It is starting from these scant provisions that the reality of European collective bargaining has to be understood and analysed. Clearly, a "normativist" approach of this kind to the study of collective bargaining may seem in stark contrast to the methodological premises and heritages mentioned up till now, in that it appears to give prominence to the "statal dimension" of collective bargaining to the detriment of its "industrial relations system" dimension. However, the decision to apply an analysis perspective of the top-down type to the study of European collective bargaining is to some extent a choice dictated by the impracticability of the bottom-up approach—an impracticability which can be laid at the door of the continued existence of obstacles which make it

---

[8] That is, matters falling within the Community's competence.

impossible to recognise in the Community bargaining system the features of a properly established and autonomous social phenomenon.

The presence of these obstacles, already discernible from purely empirical observation of the available data, is also revealed—on a different but complementary plane—by the inherent contradictions that inevitably emerge in any attempt to apply to European collective bargaining the interpretative models incorporating as their indispensable presupposition the socially rooted and widely established nature of bargaining practices: "Every bargaining system presupposes social powers . . . driven by a logic of action and interests which are socially and historically typified and recognised" (Caruso, 1997 at p. 332); which is precisely what is still lacking in the case of the supranational bargaining system.

The basic premise of the present study is that, in the theoretical recasting of the hermeneutic categories of European collective bargaining, it is not (yet) feasible to propose observing the associated dynamics with the aid of the analytical tools typical of an industrial relations system which is still non-existent in the Community context (Streeck, 1992 and 1998). Given that this is so, the methodological option has to be one which differs somewhat from the traditional approach and which must (for the time being) give primary consideration to the attitude which the Community institutions felt should be adopted towards the dialogue between the social partners: an attitude which, as is known, has basically been given expression in the provisions originally contained in the ASP.

For it is highly probable that, were it not for the intervention of the ASP provisions, the subject of European collective bargaining would not have attracted the attention it has received in the academic debate. But it is also absolutely certain that, without these provisions, the subject would now be being discussed in quantitatively and, above all, qualitatively different terms.

The quantitative effect of the ASP on developments in European bargaining is self-evident—if not in the short term, certainly in the medium and long term—and needs no further examination here.

What I would, however, point out is that the Community legislature's intervention is such as to produce a *qualitative change in the functional profiles* of European collective bargaining. Legislative measures on industrial relations systems have not always produced effects of this kind. Historically, national laws in this field have alternated between being repressive, promotional, auxiliary, supportive and other things in their stance towards collective bargaining; but it would be difficult to maintain that, for all their diversity, they have influenced or altered the function, role and structure which bargaining systems had been able to acquire autonomously on the plane of social relations: "What the state has not given, the State cannot take away" (Kahn-Freund, 1959 at p. 244). This famous pronouncement,[9] uttered by Kahn-Freund with specific reference to the "spontaneous" application of collective agreements in the British system, may

---

[9] Described as "grand but surely erroneous" by Wedderburn, 1994 now 1995a at p. 293.

be regarded as representative of a more general reality, neatly encapsulating that principle of the "indifference" of the socially typical functions of bargaining dynamics towards state intervention which may be regarded as one of the constituent elements of the very concept of collective autonomy.

What has just been described as the principle of "indifference" does not, however, apply to the relationship between Community legislation and Community collective bargaining. In contrast to what was said earlier regarding national legislative measures on collective labour relations, the ASP can quite justifiably be said to have exerted a "conformational", if not actually maieutic, effect on European bargaining in stipulating from the outset that the hoped-for developments should be channelled through "specific modes of operation" (Sciarra, 1992 at p. 739) which, as we shall see, are functionally oriented more towards the objectives of the Community institutions than towards those of the actors of Community collective bargaining. It is therefore wrong to describe the Social Chapter as promotional legislation, since it would be rather a strange promotional legislation which was more functional to the goals of the promoters (the Community institutions) than to the goals of those who are supposed to be being promoted (the European social partners).

This "heterogenesis" of the originating purposes of collective bargaining, which for the time being has been indicated apodictically only in terms of its essential characteristics, will be examined and explained in more detail later in an attempt to identify the motives which led the Community institutions to support (according to some, to invent)[10] a European bargaining system.

It is, nevertheless, useful to make some preliminary observations here. An exegetic comparison of the respective provisions is not the way in which confirmation or, possibly, refutation should be sought of the teleological approach which underlies the Community legislation concerned and distinguishes it from previous national laws in the field of industrial relations. Rather than by making such a comparison—which would probably be deceptive and in any case not conclusive—the "suspect" nature of the support given to European bargaining by the Community is better revealed by logical and chronological scrutiny of the normal historical course of events at national level. Whereas in the national context "the development of collective autonomy in a separate industrial relations system, through autonomous rule-making, procedures and judicial bodies, has always preceded heteronomous regulation . . . in the supranational context supportive legislation has preceded the separate development of collective autonomy" (Caruso, 1997 at pp. 332–333). That is to say, national supportive

---

[10] One example is Caruso, 1997, who with reference to Community collective bargaining and to the associated ASP provisions talks respectively of a "virtual legal reality" and an "instrumentation which seems totally out of proportion to the real social dimension of European bargaining". "It is one thing to create a constitutional framework within which collective bargaining can be set and operate according to its own autonomous dynamics, but quite another to think that it can be invented from nothing on the basis of institutional alchemy alone" (p.331). For similar considerations, aimed at demonstrating a "precedence of mental processes over real processes", see Caruso, 1994 at p. 223.

legislation has generally taken the form of a *response after the event* to a pre-existing social phenomenon whose autonomous dynamics it could therefore only partly influence. The ASP provisions, by contrast, coincide with or even *anticipate* the genesis of Community collective bargaining; the latter is being "born" under the auspices and protection of the ASP and, in a sort of institutional imprinting, inevitably being conditioned (if not actually moulded) by it. This chronological reversal, described as "structure before action" (Turner, 1996), may be regarded as an indicator of the real terms in which the Community legal order has hitherto measured the prospects of the possible development of a supranational bargaining system, and so as a useful pointer to an understanding of the function, and the limits of the function, assigned to European collective bargaining within that legal order.

To draw some partial conclusions, it may be said that a critical analysis aimed at evaluating the function performed by collective bargaining in the Community context cannot ignore the "twofold reversal" involved:

(a) the reversal of the historically entrenched sequence between a *prius* which is the social formation of collective autonomy and a *posterius* which is intervention by state legislation; and

(b) as a necessary consequence, a reversal of the traditional analytical approach to bargaining dynamics, consisting in attributing to the legislative intervention "anticipating" Community collective autonomy (the ASP) an importance which at this stage seems inevitably pre-eminent.

An awareness of this twofold reversal—of the *time* aspect of bargaining and of the *approach* from which it should be observed—is heuristically pertinent in that it helps to eliminate or reduce a number of recurrent misunderstandings.

It is often said that the functioning of a self-contained bargaining system at Community level is hindered by a number of "missing elements" which prejudice its full operation as a regime: the fact that there are no clear rules on representation, no fully representative actors, no defined Community collective interest and no clear rules on the normative effect of collective agreements. In short, an absence of many of the fundamental elements characteristic of, or crucial to the very existence of, any bargaining system worthy of the name.

Such observations, some of which will also be examined later, cannot be argued with; they incontrovertibly correspond to the truth and point to problematic aspects which are of undeniable importance. On the other hand, the conclusions which may be drawn from them for the purposes of a critical evaluation of the function assigned to collective bargaining in the context of the Community legal order are not entirely unambiguous. It may be said, as a matter of principle, that any bargaining system takes on a structure which is consistent with the social, industrial-relations and institutional contexts within which it operates, besides being attuned to the functions it performs or is expected to perform. This open-ended series of variants therefore has to be taken into account when the overall adequacy of a bargaining system is being assessed. For example, the formalisation of rules on trade union representation within a given system may be regarded as more essential or less essential, depending on whether or not the system concerned incorporates the *erga omnes* effect of collective agreements; definition of the criteria of representative status may be regarded as more urgent or less urgent, depending on the particular traditions of trade unionism in a given country; the establishment of "private justice" procedures may be a pillar of some systems but absent in others, without the latter being in danger of collapsing; and even a principle as fundamental as the negative freedom of association (Pedrazzoli, 1990a at pp. 371–376, 390; Kearns Davis, 1996) may be non-existent in some systems without this necessarily constituting an unacceptable restriction of the freedom of association *tout court* (Sciarra, 1990 at pp. 664–679).

In short, collective bargaining systems shape their particular structure according to the traditions. circumstances and (more relevant to our present purpose) *functions* which are particular to them. Something which constitutes a basic element of one system may well be totally absent in another system, without jeopardising the latter's rationality; something which represents a deficiency in one system may well not do so in another.

If, then, we adopt this relativising approach whereby assessments of the adequacy of bargaining systems must take account of the functions they each perform, all the "missing elements" listed above with respect to European collective bargaining are open to two different interpretations. Whereas they can be regarded as deficiencies from the point of view of an autonomous, self-contained and typically social bargaining system, they probably cease to be such when viewed from the necessarily different perspective of European collective bargaining. This is a perspective in which, as reiterated in the present study, it has to be recognised that Community collective bargaining cannot be viewed as a socially typical phenomenon comparable to anything that has gone before, but must rather be seen as an instrument of the regulatory objectives pursued by the Community institutions. Consequently, the uncertain representative legitimacy of the actors of bargaining, the absence of rules on procedures and enforcement of agreements and the actual difficulty of identifying any collective European interest underlying supranational industrial relations activity[11] are not temporary shortcomings of an as yet incomplete Community bargaining system, but telling indications of a different functional perception of European collective bargaining—a different functional perception which is deducible both from the "normative" (as opposed to social) manner of its genesis and, as we shall see, from observation of the more recent circumstances in which it has developed.

---

[11] "the social dimension is, therefore, not, as is often argued, one in which cross-national coalitions of workers and employers, unions and employer associations can be expected to confront each other at the European level around alternative, internally consistent visions of Social Europe" (Lange, 1992 at p. 236).

3   THE "FUNCTIONAL SINGULARITY" OF EUROPEAN COLLECTIVE BARGAINING
AND INTERPRETATIVE TOOLS: AN INTERIM SUMMING-UP

For reasons of clarity, this is a good point at which to distil the essence of the basic thesis to which the whole range of evaluations presented so far can be referred. This thesis—hinted at repeatedly and now set out explicitly—seeks to demonstrate the radical difference in structure, content, procedures and, above all, functions which exists between Community collective bargaining and the socially typical bargaining systems that have evolved at national level.

To confirm the plausibility of this working hypothesis, I would also point out that its assertion of the difference in function of the two forms of bargaining (if that at Community level can actually be called such)[12] has its basis in a series of composite assessments which, however, share a common presupposition to be found in the (scant) stock of qualitative and quantitative information so far offered by Community bargaining experience. These assessments, apparently promiscuous, can be roughly grouped into two separate schemes.

(A)

The first scheme (which has featured the most prominently up until now) comprises what may be called "first-order" deliberations in that they are the result of a non-value-based comparison of the objectively observable *facts*. In the preceding pages an attempt has been made to demonstrate that, even at this first analytical level, the differences between national and supranational bargaining experience are enough to corroborate the assertion that they have essentially different functions.

It could be said, however, that first-order observations are not sufficient. It might reasonably be objected that they prove nothing, since they are derived from an unsustainable juxtaposition of phenomena which cannot be compared because they are being observed at different stages in their respective growth and development. This kind of viewpoint does not totally refute the difference in structure and functions between the two forms of bargaining, but interprets it as a purely incidental result of Community bargaining's recent "date of birth". This last fact is thought to be sufficient to explain the difference (or rather, from this viewpoint, the non-difference) between the two, which it is believed will in any case disappear as the Community bargaining system matures: it is therefore just a matter of time.

However, the issue can and should be presented in quite different terms.

---

[12] "Few of the relationships between management and unions in the Social Chapter can properly be called collective bargaining" (Wedderburn, 1997 at p. 29). Strictly speaking, we can talk of collective bargaining only in the presence of a number of elements which distinguish a bargaining system from a mere succession or superimposition of isolated agreements. For a clarification of the concepts, Kahn-Freund, 1954b is still essential reading.

The notion that what lies behind the still uncertain physiognomy of Community collective bargaining is a kind of "portrait of collective autonomy as a young man" does not seem sustainable, and it is therefore not enough to wait patiently for time to pass until it is possible to discern in the former the semblance of the latter. If that were so, the functional difference that has been referred to would amount to no more than a hasty or premature conclusion based on the failure to find in the Community bargaining system something which that system, because of its youth, cannot offer as yet.

However, a "continuum-based" interpretation of this kind, which, in the conviction that like any other bargaining system Community collective bargaining will inevitably take time to mature, underestimates the significance of the differences found on the factual plane, can be countered by a substantial series of observations on a different but complementary plane—a different (more indirect or second-level) plane of analysis within which can be found the elements to confirm or refute, definitively, the assertion that Community bargaining cannot be likened to the idea of collective bargaining as it has evolved historically in the national context.

(B)

These further deliberations can be grouped, as already indicated, into a second observational scheme to be used in the analysis of Community bargaining.

Continuing the terminology used for those described under *A)* as non-value-based or "first-order", these will be called value-based or "second-order" observations. They comprise observations which go beyond mere "naturalistic" recognition of the *facts* of bargaining and seek to take a fresh look at the bargaining reality through the lens of some established *interpretative models* developed on the basis of those facts.

This operation, as stated earlier, in no way implies the use of type-defining methods, which, as is generally recognised, are especially unconvincing in regard to the analysis of collective labour relations. Instead, it follows a line of research in which the attempt to understand phenomena which are difficult to typify—as collective phenomena are, by definition—adopts a relativistic approach which imposes a constant need to establish links and distinctions.

It should be noted in this connection that, as regards both their autonomous evolvement and their relation to statutory law, bargaining systems elude "attempts at organic rationalisation" and demand, on the contrary, a "multiplicity of reconstructive techniques"[13] (Mariucci, 1985 at p. 444). And Community collective bargaining, in a multi-tiered panorama of subjects, structures and functions in which a multiplicity of bargaining systems co-exist and intermesh, still lacks a "dedicated" reconstructive technique capable of demon-

---

[13] Vardaro, 1985b at p. 438 also talks of a "diversification of the legal representations of the collective agreement" and of the need to "adopt a 'plural' reconstructive model".

strating its very particular features on the structural and functional plane. Here the need for a new theoretical framework for European bargaining which does not aspire to being prescriptive, but merely descriptive of the true terms in which it was perceived by those who, more than any others, have encouraged its birth: the Community institutions, the real "midwives" of Community bargaining.

It was stated earlier that the functional singularity of Community bargaining as compared with previous bargaining experience becomes obvious as soon as an attempt is made to superimpose on the former some of the main observational schemes developed with reference to the latter. It is now time to make these assertions more explicit by specifying which established interpretative models this referred to.

For the purpose in question, it was decided attention should be focused on two of the tools most widely used in the legal analysis of collective labour relations: a general and fundamental concept of collective labour law, i.e. *collective autonomy*; and a tried and tested model of industrial relations activity, i.e. *pluralism*. A "targeted" analysis of the concepts and models concerned will reveal the total unsuitability of the latter for representing the dynamics of European bargaining and of the former for representing the terms in which such bargaining relates to the Community legal order.

The choice decided upon nevertheless warrants (or even demands) at least some brief justification, given the numerous (and no less relevant) other methodological possibilities that could have been used. Obviously, collective autonomy and pluralism are not the only methodological options available to a labour lawyer intent on the systematic representation, interpretation and rationalisation of collective bargaining dynamics. The history of the conflict between the possible methodological alternatives for analysing bargaining systems can, in fact, be identified with the very history of labour law *tout court*.[14]

However, it is not by accident that collective autonomy and pluralism were selected from the labour lawyer's stock of methodological tools, to be used with reference to the arguments which concern us here. They are particularly well suited to the purposes of the present study, which is essentially designed to show that the traditional interpretative tools, although firmly established, prove to be of little use in developing a unitary frame of reference for the roles and functions of European bargaining. The decision to concentrate attention on collective autonomy and pluralistic models is supported by several circumstances.

First, there is (on an objective plane) solid and widespread acceptance of collective autonomy as an explanatory concept for the legal significance of collective bargaining phenomena, and of pluralistic models as general observational schemes for the sociological, legal and politico-economic rationalisation of a non-unitary social and political reality. This is not, of course, intended to give the false impression that they have a monopoly; it is, however, undeniable that,

[14] For a re-examination of some institutions of Italian trade union law in the light of the basic methodological options which have been compared in relation to each of them, see the articles in D'Antona (ed.), 1990.

although not hegemonic, they constitute a widely accessible basis for discussion and comparison.

Secondly, there is an incidental fact, specific to the issues in question, which cannot be ignored. It relates to the present state of the art of the copious literature accumulated on the subject, and consists in the frequency with which the concepts and models concerned are featured with reference to the bargaining activity carried on by the social partners at Community level.

And lastly (on a subjective plane), there is the fact of an unavoidable methodological choice of a personal nature, which may be said to be "dictated by the burden of explanation or at least awareness of the hermeneutic procedure used" (D'Antona, 1990 at p. 224).

The adoption of the above-mentioned hermeneutic schemes may well appear somewhat unusual, given that collective autonomy and pluralism are used here not in order to affirm their relevance to the analysis of supranational bargaining, but for the sole purpose of demonstrating that they are unusable in the particular case in point. Odd though it may seem, this confirms the basic assumption that has been stated several times: the more they are regarded as generally valid and appropriate for understanding the various forms of trade union organisation and collective bargaining activity, the more the inconsistencies and incongruities produced by these heuristic tools in relation to the particular reality of European bargaining processes confirm the need to develop a new and different theoretical frame of reference for those processes. If, in short, at the end of the observations which follow, collective autonomy and pluralism prove inadequate for explaining, reflecting, containing or interpreting Community collective bargaining, the inevitable conclusion will be that other interpretative schemes are needed.

This will lead, by way of conclusion, to the advancement of a radically alternative interpretative proposal (Chapter 6, section 2 below).

4

European Collective Bargaining and Hermeneutic Categories: The Need for a New Theoretical Framework

1 PRIVATE LAW CLASSIFICATION OF COLLECTIVE AGREEMENTS AND TRADE UNION "AGENCY" IN THE COMMUNITY SYSTEM

AS INDICATED IN earlier chapters, the observations which follow are aimed at demonstrating why European collective bargaining is *not* to be viewed as evidence of a true European social, and therefore legal, pluralism, but rather as a normative construction of the Maastricht ASP; in this sense, they constitute the *pars destruens* of my argument. To support this viewpoint I have chosen to illustrate the functional peculiarity of European collective bargaining on the basis of a process of reasoning *a contrario*, i.e. by seeking to show that the categories used in the legal conceptualisation of previous collective bargaining experiences at national level cannot feasibly be applied to explaining European bargaining. The particular categories used to demonstrate this unsuitability will be the concepts of collective identity, employee representation, the pluralist model of industrial relations, collective autonomy and neo-corporatist models.

There is no doubt that one of the major methodological options of collective labour law which still constitutes an obligatory element of any analysis of collective bargaining phenomena, just as it did almost ninety years ago, is represented by the well-known schools of thought which, adopting a variety of approaches, have sought to relate collective organisation and, above all, action to the common law of contract. Starting from the early decades of the twentieth century these tendencies, although emerging at different stages and "lasting" for different lengths of time, have, as is widely known, been a feature of more than one legal system in continental Europe.[1] The debate that grew up in French

---

[1] For a historical approach to the debate on the civil law reconstruction of collective organisation and collective agreements, see Rusciano, 1984; Caruso, 1989; Romagnoli, 1974; Mengoni, 1975 now 1985; Vardaro, 1985a. For an impassioned defence of the inherently private law nature of collective industrial associations and their activities, see Santoro Passarelli, 1969; and also by the same author, the now standard work on collective autonomy, Santoro Passarelli, 1959. On the significance to be attributed to the development of private law conceptions of the collective industrial association and of collective bargaining in Italy and other European countries and, in particular, the reasons for the longer-lasting success of the former, see the admirable comments by Vardaro, 1984 at pp. 47–64.

doctrine on the subject of the legal nature of *conventions collectives*, for example, was certainly no less intense than that in Italy or Germany.[2] Whole generations of French labour lawyers applied themselves to the disagreement between the *contractuel* versus *réglementaire* nature of collective agreements, before finally reaching widespread acceptance of the *dualistic* hypothesis[3] put forward in a now classic article by one of the founding fathers of labour law in that country (Durand, 1939).

This is certainly not the place to trace the steps of the importance which the private law theory of collective labour law came to assume, becoming so "universal" during a particular period in history that it was "elevated to the rank of a legal meta-institution of collective labour relations . . . an obligatory topos of any study (whether descriptive or prescriptive) of collective bargaining" (Vardaro, 1984 at p. 67). And it is even less the place to make evaluations or judgements which would require supporting arguments far beyond the scope of the present book.[4]

The only reason for mentioning these circumstances surrounding the private law classification of collective agreements in many European legal systems is as the context for an initial partial conclusion of my line of argument here, which can be summarised as follows: a reconstruction of European collective agreements based on theoretical schemes of the common law of contract and the concept of agency would find less room to accommodate it than it was or still is possible to find in the case of national collective agreements, in relation to which those interpretative schemes were developed in the past. In short, the solution of what—alluding to the technical legal classification of Community collective agreements—has been called "an unsolved riddle . . . which legal scholars do not know how to answer" (Romagnoli, 1995a at p. 255) does not seem to lie in a common law of contract which would, moreover, be difficult to define.

It is true (even if debatable) that the agents of Community bargaining can be regarded as mere associative projections of bargaining agents as they operate in national systems. It is also true (but likewise debatable) that the effects of the agreements they sign are destined to reverberate, in some way, within individ-

---

[2] See, as respective examples, Messina, 1907 now 1986; and Lotmar, 1900 now 1984.

[3] "Lors de sa conclusion, la convention collective est traitée comme un contrat . . . Lors de son application la convention collective est traitée comme un règlement" (Lyon-Caen, G., Pélissier and Supiot, 1994 at pp. 753–754). In similar terms, see also Despax, 1989 at Part I, sect. 3, ch. 1. There is a good deal of similarity between the "dualistic" thesis almost unanimously accepted by French doctrine and the likewise classic description of the collective agreement as a "hybrid" which is a contract in body and a law in spirit, provided in Italy by Carnelutti. More generally, on the relationship between labour law and civil law in France, see the collected articles in the special issue, with that title, of *Droit social* No. 5, 1988, and in particular Langlois, 1988, who returns there to some of the issues already discussed in an earlier article (Langlois, 1975) regarding the lasting centrality in the field of collective labour law of the civil law concept of agency.

[4] On the other hand, Giugni's well-known article on "the actors of collective labour law" is certainly "evaluative" and, indeed, explicitly concerned with considerations of legal policy: expressly extending the evaluation to other legal systems as well as the Italian one, it states that "civil-law reasoning carries within it implied conservative values and effects of institutional viscosity which can, in fact, make it inadequate when applied to new social matters" (Giugni, 1970 now 1989 at p. 204).

ual national systems. And it is therefore true—this time necessarily debatable—that in such a context it would be possible to view the idea of Community bargaining as just a further level of the national bargaining system, and therefore to use the conceptions particular to each national system in order to absorb the new European instance into national interpretations of the collective agreement possibly based on the private law concept of agency. It would merely be a matter of adding one more level to those already existing in each national system and attributing to the European trade union organisations the status of representative agents of the national associations affiliated to them and therefore, in the final analysis, of Community employees.

However, it can be objected (and it is this which makes the whole thing debatable) that a rationalisation of this kind fails to take account of an element which it seems quite impossible to ignore: the fact that, in the case of *Community* collective bargaining, the legal order of reference happens to be, in the first place, the *Community* legal order, within which the use of the concepts of agency and the common law of contract would be at the very least perplexing, for the simple reason that in that legal order even the identification of such a law would cause enormous difficulties. In the absence of a specific "legal status for European collective agreements" (Jeammaud, 1998 at p. 71), what would be the EC common law of contract to be used in a purely "contractualist" or "agency-oriented" reconstruction of such agreements? What contract law would European agreements be subject to? According to what legal rules would they be considered as a legitimate expression of European employees' interests and wishes? Would it be possible to regard European collective agreements as directly applicable[5] to the individual employment contracts of those who are members of the affiliated organisations, as some authors argue (Franssen, 1998)?[6] And if so, according to what private law of contract?

Even setting aside such external considerations, however, purely on the different plane of an internal evaluation it can be said that careful scrutiny of the structural and functional characteristics of Community bargaining is enough to exclude or limit the validity of interpretative constructions derived, *mutatis mutandis*, from the civil law doctrine of contract and agency.

There is certainly no need to remind ourselves that, since the first reconstructions developed at the beginning of the century by both Italian and German doctrine, the operation of "hooking" collective labour law onto the common law of contract has always been fundamentally based on the private law concept of, and behind this the actual idea of, bargaining agency; on the presupposition, therefore, of the existence of a legally effective relationship between a representative agent (the trade union) and a principal being represented (the employee). And it is precisely the absence, or at any rate the extremely tenuous nature, of such a relationship, the essential presupposition of all private law interpretations of

---

[5] That is, without the two modes of implementation provided for by Article 139(2) TEC.

[6] For an answer in the negative, see Sciarra, 1995b at p. 329, who states: "No individual employee or employer in the member countries could claim to enforce them directly".

bargaining phenomena, which would seem to advise against any attempted reconstruction of Community collective bargaining in that direction.

Not only does there not seem to exist between Community employee and Community trade union organisation a relationship of representation structurally comparable to that between national employee and national union on which private law models of bargaining have always been based; neither does it actually appear possible, in functional terms, to class the negotiating activity carried on by the Community social partners as representation *tout court*, even allowing for the many different constructions which can be put upon this very general category.[7] A number of considerations which are relevant on various planes seem to support these conclusions, both in their "weak" version (non-comparability of the relationship of representation between Community employee and Community trade union organisation to the relationship of representation between national employee and national union) and in their "strong" version (impossibility of classing the relationship between Community employees and trade union organisations as representation). The degree of credit given to these considerations, which are set out below, will determine the possibility, or otherwise, of fitting Community collective bargaining into the framework of the common law of contract. Given that the application of civil law categories to collective bargaining has always been justified and used with reference to the notion of agency,[8] if (as I shall attempt to demonstrate) that concept cannot describe the relation between a Community employee and the negotiating activity performed by a Community trade union organisation, then the logical conclusion will be that such activity cannot be related to those categories. But let us take things in order.

The considerations invoked in support of the hypothesis presented here can be summarised as referring to:

(i) the structure and forms through which collective bargaining can feature in the Community legal order; and
(ii) the overall developments which have taken place in the past few years in regard to the role of the union in the context of several European systems.

(i)

The instances of bargaining envisaged by the ASP, and now by the EC Treaty, are conventionally viewed as classifiable into three types.

As regards the first (implementational or transpositional) type, the reasons why it can be excluded from the notion of European collective bargaining and,

---

[7] For a definition of the concepts relating to collective industrial representation, see Caruso, 1990b and 1992 at Part II, ch. III, sect. I; also, the interesting suggestions put forward by Borenfreund, 1991 and 1997.

[8] See, along these lines, Mengoni, 1990 at p. 16, according to whom the "element of connection with civil common law [is] related to the private-law concept of agency".

consequently, from the scope of this study have already been discussed in Chapter 3, section 2 above.

The other two types, however, involve forms of collective bargaining which can properly be described as *Community* bargaining. As stated earlier, they concern the hypotheses envisaged by Article 138 (2–3–4) and Article 139(1) TEC, distinguishable from each other depending on the "voluntary" or "induced" origin of the bargaining procedure entered upon by the social partners (see Table I below).

What must be stressed at this stage, in common to both hypotheses, is the "price" which supranational collective agreements have to pay in order to acquire "visibility" in the Community legal order: a price consisting in the limitation of the range of issues within which such agreements are deemed to "merit" legal effectiveness at Community level. A pre-defined range coinciding with the scope of Community competence, which as in other fields is, of course, very restricted in the field of social matters.[9] This conclusion is axiomatically imposed by the very structure of the rules provided for. As stated earlier, examination of Articles 138 and 139 TEC leads to a twofold hypothesis:

(a) either the bargaining process may take place on the occasion of or during the course of an initiative on the part of the Commission ("induced" negotiation), in which case coincidence between Community competence and the content of collective agreements is *in re ipsa*; or

(b) the social partners initiate an autonomous bargaining process to which the Community institutions remain extraneous as regards both its genesis and its progress ("voluntary" negotiation). In this second case, the agreement reached between the social partners can then acquire legal force within the Community system (through a Council decision) only to the extent that the associated content falls within the Community's competence,[10] since it is only where this is so that the signatory parties may actually request "implementation" of the agreement by a Council decision.

It is true that the required coincidence between the content of a collective agreement and the scope of the Community's competence may be lacking in the case of agreements "with unrestricted content" (Guarriello, 1992 at p. 233), in respect of which no request is made for their implementation by way of

[9] For an analysis of Community competence in social matters, see Shaw, 1994; Whiteford, 1995; Szyszczak, 1995; Barnard, 1996; Bercusson, 1996; Arrigo, 1996; Nielsen and Szyszczak, 1997. For a critical analysis of Community social competence up to the Maastricht Treaty on European Union, see Davies, 1992.

[10] Even a voluntarily based collective agreement could therefore be implemented by a Council decision, provided it deals with matters falling within the Community's competence. Contrary to this reconstruction, Betten, 1998 argues that negotiations which are initiated voluntarily (i.e. those initiated without waiting for a Commission proposal) can never fall within the ASP: "An agreement by social partners not based on an initial Commission proposal would fall outside the context of Community law. The Maastricht Agreement on Social Policy clearly implies that the social partners can take a proposal away from the Commission. If there is no such proposal, there is nothing to take away" (at p. 29).

intervention by the Community institutions. Where this is the case (as will be discussed in more detail in Chapter 5, section 1 below), such agreements have absolutely no legal significance at all for the Community legal order. It seems rather superfluous that the social partners are granted "authorisation" to implement an agreement concluded at Community level "in accordance with the procedures and practices specific to management and labour and the Member States" (Article 139(2) TEC). This apparently harmless provision was, nevertheless, regarded as a potential source of unwanted misunderstandings, given that the Member States indicated the need to annex to the ASP a Declaration on the matter,[11] clearly intended as a precaution to exclude any possible spillover of the provision in question towards the adoption of more binding forms of legislative support of the bargaining activity of the Community social partners.

As described so far, the situation can be represented schematically as shown in Table 1.

Leaving a more searching appraisal of these provisions until later (Chapters 5 and 6), it may be pointed out in the meantime that the social partners' bargaining function as thus "recognised" by the Community institutions can essentially be identified as one directed at *assisting the adoption of a Community normative provision.* Support for bargaining it may well be, but it is certainly not disinterested support.

If that, put at its briefest, is the image of the social partners' organisations and collective bargaining which appears on the Community institutions' screens, we need to examine—returning to the discourse from which we started out—whether and to what extent these new scenarios are compatible with a private law reconstruction of supranational bargaining and with an associative idea of representation.

On the basis of what has been said so far, the answer can only be in the negative.

Dispossessed of the authority to delimit autonomously the scope of their own bargaining activity, and therefore restricted in the actual definition of the interests to be protected, the European social partners' organisations seem to have gained the legitimacy and standing accorded them by the Community institutions mainly on the basis of a Commission strategy, even if one which could be appreciated, and less by virtue of their capacity to represent the rights and interests of their respective "members" (if they can still be referred to as such). In short, the structure of Community bargaining contains no visible signs of the

---

[11] "The eleven High Contracting Parties declare that the first of the arrangements for application of the agreements between management and labour at Community level—referred to in Article 4(2)—will consist in developing, by collective bargaining according to the rules of each Member State, the content of the agreements, and that consequently this arrangement implies no obligation on the Member States to apply the agreements directly or to work out rules for their transposition, or any obligation to amend national legislation in force to facilitate their implementation", *Declaration on Article 4(2)*, now *Declaration 27* of the Treaty of Amsterdam. See also, for an authentic interpretation of the Declaration concerned, the *Communication of the Commission on the application of the Agreement on Social Policy* (COM(93) 600 final of 14.12.1993, at para. 37).

Table 1: (1) "Voluntary" and "Induced" European collective agreements (2) "Weak" and "strong" implementation of such agreements

(1) Two possible origins of negotiation between the European social partners:

"Voluntary" . . . →

. . . and "Induced" negotiation →

Should management and labour so desired, the dialogue between them at Community level may lead to contractual relations, including agreements (Art. 139(1) TEC)

. . . before submitting proposals in the social policy field, the Commission shall consult management and labour on the possible direction of Community action. If, after such consultation, the Commission considers Community action advisable, it shall consult management and labour on the content of the envisaged proposal. Management and labour shall forward to the Commission an opinion or, where appropriate, a recommendation. On the occasion of such consultation, management and labour may inform the Commission of their wish to initiate the process provided for in Article 139. The duration of the procedure shall not exceed nine months, unless the management and labour concerned and the Commission decide jointly to extend it (Art. 138(2), 138(3) and 138(4))

EUROPEAN COLLECTIVE AGREEMENT

(2) Two possible ways of implementing a European collective agreement:

"Weak" . . . →

and "strong" implementation →

in accordance with the procedures and practices specific to management and labour and the Member States (Art. 139(2))

in matters covered by Article 137, at the joint request of the signatory parties, by a Council decision on a proposal from the Commission.
The Council shall act by qualified majority, except where the agreement in question contains one or more provisions relating to one of the areas referred to in Article 137(3), in which case it shall act unanimously (Art. 139(2))

characteristic features of the original associative dimension of collective activity; as a result, the idea (ingrained in that dimension) of the representation of a collective body of employees has little prominence. The form of collective activity outlined by the ASP therefore lacks not only legal form but also any reference to the logical category of representation itself: to this "formula encapsulating a clutch of power and consensus relationships as differentiated between those being represented and their representatives" (Caruso, 1992 at p. 194) which in any event presupposes acting in the name, on behalf of and in the interest of others.

Now, whether we choose to regard the activity of representation as a manifestation which confers legal significance on a pre-existing group, or choose to believe that the identity of the group as such is actually created as a result of that representation (Borenfreund, 1991),[12] the procedures for collective action recognised by the Community legal order do not allow room for the relationship between Community employee and Community trade union organisation in either scheme. The European unions do not constitute the expression of a "communion naturelle d'intérêts" (Borenfreund, 1991 at p. 687) ascribable to the collectivity of Community employees—and in this specific sense, therefore, do not represent them—since the interests for which their bargaining activity is prescribed are, as we have seen, largely determined heteronomously[13] and essentially related to overcoming the Community's regulatory difficulties. It necessarily follows from this that the activity of the European trade union organisations does not "construct" the collectivity of Community employees in legally effective terms, nor does it delineate a collective interest specifically ascribable to them; not, at least, as long as it remains exclusively tied to the procedures laid down by the ASP.

What those procedures provide for is a trade union organisation and, above all, a collective bargaining which (in the particular sense just described) do not represent Community employees.

(ii)

Nevertheless, as is perhaps obvious, these conclusions are no reason to belittle the role of Community trade union organisations and collective bargaining and dismiss them both as instruments which serve purposes extraneous to them.

Recording the progressive distancing of the trade union from its original associative dimension towards the assumption of an institutional function does not

---

[12] See also Supiot, 1994 at p. 125, who, from a historical perspective, defines "fraternité" between employees as one of the "liens sociaux susceptibles de faire accéder un groupe à la vie juridique". See also p. 33 in the same text.

[13] Even in the early 1970s, in relation to the limited range of matters falling within the competence of the Joint Committees (the first embryonic manifestations of a European social dialogue), reference was already being made to collective agreements being "encadrées ou prisonnières" (Lyon-Caen, G., 1973–74 at p. 28), restricted in the choice of bargaining issues.

amount to envisaging a sort of "Franco dictatorship model" of trade unionism. Far from being an exclusive prerogative of the Community legal order, the gradual affirmation of the institutional logic of the trade union is nowadays becoming a feature common to many European systems (Romagnoli, 1996).[14]

Indeed, it is on the basis of developments at national level that the eclipse of the logical category of representation, and of the associative dimension of the trade union which was originally its natural *pendant*, started to shake the legal edifice which private law conceptions of the collective agreement had successfully built up from them, causing it to totter. When, in the national context, the trade union began to be assigned a type of function broadly definable as "public" (D'Antona, 1987), the concept of representation, which until then had maintained an undeniable centrality, was forced to give way to the different concept of representativeness,[15] which represents, if not an actual negation of the former, a "heteronomistic alternative" (Scarpelli, 1993a at p. 134) in the sense that it seems oriented more towards selecting union organisations capable of performing the new "public" functions than towards consolidating the associative relationships between those being represented and their representatives.

Nor did this situation escape the attention of alert observers from the different perspective of sociological analysis, where it is the subject of well-known and respected reconstructions representing it in terms of a conflict between the trade union as a "*mouvement social*" and the trade union as an "*agence sociale*": "Ces deux dimensions restaient jusqu'à présent fortement articulées, elles étaient même indissociables: c'est en tant que mouvement social que le syndicalisme voyait ses prérogatives d'agence sociale élargies. L'institutionnalisation du fait syndical marque une nouvelle étape, beaucoup plus récente: elle correspond à une autonomisation de la fonction d'agence sociale qui se dissocie de son support d'origine, le mouvement social" (Rosanvallon, 1988 at p. 38).[16]

Nothing radically new, therefore—to all appearances, at any rate.

In point of fact, the "collective bargaining without representation" of the Community system cannot be likened entirely to the processes of institutionalisation of the trade union which have just been mentioned. What in the national context constituted the non-exclusive outcome of a lengthy historical evolvement constitutes, in the Community context, the exclusive trade mark of the supranational trade union organisation and collective bargaining. In short, European collective bargaining has been born with the characteristics which

---

[14] Who represents this change as a transition from an ethic of consensus, on which the self-government of groups is based, to an ethic of responsibility for everything to do with the institutions (Romagnoli, 1996 at p. 13).

[15] In the case of France and Spain see, respectively, Verdier, 1991; Borenfreund, 1988; and Escudero Rodriguez, 1990; Casas Baamonde, 1990.

[16] A concept which is directly translatable into legal terms. See Borenfreund, 1991 at p. 689, according to whom: "L'action du mouvement syndical contribue autant sinon plus à une meilleure gouvernabilité de la société, qu'à une expression immédiate des aspirations des travailleurs"; and Scarpelli, 1993b at p. 167, who talks of an "attribution of legally based powers 'different' from the power which derives from the coalition of private individuals for the purposes of self-protection".

national bargaining did not acquire until its "mature" phase, and without having first passed through dimensions or functions other than those which the Community system deemed could or should be reserved for it:[17] a circumstance representing one of the presuppositions which confirm the need to apply to Community bargaining cognitive schemes and legal categories different from those valid for national bargaining.[18]

2 COLLECTIVE AUTONOMY AND EUROPEAN COLLECTIVE BARGAINING: THE MANY REASONS FOR AN INCOMPATIBILITY

Having demonstrated the reasons for rejecting a "Community projection" of the civil law categories used in the reconstruction of employee representation and collective bargaining, we now turn our attention to other established observational schemes which at first sight could appear better able to "contain" the bargaining phenomena featuring in the Community system.

The purpose, as already indicated, is to assess the degree to which the category of collective autonomy and the pluralist observational scheme (both frequently referred to in attempted systematic reconstructions of Community collective bargaining) represent interpretative tools which are really consistent with the latter's specific structural and functional characteristics. This operation does not involve an analytical study of the categories, schemes and models concerned, which would have little meaning, nor a critical assessment of their overall scientific plausibility, but an attempt to verify, systematically, the (few) correspondences and (many) differences that can confirm or refute the claim that Community bargaining may be interpreted in terms of collective autonomy and pluralism.

In the case of collective autonomy, approaching the subject undeniably prompts a sense of uneasiness, since it could perhaps be described as a victim of its own success. In the course of its now lengthy existence,[19] many scholars have used it as an almost obligatory reference element of numerous doctrinal inter-

---

[17] According to a recent reconstruction of the trade unions' "pouvoir de représentation" (Borenfreund, 1997 at p. 1007), "dans l'esprit de ses fondateurs, le syndicalisme entendait même s'identifier avec le groupe . . . Cette vision quasi fusionnelle s'est peu à peu éteinte, mais il ne fait aucun doute que les collectivités de salariés ont joué un rôle sensible dans la naissance et la consolidation du pouvoir de représentation que la loi confère aux syndicats". These remarks were made with reference to a particular national system (the French one) but are perfectly applicable to other national systems. Could we also refer them to European unions and collective bargaining? Probably not.

[18] Similarly, as long ago as 1973 (but the author stated that the study dated from 1971), Lyon-Caen, G., 1973–74 at p. 593, according to whom: "La convention collective européenne, ou ce que l'on appelle ainsi, ne peut pas avoir beaucoup de points communs avec la convention collective du travail jusqu'à présent pratiquée".

[19] Which as far as Italy is concerned can be traced back, in its original private law formulation, to Santoro Passarelli, 1949 now 1961. For a critical historical assessment of the concept of collective autonomy in the French doctrine and legal system, see Yannakourou, 1995 at Part I, sect. I, ch. II.

pretations and/or legal policy operations which, in all the diversity of their respective approaches, have always kept to the name of the "thing" they interpret so differently, grouping together under this one name a multitude of sometimes mutually conflicting topics.[20] As a result, with the passage of time collective autonomy has become a concept conveying, and widely used with, so many different meanings that by force of circumstances it has lost almost all truly connotational specific value.

That is to say (and this constitutes a first preliminary observation) that to refer to collective autonomy *sans phrases*, without further qualification, probably has little meaning, since this expression has now become no more than a synonym of trade union activity or collective bargaining. Consequently, any discourse such as the present one which hopes to determine whether or not Community bargaining may be regarded as a manifestation of collective autonomy cannot be developed with reference to collective autonomy viewed as a single concept, but has to be pursued through the prior identification of some of its constituent elements.

According to a recent, intentionally "minimalist", definition, collective autonomy can be represented as the "power of autonomous determination of working conditions and terms and conditions of employment, the exercise of which is the typical and fundamental, though not exclusive, function of the trade union organisation".[21]

This definition directly features some of the elements which can usefully be taken into consideration for our present purposes: in particular, the *quasinormative status* attaching to acts which are an expression of collective autonomy; and also other elements of perhaps less importance such as the relation between the exercise of collective autonomy and the historically familiar face of the trade union.

With some forcing, it would also be possible to extract from the same definition a further element which is certainly equally essential to the concept of collective autonomy, namely its *originating or pre-statal nature*: it has to be agreed that, as pointed out by Mariucci, 1985 at p. 443, "within the matrix of collective

---

[20] On the same point, see Liebman, 1990 at p. 49. Aliprantis, 1980 (at p. 29), recording notes by Zöllner and Adomeit, writes that it is possible to count up to eight different definitions of collective autonomy.

[21] *European Employment and Industrial Relations Glossary: Italy*, London/Luxembourg: Sweet & Maxwell/Office for Official Publications of the European Communities, 1991. Further "national" definitions of collective autonomy given in other volumes in this impressive series (edited by T. Treu and M. Terry for the European Foundation for the Improvement of Living and Working Conditions) follow more or less the same line, variously singling out: the relation with state sources of regulation ("the term is used in the context of examining what role is or should be played by the autonomous determination of rules as against their 'heteronomous' (i.e. external) determination by a constitutionally competent authority", *France*); the "immunity" of the trade union and employers' association and the importance of the position of the individual ("power to draft internal rules on organisation . . . It is founded in the principle of personal autonomy", *Spain*); and express constitutional recognition ("The Greek Constitution establishes collective autonomy and subjects it to state regulatory powers", *Greece*).

bargaining as an originating phenomenon of autonomous regulation, there is something which cannot be related to the state legal order".

However, there are other characteristics or, more accurately, requirements of collective autonomy which are missing from the definition concerned and which are relevant not only to its description but also, more fundamentally, to its very existence. These include: what has been called, alongside collective autonomy as a function, *collective autonomy as a freedom* (Giugni, 1970 now 1989); the central importance of the *self-protection and conflict* dimension (Wedderburn, 1994 now 1995a at p. 298; 1995b at p. 406); and lastly (an element which is surely quite impossible to ignore), *autonomous determination of the aims and content of collective bargaining and of the employers and employees covered by it.*

It is with reference to these constituent elements that the operation of comparative "verification" mentioned earlier will now be carried out in order to assess the "compatibility" of the characteristics of Community collective bargaining with those of collective autonomy.

2.1 A collective autonomy without employees?

In some recent historical critiques of collective labour law, the "*invention du collectif*" is dated from the beginnings of the collective identity and legal personality acquired by groups of workers identified on the basis of their shared position of subordination within an employment relationship (Supiot, 1994 at p. 111).

Some years before this, a similar idea of necessary interpenetration between the individual dimension and collective dimension of labour law had been advanced in Italy, in the context of a more systematically reconstructional proposal which explicitly sought to eliminate what was considered an artificial conventional division, and to refer both dimensions to a single case (employment in a position of subordination), treating them alike as its constituent elements (Pedrazzoli, 1985).

These two publications, which in some ways—despite the difference in their underlying approach—are complementary to each other,[22] provide the cue for a discourse on "Community" collective bargaining starting from its foundations.

The lowest common denominator of the doctrinal reconstructions concerned (in terms of relevance to the purposes of the present study) can be summed up, in what is perhaps an oversimplification, as their shared reference to a *typified personal situation as forming the foundation of collective autonomy.* In this sense, the typification of the employee's personal situation through the category

---

[22] Sometimes assuming tones of total agreement: "The case of bargaining typical of the subordinate employee and collective organisation go hand in hand, since in terms of legal categories neither is conceivable without the other" (Pedrazzoli, 1985 at p. 343). "L'individuel et le collectif ne sont donc séparables l'un de l'autre, car il s'agit des deux dimensions d'une même relation juridique" (Supiot, 1994 at p. 139).

of subordination may be regarded primarily as the logical and chronological presupposition of the creation of a collective legal personality; to put it another way, as an indispensable constituent element of collective autonomy.

Alternatively, in what might be termed a more radical version, the connection between the normative typification of the subordinate employee figure and the legal significance acquired by the collective dimension is no longer represented in terms of a linear chronological sequence, but taken to the point of "fusing" the two into a single concept of employment in a position of subordination in which the collective dimension co-exists with, without blotting out, the individual dimension.

It is, in fact, undeniable that labour law, viewed as a corpus of social legislation, contributed historically to the definition of a social and legal identity for employees as *hommes situés*,[23] as well as to the emergence of a collective identity relating to them.[24] But by a sort of reverse route, the progressive development of a collective identity for individuals who share a common situation of subordination helped to shape the legal categories of (collective) labour law, including collective autonomy.

Obviously, the possible doctrinal reconstructions directed at providing a *juridical* rationalisation of the historical processes which led to the emergence of a collective dimension of the employment relationship and labour law extend beyond those mentioned here.[25] However, a first conclusion could be formulated as follows: in the legal development of a collective identity for employees or a collective dimension of labour law it remains essential—in all the various options possible—for it to have reference to a typical figure of the subordinate employee, whose normative typification may constitute, depending on the different options, either the historical and logical *presupposition* of collective autonomy or the *product* of the latter's typifying function.

It may also be said (as a second conclusion perhaps more directly relevant to our present purposes) that the normative typification of the employee figure, which is equally essential to the development or the explanation of a legally effective collective identity, resides fundamentally in the fact that the collective group of employees shares a common legal position: hence, subjection to an equal power or enjoyment of equal rights.

---

[23] All kinds of names and descriptions may be used for this bond of identity. According to Supiot (as already mentioned in n. 12 above), it can be described in terms of "fraternité"; a fraternity which, in the vivid language used by that author, "se noue dans la paternité mythique que représente la Loi, la Loi qui nous définit, et qui fait de nous ce que nous sommes" (Supiot, 1994 at p. 83).

[24] In similar terms to those used by the doctrine mentioned in the preceding footnote, the shaping effect of legal rules on the creation of a collective identity for employees is emphasised by Jeammaud, 1994 at p. 347, according to whom it must not be forgotten how much the "collective fact" owes to the constitutive effect of legal rules, without which the social fact, which is assumed to "precede the law", would not be what it is.

[25] Analysis of the dynamics and processes which underlie and originate collective action on the part of employees, and not just employees, continues to be the subject of a copious literature including, and perhaps above all, publications outside the legal literature. See Birnbaum, 1990; Crouch, 1982; Crouch and Marquand, 1995; and the classic work by Olson, 1965.

Drawing together the comments made so far, the underlying path of logic is as follows: (1) given the initial question of verifying whether or not Community collective bargaining can be regarded as a manifestation of collective autonomy, (2) it is discovered that, in the various doctrinal reconstructions of the latter which have been put forward, collective autonomy implies reference to a typical employee figure, and (3) it is concluded (although admittedly forgoing any more searching and complex debate on the matter) that the normative typification of the employee figure presupposes that the employees concerned possess uniform rights. Examining the possibility of anchoring Community bargaining to the concept of collective autonomy leads, in fact, to the definition of a presupposition whose recurrence appears to dictate the answer to the initial question: *uniformity of the rights of Community employees*, which is, however, anything but the case in the Community context.

If, as it has been said, "l'identité collective des salariés est étroitement liée à la spécificité et à l'uniformité des droits qui leur sont reconnus" (Supiot, 1994 at p. 90), it has to be asked whether and to what extent it is possible, in the Community context, to talk of collective identity and collective autonomy. For the reasons given below, it would appear that the answer has to be extremely doubtful.

If we subscribe to the idea that the law "constructs" collective identity through a normative typification of the employee figure which operates on the basis of the recognition of uniform rights for the employees concerned, all this seems untenable in the Community system, where there is no evidence at all of a uniformity of rights which could endow it with the "fraternity" of Community employees (see footnotes 12 and 23).

If, on the other hand, we subscribe to the equally reasonable reconstructions according to which collective autonomy itself contributes to the legal typification of the employee and qualifies this figure as such, it is once again the provisions of the Community legal order which militate against the possibility of talking of a Community collective autonomy, as will be shown by an analysis of those Treaty provisions which fundamentally undermine the very presuppositions of the typifying function hypothetically attributed to collective autonomy. For those provisions, as they have been worded (and also as they have been interpreted by the Community institutions on the first occasions of their application), do *not* guarantee the social partners who sign European collective agreements autonomous determination of the circle of employers and employees to be covered by a given agreement, nor preservation of the content regarding which the agreement has been concluded; nor, in the case of "weak" agreements, any effectiveness other than that which the social partners themselves are able to give it. In these circumstances it seems, frankly, rather difficult to talk of a typifying function contributed by collective autonomy.

Unlike what has happened historically in national systems, therefore, in the Community context uniformity of rights does not represent a catalyst that can bring about the typification of a Community employee figure and the creation of an associated collective identity on which to base a collective autonomy of transnational effect and dimension. However, that does not mean we have to accept the "disappearance" of employees from the stage on which attempted reconstructions of a notion of Community collective autonomy are presented; nor does it exclude the possibility of identifying different factors (other than subordination and uniformity of rights) to support a possible normative typification of the Community employee, on the basis of which a collective identity can then develop and the collective autonomy of Community employees can acquire a more definite legal significance.

It is simply a question of identifying any such factors.

The paucity of the quantitative dimension of what could, inappropriately, be called the Community collective bargaining system has already been mentioned several times. As a result, any legal factors which may help to identify a typical Community employee figure (and thus act as the "combining elements" or "catalysts" of a possible collective identity for Community employees) have to be sought in the area of Community positive law, and this, as is well known, offers little promise to anyone hoping to find in it the features of a systematic organic structure, which is non-existent, at least as far as labour law is concerned.[26] Nevertheless, an evolutive interpretation of some of the principles it contains might lend itself to providing a potentially adequate reference basis for identifying the legal presuppositions to assist the establishment and consolidation of a Community collective autonomy.

(i)

The first such principle is the freedom of movement for workers, already indicated by some authors as a possible "flywheel" of collective autonomy in the Community legal order: "Full implementation of the principle of freedom of movement for workers . . . implies, among many other things, recognition in the Community system of the role of collective bargaining between the social partners" (Aparicio Tovar, 1996b at p.173).[27] As regards the identification of factors capable of explaining the formation of a collective dimension of labour law, in other words, freedom of movement could be the functional equivalent, in the Community context, of what subordination has been in the national context.

For the time being these remain no more than suggestions, as yet to be developed and not supported by consistent Community attitudes; not even on the part of the Court of Justice, of which it has been said (probably too harshly) that it "was never interested in social policy as such, for example in transforming

[26] D'Antona, 1996 prefers to talk of a "communitisation" of certain areas of labour law, and not the creation of a common Union labour law. On the present non-existence of a European labour law, see Däubler, 1998.

[27] However, the same author feels compelled to add, immediately, that "a statement of this type, although certainly not unjustified on the legal plane, has not yet met with any correspondence in the realm of fact".

individual rights to labor market participation into collective rights to individual or social citizenship" (Streeck, 1995b at p. 399).[28] Such suggestions are also seriously undermined, in other ways, by the absence of a legally effective concept of the Community employee, which, again, the case law of the Court of Justice—with its "minimalist" decisions—has done little to help delineate.[29]

Nevertheless, there are other pointers (discernible not just in the Treaty provisions but also in the evolvement of secondary Community law) which give grounds for not underestimating the possibility of arriving at a more definite conceptualisation of Community collective autonomy as a result of factors including the identification of several potential *constituent elements of the Community employee concept.* Purely by way of example, and without in any way claiming to present an exhaustive argument, two regulatory developments can be cited which appear to lend some significance to this approach: Directive 91/533/EEC of 14 October 1991 and Directive 94/45/EC of 22 September 1994.

(ii)

The first of these, so little "trumpeted" by the Community institutions themselves and greeted with such lukewarm interest in the literature that it has earned the name of "the Cinderella Directive" (Clark and Hall, 1992), regulates the employer's obligation to inform employees of the conditions applicable to the contract or employment relationship.

At first sight the provisions contained in the Directive are not, in fact, particularly significant,[30] either in absolute terms or in relation to the prevailing national rules on the matter, and consequently seem to justify the lack of attention they have generally attracted. Correlatively, the claim that is possible to balance on the weak shoulders of the Directive concerned the enormous rock of Community collective autonomy should, it might seem, be received with a scepticism bordering on disbelief.

[28] Although the statement cited was formulated by the author concerned in general terms, it seems perfectly possible to refer it to the point under consideration.

[29] The Court's case law in the matter of defining the Community employee concept is censured by Supiot, 1994 at p. 24, who draws attention to the clearly economic bias of its approach; "Le fait que la terminologie communautaire se réfère au travailleur plutôt qu'au contrat de travail ne doit pas être interprété comme une préférence accordée à une analyse statutaire du rapport de travail, mais bien au contraire comme une réduction du salarié à sa qualité d'offreur de services sur le marché européen . . . L'idée d'échange économique (prestation de travail contre rémunération) est première, et la notion de travailleur lui est subordonnée".

[30] The Directive obliges an employer to inform employees of the conditions applicable to their contract or employment relationship, and in particular: the identities of the parties; the place of work; the title, grade, nature or category of the work for which the employee is employed; the date of commencement of the contract or employment relationship; in the case of a temporary contract or employment relationship, the expected duration thereof; the amount of paid leave to which the employee is entitled; the length of the periods of notice to be observed by the employer and the employee should their contract or employment relationship be terminated; the initial basic amount, the other component elements and the frequencies of payment of the remuneration to which the employee is entitled; the length of the employee's normal working day or week; and the collective agreements governing the employee's conditions of work.

Nevertheless, bearing in mind what was said earlier regarding the need to identify within the Community system the elements (or traces) of a common normative status for Community employees, the Cinderella Directive 91/533/ EEC seems to have some small grounds for revenge over its more ambitious bigger sisters. Setting aside its substantive provisions, which do not seek to influence the actual terms and conditions of employment relationships, it is the envisaged objective served by the Directive in question which justifies the importance given to it here: in defining a "minimum regulatory aspect, common to all types of employment within the Community system" (Romei, 1996 at p. 457), Directive 91/533 represents a worthy attempt to apply uniformly to the employment relationships of all citizens of the European Union a canon of legal civilisation regarding the employment relationship, consisting in informing Community employees of the legal terms governing their employment. Admittedly, uniformity of the rights concerned remains quite another matter, but this in no way detracts from the fact that it is possible to discern in this directive a tendency towards the uniform treatment of employment relationships which cannot be ignored.

(iii)

The second expression of secondary Community law which lends itself to being included among what were earlier called "constituent elements", i.e. normative factors capable of helping to define the legal outlines of the typical Community employee figure, is Directive 94/45/EC on the establishment of a European Works Council or a procedure in Community-scale undertakings and Community-scale groups of undertakings for the purposes of informing and consulting employees.

In contrast to what happened in the case of Directive 91/533, this European Works Council Directive immediately commanded the attention of the international academic community and quickly became the subject of an abundant literature.[31]

The interest aroused by the Directive seems justified by a number of elements relating both to the content of its provisions and also, perhaps mainly, to the

---

[31] On the content of the Directive, see Blanpain and Windey, 1994; Richard, 1995; Heerma van Voos, 1995; McGlynn, 1995; Carlin, 1995; Rodière, 1995; Falkner, 1996; Cruz Villalon, 1996; Colaianni, 1996; Schulten, 1996; Streeck, 1997a and 1997b; Knutsen, 1997; Lorber, 1997; Wheeler, 1997; Lyon-Caen, A., 1997b; Blanpain, 1998a and the entire issue of the *Bulletin of Comparative Labour Relations*, Vol. 32/1998. On the specific problems posed by the transitional phase with reference to agreements already in existence before the Directive's entry into force (Article 13), see Laulom, 1995 and Teyssie, 1995.

For the first references to the labour law problems raised by the internationalisation of companies, see Wedderburn, 1972b. For a pioneering study carried out in the 1970s by the Wharton Industrial Research Unit of Pennsylvania University as part of a comprehensive project on "Multinational Industrial Relations", see Northrup and Rowan (eds), 1979.

(then) new "eleven-State" decision-making procedure, which was tried out (with some degree of failure)[32] for the first time on that occasion.

For our present purposes, however, we need emphasise only one particular aspect to which no great importance has yet been attributed. From the point of view of a quest for the few normative fragments capable of forming the basis of a collective autonomy which is firmly *hinged* on the collective identity of Community employees—and not merely *projected* upon them by the "benign presence of the Commission" (Wedderburn, 1995b at p. 406)—Directive 94/45 /EC may be regarded as a key potentially able to open up several interesting prospects.

Leaving the reader to refer to the copious literature cited for a detailed scrutiny of the relevant provisions, it is sufficient to record here that Directive 94/45 essentially provides for the establishment, in companies with undertakings in more than one Member State, of transnational representative bodies entitled to be informed and consulted (but not to negotiate collective agreements) on issues of *cross-border* interest. The negotiation of an agreement is provided for only in the phase leading up to the establishment of a European Works Council. Forbearing to express any opinion on this very strange provision (whereby it is possible to establish by way of bargaining a body which is not able to bargain), it may be said that the Directive's potential implications extend far beyond its substantive provisions, which not everyone considers to be adequate (McGlynn, 1995). In addition to, and perhaps even more than, the fact of the establishment of a significant number of European Works Councils[33] possessing somewhat limited powers, the latter could be viewed, and indeed function, as possible vectors of processes and mechanisms different from those specifically envisaged and extending beyond them:[34] like a kind of laboratory for experimenting with a Europeanisation of the actors and the formation of a "collective identity" (Hyman, 1996) or a possible European collective interest shared by Community employees who are represented as such; in short, as the precursors of possible forms of Community collective autonomy.[35]

---

[32] As is known, the social partners, consulted by the Commission "on the content of the envisaged proposal" (Article 3(2) of the ASP), informed the Commission "of their wish to initiate the process provided for in Article 4" (Article 3(4) of the ASP) but failed to reach an agreement and so reactivated the ordinary institutional (eleven-State) decision-making procedure.

[33] The number of Community-scale undertakings affected by the Directive is estimated at around 1150 (source: *European Trade Union Institute*). For a report on the current situation regarding agreements, see the information published in the *Supplement* of *EIRObserver*, No. 4/1998.

[34] It is, for example, possible to read in this light the voluntary negotiation of agreements to establish European Works Councils by a not inconsiderable number of British companies formally excluded from the scope of the Directive under the UK "opt-out" provided for by Protocol 14 on Social Policy annexed to the Treaty on European Union (although following the conclusion adopted at the Amsterdam European Council the Directive now applies to the UK: see the "extension" Directive 97/74/EC).

[35] The potential aptitude of European Works Councils to foster the formation of a European collective interest is denied by Wolfgang Streeck, who nevertheless concedes that this effect could ensue

It is perhaps possible to reconstruct, around the fragments of Community law identified under *(i)*, *(ii)* and *(iii)*, a typical Community employee figure in which all Community employees can recognise and identify themselves as a collectivity, and to which a series of common interests can therefore be referred. Only in those circumstances, as argued here, is it or would it be possible to talk of Community collective autonomy. Although what we have are as yet no more than a few potential starting-points, they are possibly enough to suggest that this is a path which could be worth pursuing in the future.

3 PLURALISM AND COLLECTIVE AUTONOMY IN THE COMMUNITY SYSTEM

Although, as I have attempted to demonstrate above, a discourse on collective autonomy (including Community collective autonomy) cannot help but consider the individual dimension which inevitably underlies it, from now on we must shift our attention to a legal analysis of its "collective" aspects. With respect to these aspects too, therefore, an analysis will now be made to verify the "Community-compatibility" of several cardinal concepts of collective labour law.

It is well known that, in the field of legal analysis of industrial relations, starting from a certain period in history a very particular importance came to be assumed in Europe by the doctrinal approaches and reconstructions of the Anglo-Saxon mould—if not to say simply British mould, if we regard Kahn-Freund as British and make an exception for the influence exerted during the 1950s and 1960s by the Madison institutionalist school.[36] This is certainly not meant to imply that within the British system a complete concept of collective autonomy was developed which was subsequently imported into other European systems. Apart from the fact that it would not be true,[37] it would not even be relevant to our purpose here, which is not to analyse the evolution of the various national industrial relations systems but to ascertain whether, and to what extent, Community collective bargaining may be regarded as an expression of collective autonomy.

Consequently, the consonance of interests (and, in some respects, outcomes) which it seems possible to record between the "pluralist doctrine of collective

for the other side of industry: "European works councils seem to offer European multinational companies an opportunity to develop a multinational corporate identity and comprehensive, non-parochial human resource management" (Streeck, 1997a at p. 657).

[36] In Italy, the influence of Anglo-Saxon doctrine on developments in the collective labour law debate is widely recognised: see Tarello, 1972; Treu, 1979; Balandi and Sciarra (eds), 1982, in which see, in particular, Ballestrero, 1982 for an evaluation of the influences respectively attributable to the British and to the North American model.

[37] It is, in fact, interesting to note that, in the *Glossary* series mentioned earlier (see n. 21 above), there is no entry under "collective autonomy" in the UK volume, whereas the latter, significantly, contains an entry under the term "voluntarism", which does not appear in any of the other national volumes.

bargaining"[38] and other European labour law doctrines, notably Italian doctrine[39] is mentioned only in order to emphasise its objective significance and in the belief that it was during that fruitful stage of collective labour law and industrial relations studies that a series of concepts, methods and conclusions were developed which remain, to this day, valid and useful for the purposes of formulating a theoretical construct of Community collective bargaining. In pointing to the significance of British doctrine in the field of collective labour law we introduce into our study a number of issues—pluralism, the role of legislation in shaping industrial relations systems, the significance of the constitutional (non-)recognition of the principle of freedom of association, and the very concept itself of collective bargaining—which no study of collective bargaining, including this one, can ignore.

There would seem no doubt that, above and beyond its multifarious interpretations and the alternating fortunes it has undergone, pluralism—viewed as a fundamental category of a general theory of society—constitutes the general reference model for any study of industrial relations and for the conceptualisation of collective labour law. In the sections which follow attention will therefore be focused on those aspects of the pluralist doctrine which are thought to be most relevant to the purposes of the present study.

3.1 Social pluralism and rationalisation in terms of collective labour law

In the years following the Second World War, when legal doctrine found itself confronted with the need to identify explanatory schemes capable of containing a growing phenomenology of collective bargaining (which even at the beginning of the century had begun to present an obvious contradiction to several dogmas of the legal system and legal scholarship of the day),[40] there was an inevitable upsurge of interest in the pluralist reconstructions developed in the field of *sociology*, within which it was clearly possible to find lines of reasoning consistent with the aims pursued on the plane of *legal* reconstruction.

[38] The quotation marks are needed because, although it perhaps makes more sense (while paying close heed to the different phases involved) to talk of a British collective bargaining "model", it is not possible to talk in outright unitary terms of a British pluralist "doctrine". On the contrary, conflicts of views within the pluralist school remained a constant factor in the British doctrinal debate up to the end of the 1970s. For a reconstruction of the terms of the debate, see Hyman, 1978.

[39] On the methodological renewal undergone by Italian labour law doctrine during the period concerned and the part played in that renewal by comparative labour law studies related, in particular, to the countries with common law systems, see Giugni, 1989, who refers to a gradual change which matured (in Kahn-Freundian fashion) into "a mixture of continuity and renewal" (his Introduction at p. 11).

[40] There is certainly no need for a reminder here that the emergence of trade unionism and, in particular, the first experiences of collective bargaining coincided with the decline of several of the dogmas which up till then had dominated legal scholarship: the unitary, complete and statal nature of law. On this subject see Bobbio, 1960, who (not by chance) cites among the exponents of what he calls the "reaction to legal fetishism" Eugen Ehrlich, the German legal sociologist who found confirmation of his theses concerning the normative autonomy of social groups, as is known, in collective labour law.

Indeed, it would have been strange if it had been otherwise: that is, it would have been strange if a labour law doctrine at grips with a need for legal rationalisation of the phenomena of autonomous regulation in industrial relations had neglected to consider the starting-points offered by a sociological science which formulated the reality of a complex society articulated into systems each endowed with their own autonomy,[41] and also by a political science which postulated the dismantling of the monolithic conception of the state as the sole interpreter of social interests and demands, of neo-Hegelian derivation.[42]

Even before the labour lawyers, however, it was the Madison institutional economists[43] and the industrial relations scholars of the Oxford school[44] who took up these suggestions,[45] through the development (mainly by the latter) of a series of theoretical reconstructions of the structure and activity of collective bargaining institutions which, explicitly based on the assumptions of pluralist doctrines,[46] "transcend the pragmatism and empiricism that had hitherto characterised the study of industrial relations" (Hyman, 1994 at p.166).

It is known that the evolutive parabolas successively traced by the various exponents of the pluralist school of industrial relations were far from coincident; on the contrary, they exhibited marked deviations and critical about-turns, not only between its different exponents but also between different phases in the development of an individual intellectual path.[47]

The divisions within pluralist doctrine mainly related to the contrast between the "pragmatic" and the "radical" perspectives. The *pragmatic* pluralists extolled the systemic stabilising function of the pluralist method, holding that "régimes which allow wide scope to pressure group activities have been more stable than other forms of government" (Clegg, 1975 at p. 309);[48] whereas the

[41] See, by way of example, Parsons, 1951 and 1971.

[42] See, by way of example, Laski, 1919 now 1968; Laski 1921; Duguit, 1928; Dahl, 1956. On the work of Laski and the British pluralists, see the collection of writings edited by Hirst, 1989 and, more recently, Wedderburn, 1996. In a recent article analysing the Community idea of democracy, the contribution made by the British pluralists from the early years of the century up to the pre-war period is expressly recorded by Ward, 1996, who also pauses to reflect on the relationship between "Community" democracy and social policy instruments.

[43] Commons, 1923 now 1968; Perlman, 1928.

[44] Flanders and Clegg (eds), 1954; Flanders, 1968; Fox and Flanders, 1969; Clegg, 1975.

[45] The *trait d'union* between these two schools of thinking is evident in the systemic conceptions developed by Parsons, 1951 and, with specific reference to industrial relations, by Dunlop, 1958, in which there is an identifiable emphasis on, respectively, Wisconsin institutionalism and Oxford pluralism (Vardaro, 1984 at p. 96, n. 5).

[46] Although (as Lewis, 1979 points out) a scholar who is regarded as the leading theorist of industrial relations pluralism, Allan Flanders, "did not make use of the term in his own writings" (at p. 210, n. 40). Partly correcting this statement, Hyman, 1978 adds that Flanders used the word "pluralism" for the first time only in 1966 and that another leading exponent of the Oxford school, Hugh Clegg, "does not appear to have used the term in an academic publication before his defence of pluralism in 1975" (p.23).

[47] As was the case with the "abjuration" of pluralism by Fox, 1973 and 1974: the same author who only a few years earlier had co-authored, with Flanders, an article which is considered one of the classics of the literature on industrial relations pluralism (Fox and Flanders, 1969).

[48] A stabilising function of this kind, or "the aim of eliminating the causes of disorder", is attributed to collective bargaining by Fox and Flanders, 1969 at p. 160, according to whom: "If, then, we

radicals held that, in its apparent procedural neutrality, pluralism conceals the actual imbalances of power between social groups,[49] to the point of being reducible to the status of an "ideology of far-seeing managers" and at risk of becoming a "shameful myth" (Fox, 1973 at pp. 103 and 120).[50]

In the contributions which followed the emergence of this conflict of views it is, in fact, possible to discern (even on the part of those who continued to avow their convinced support of pluralism) a kind of substantive recognition of the validity of the criticisms levelled against it which in a way "defused" the situation by marginalising the objections raised against the pluralist method as a whole to just *one* possible view of pluralism, i.e. its prescriptive aspect, in an obvious attempt to salvage its plausibility as a descriptive tool of industrial relations. Consequently, in the final versions supplied by its most notable pragmatic exponents, pluralism is no longer presented as an ideology or moral doctrine which "salves consciences and legitimises the existing industrial relations situation" (Fox, 1973 at p. 116) but is, in fact, regarded mainly as a scheme for observing the reality of collective labour relations (Kahn-Freund, 1977 at p. 15),[51] and as "an incomplete moral philosophy. It presupposes other values besides those of the pluralist ethic" (Clegg, 1975 at p. 316).

The debate over the prescriptive or descriptive nature of industrial relations pluralism is certainly one of passionate beliefs; among other things, it might be said that it bears the signs of a period of political commitment and fervour which has nowadays been rather forgotten.[52]

For our more direct purposes here, however, it is relevant only in that it helps to delineate more clearly the importance which the pluralist doctrine assumed and, inevitably, still retains for understanding the phenomena of normative

seek to construct a simple model of collective bargaining as a social process we must describe the input as conflict and disorder, just as we must describe the output as rules, including their application and adjustment".

[49] Which Fox caustically calls "romantic" pluralism: "What pluralists describe as free and par- ity- based joint regulation is nothing more than bargaining in a situation of necessity"; "The entire structure may be seen as a confused and eulogistic view of 'responsible' behaviour [on the part of employees] as a variant of the 'consolation prize' technique" (Fox, 1973 at p. 111).

[50] For a radical Marxist-type criticism of the pluralist model, see also Goldthorpe, 1974.

[51] In what is probably the most famous footnote in the history of labour law, Otto Kahn-Freund commented on the dispute over the descriptive or prescriptive nature of pluralism by saying :"I con- sider pluralism as a method of explaining what happens in a non-totalitarian society, not as an ideo- logy" (Kahn-Freund, 1977 at p. 15, n. 30). This subscription to a "purely" descriptive view of pluralism is regarded as not entirely convincing by Wedderburn, 1983 at pp. 61 and 68, who main- tains that, on the contrary, Kahn-Freund's view of pluralism remained, even in the latter part of his life, far more prescriptive and "ideological" than he chose to reveal.

[52] Recently, however, these signs of a debate which seemed lost in the mists of time have returned in the writings of those who see themselves as advocates of what has come to be called *critical legal pluralism*: "This notion that the law of the workplace is ultimately shaped by power relations, how- ever overtly or subtly exercised, makes it necessary to move beyond the basic descriptive claims of legal pluralism to a theoretical position with greater explanatory ambitions, a position which may be called critical legal pluralism" (Arthurs, 1998 at p. 30).

autonomy of social groups. And it is in that particular guise that it commanded consideration by labour lawyers, in Europe[53] but also elsewhere.[54]

The problem for labour lawyers who recognised in the pluralist paradigm the industrial and sociological presuppositions of the norm-creating nature of collective bargaining was the question of how to translate all this into legally effective terms. In this sense the pluralist labour law doctrine of the 1950s and 1960s was in a line of continuity with the legal sociology ideas of the early years of the century and with the jurist who, in that context, had emphasised the "law-creating function of autonomous collective organisations (trade unions and employers' associations) through the process of collective conflict, collective bargaining and the making of collective agreements" (Lewis, 1979 at p. 205):[55] a continuity represented by the figure and personal history of Otto Kahn-Freund.

But although there was essentially only one problem, the solutions provided in the context of the various systems inevitably differed, since they each had to ensure maximum consistency with their respective cultures and national legal and academic traditions. To take a simplified example, in a system like the German one, traditionally careful to preserve the role of the state as the authority within which special interests are adjusted in the general interest, the preferred route is the doctrine of the delegation of powers, in accordance with which the source of the normative power granted to the social partners is to be found in positive law or in the Constitution.[56]

In France, where the statist tradition is also strong and deeply rooted (if not more so), the legal effect of the normative power of collective bargaining could not, for those same reasons, be related to the concept of norm-creating

[53] One of the earliest and most important articles written by Kahn-Freund on the pluralist structure of the British system (Kahn-Freund, 1954a) was published in a volume edited by Flanders and Clegg. The relationship which developed from the 1950s onwards between Kahn-Freund and the exponents of the Oxford pluralist school of industrial relations is recorded by Clegg, 1983.

[54] With reference to North American industrial relations systems, it has recently been written that "Several generations of North American labour law and industrial relations scholars regarded collective bargaining as the central pillar of industrial relations policy, and industrial pluralism as the dominant theoretical perspective within which collective bargaining was to be understood" (Arthurs, 1998 at p. 23).

[55] The reference is to Sinzheimer and his analysis of the normative effect of collective agreements, which is, according to Kahn-Freund, "Sinzheimer's most individual contribution to the practical realisation of the principle of autonomy in labour law" (quoted by Wedderburn, 1994 now 1995a at p. 301). On the Weimar period, see Lewis and Clark (eds), 1981; Arrigo and Vardaro (eds), 1981. For a more comprehensive analysis "of the profound changes produced in the actual way of understanding labour law by the impact [of the] Weimar jurists on the Anglo-American environment", see Vardaro, 1982.

[56] Several references to the German theory of the delegation of powers are to be found in Kahn-Freund, 1976 at p. 268; for various critical comments on the theory of the delegation of powers, see Aliprantis, 1980 at pp. 32–35 and Lyon-Caen, G., 1973–74 at pp. 590–591, according to whom such an approach "restricts the bargaining organisations' room for manoeuvre". In the same article the author also refers to an attempt to apply the theory at Community level made by G. Schnorr in a report drawn up for the EEC in 1969 (*Possibilités de conventions collectives sur le plan européen*). The possibility of using the 1960s and 1970s legal literature on European collective agreements for the purposes of evaluating the current situation is excluded by Grandi, 1993 at p. 468.

autonomy and instead had to be mediated through reference to categories of statal derivation such as *l'ordre public social*[57] or, according to others, *pouvoir*.[58]

And in Italy, the formulation of the theory of *ordinamento intersindacale*[59]— unanimously seen as marking the "definitive grafting of Anglo-Saxon adversarial pluralism onto Italian legal culture" (Carabelli, 1986 at p. 37)—necessitated recourse to the *auctoritas* accorded by the Italian legal environment to the doctrine of Santi Romano, in order to make the norm-creating autonomy of the social partners less "radical" than it might have appeared if presented in other forms (Ballestrero, 1982 at p. 151).

In fact, it does not seem to provide a simplifying interpretation of the relationship between pluralist industrial relations models and the rationalisations provided in the legal sphere if we identify, behind the developments in European labour law doctrine in the face of the need to provide a plausible conceptualisation of collective bargaining's normative function, one and the same requirement: that of "enabling the facts to enter the law" (Ballestrero, 1982 at p. 150). Meaning, by *facts*, those entrenched and widespread bargaining practices for which the pluralist models had, for their part, provided an effective rationalisation on the sociological plane of industrial relations but not yet (nor could they have done) on the legal plane. In short, the purpose of the arguments set out above is to demonstrate that, from a certain phase onwards, pluralist-based rationalisation of the collective bargaining reality influenced the evolvement of labour law thinking, turning it towards the *legal conceptualisation of a notion of collective autonomy rooted in a socially typical industrial relations practice*.

All this leads us to conclude that, if stripped of its pluralist presuppositions, the concept of collective autonomy laboriously constructed by labour lawyers is in danger of becoming a "virtual" concept: possessing an apparent coherence but lacking, like all virtual realities, any reference to the world of happenings. In other words: for it to be possible to talk of collective autonomy, the phenomenological dimension in which its legal conceptualisation originates remains an essential consideration.

Hence it would appear, once again, that the Community bargaining reality cannot be related to the schemes or even the idea of collective autonomy. As was argued earlier with regard to the "individual" presuppositions of collective autonomy (section 2.1 above), any reconstruction which founded the legal ratio-

---

[57] "Le public et le collectif se trouvent étroitement liés dans la culture juridique française. L'autonomie collective ne s'y est pas développée contre ou en dehors de l'hétéronomie, mais bien au contraire en son sein, dans une aire garantie par l'Etat" (Supiot, 1994 at p. 137).

[58] See Yannakourou, 1995 at pp. 72–77. Also, an analysis of the French system (but with the aim of developing a general theory) was used as the starting-point for formulating the theory of *réception*, which seeks to interpret the relationship between systems from the viewpoint of a positivist approach of the Kelsenian type (Aliprantis, 1980).

[59] The theory of *ordinamento intersindacale*, elaborated by Gino Giugni, builds on previous *ordre juridique* theories to assert the inner legal value to be attributed to the autonomous social norms produced within the industrial relations system (Giugni, 1960).

nalisation of collective autonomy on a socially entrenched and widespread bargaining phenomenology would be difficult to transpose into the Community context, where, by contrast, it seems more accurate to talk of the mere utilisation of subjects external to the "public" institutional machinery for the purposes of resolving regulatory problems which are internal to it.

5

An Unhappy Alternative

1 "INCONSEQUENTIAL" COLLECTIVE BARGAINING

EVEN IF IT were to be assumed that the phenomenological dimension of Community collective bargaining is, or will become, such as to justify relating it to a pluralist model of collective autonomy, there are still certain "variances" which such a categorisation would inevitably encounter.

The incompatibility of Community bargaining with the pluralist model—and therefore, in line with what was said earlier, with the very notion of collective autonomy—is, in fact, confirmed by the particular connotation taken on in the Community context by a number of elements which may be considered natural corollaries of labour law pluralism, at least as concerns the conceptions which will be discussed here. These latter are: the principle of freedom of association (or its equivalents); the role of conflict as a constituent element of collective autonomy; the inherent rule-making function that is acknowledged for manifestations of collective autonomy; autonomous determination of the aims of collective bargaining and the circle of employees and employers to be covered by it; the possibility of relating individual acts of negotiation to a self-regulated bargaining system in its dynamic dimension; and still other elements whose evaluation will attest further to the need, as mentioned several times, to identify for Community collective bargaining hermeneutic schemes other than those (impracticable in this case) of pluralism and collective autonomy.

This is what will be discussed in the present chapter, which attempts to contextualise analysis of the above-mentioned elements within the normative system outlined by the ASP provisions now embedded in the Treaty.

In this connection, it is useful to clarify here what is meant by the expressions "inconsequential collective bargaining" and "tied collective bargaining" (see sections 1 and 2) that will be used. The thesis to be argued holds that only collective agreements implemented by way of a Council decision ("strong" agreements, see Table I above) have any relevance within the Community legal order, while European collective agreements implemented in accordance with the procedures and practices specific to management and labour and the Member States ("weak" agreements) remain excluded from the sphere of Community legal relevance. According to this thesis, therefore, European collective agreements which are not incorporated into a Council decision have to be regarded as *inconsequential* as regards the Community legal order.

Given that such a thesis as formulated in these terms is in danger of appearing excessive or even arbitrary,[1] it is necessary to present a number of arguments to support its validity.

1.1 The normative function of collective bargaining and the (non-existence of the) principle of freedom of association in the Community legal order

"Agreements concluded at Community level shall be implemented . . . in accordance with the procedures and practices specific to management and labour and the Member States, [but] this arrangement implies no obligation on the Member States to apply the agreements directly or to work out rules for their transposition, or any obligation to amend national legislation in force to facilitate their implementation".[2]

From this normative "minisystem" it is possible to deduce the contractual hypothesis here termed as "inconsequential" within the Community legal order.

A European collective laissez-faire?

There has already been occasion to point out the ineffectively concessive tenor of the provisions concerned,[3] which grant what did not need to be granted (the conclusion of collective agreements between the social partners and their implementation in accordance with the means autonomously available to the latter) but neglect to give formal confirmation of what does, by contrast, need formal confirmation: the principle of the freedom of association, which Article 137(6) TEC even expressly excludes from the ambit of Community competence, like all matters relating to "the right of association, the right to strike or the right to impose lock-outs".[4]

The next step in the task of verifying the real autonomous and pluralist nature of Community collective bargaining is to determine whether the attitude adopted by the Community legislators on the occasion in question may be regarded benignly as an instance of collective laissez-faire (Kahn-Freund, 1959

---

[1] And indeed is not universally shared. For some theses which, on the basis of different arguments, tend to attribute a Community legal relevance to European collective agreements not implemented through a Council decision, see Jeammaud, 1998; Franssen, 1998; and Bercusson, in the report prepared for the European Parliament, *Trade Union Rights in the EU Member States*, European Parliament/Directorate-General for Research (Social Affairs Series W–12), December 1997 at p. 92.

[2] Article 139(2) TEC (ex Article 4(2) ASP), and Declaration 27 of the Treaty of Amsterdam.

[3] In a similar vein see Lyon-Caen, A., 1997b at p. 367, according to whom the significance of the provisions concerned "à première vue inutile . . . demeure avant tout politique".

[4] The formally equal footing on which this provision places the right to strike and the right to impose lock-outs is seen by Scarpelli, 1993b at p. 163 as confirming the difference between the planes on which Community law and national labour law are situated," [the latter] being a system of law which is by definition asymmetric, and biased to favour the part of the employee as regards being able to countervail the owner of the means of production in the operation of employment relationships". The symmetry between strike and lock-out accorded by this provision is also criticised by Lyon-Caen, A. and Verdier, 1995.

at p. 224) or whether, rather, the absence of any "state intervention" in the application of weak argreements is more correctly to be interpreted in other, less noble, terms.

According to a perhaps somewhat mannered view of the relationship between the industrial relations system and the state legal order, mature pluralism and abstention of the law not only support each other but presuppose each other.[5] Such positions, as is well-known, were based on sociological observation and the subsequent juridical rationalisation of what for decades constituted the fundamental characteristic of the British industrial relations system: to wit, collective laissez-faire.[6] The elevation of that system to the role of paradigmatic model of a pluralist industrial relations system consequently brought about a proliferation of labour law doctrines formulated on its basis, making collective laissez-faire a heuristic instrument which is also applicable, and has been applied, in the context of systems other than the one in which it had originally been formulated.

In its dual guise of a constituent element of a reputedly "very efficient" collective labour relations system (Giugni, 1960 at p. 95) and a (widely shared) labour law doctrine based on observation of that system, abstention of the law—understood here as the absence of regulatory interventions of a normative nature[7]—thus became one of the traditional canons of collective labour law, frequently cited as a paradigmatic manifestation of an attitude which gives full recognition to the social partners' collective autonomy. Since the issues involved are obviously ones which are central to collective labour law, all that will be added here are a few brief "notes in the margin" considered useful for the purposes of ensuring that the problems being examined are stated correctly.

In the first place, it seems true to say that some of the assumptions generally ascribed to or deduced from the British model of collective laissez-faire need to be partially reconsidered, at least in the light of the conclusions reached by more perspicacious commentators. These offer a threefold series of observations belying what was referred to above as the "mannered" version of collective laissez-faire.

First, the myth of total abstention is refuted and its dissemination is imputed to the writings of "less than well-informed" commentators (Wedderburn, 1994 now 1995a at p. 318).[8]

[5] A view regarding which it is customary to quote the classic statement made by Kahn-Freund in his "first" English phase: "There exists something like an inverse correlation between the practical significance of legal sanctions and the degree to which industrial relations have reached a state of maturity" (Kahn-Freund, 1954a at p. 43).

[6] On the evolution of the legal policies on the matter adopted by successive British governments over the period 1960–1991, cf. McCarthy, 1992.

[7] On the terminological ambiguity which has led to abstention of the law being interpreted *solely* in the sense of non-intervention of a legislative nature, disregarding the fact that it originally also included an absence of intervention by the courts, see the detailed comments by Ballestrero, 1982 at p. 157.

[8] "Collective bargaining has never anywhere operated free from some legislative framework" (Wedderburn, 1994 now 1995a p. 318).

Secondly, the idea is negated that legislative abstentionism must be regarded as a value in itself, functional to the development of an autonomous collective bargaining system, as shown by an author who urges that we must "no longer fall into the trap of thinking that reflexive law requires abstentionism" (Collins, 1997 at p. 308).[9] These observations had already, in fact, rightly been placed on the agenda of the British debate on legal policy some time earlier: referring to the work of the Donovan Commission, it was stated that "the citadel to be protected was not non-intervention in the abstract, but concrete trade unionism"; and it was added, with reference to the dispute between proponents and opponents of legislative intervention, that "being for or against it generally is rather like being on principle for or against orange" (Wedderburn, 1994 now 1995a at pp. 295–296).

Lastly, comments are expressed on the subject of the historical and political reasons identifiable as the source of the "tendentionally" abstentionist characterisation of the British system, and also the present-day validity of a system structured in this way. As regards the first, it is pointed out that "the traditional framework of British labour law really rested upon a middle class acquiescence in the current balance of industrial power" (Wedderburn, 1972a at p. 270).[10] And even as regards the second, there is certainly no concealment of perplexities towards a system which does not guarantee any forms of "positive" protection other than traditional common law immunities. Far from being the subject of proud and insular claims, the British system of immunities and privileges is, in short, presented not in terms of an alternative to protection of the "constitutional" type but as an expedient solution justifiable only on account of reasons of a historical nature which nowadays are perhaps no longer capable of justifying it.

On the other hand, even within those doctrinal reconstructions which most passionately supported the validity of abstentionist options there is nothing immutable about the evaluation of the relationship between the state legal order and the industrial relations system: the "conversion" of Kahn-Freund in later years and the legislative adjustments called upon to ensure "order" in a bargaining system which was considered disordered (Kahn-Freund, 1979) confirm the inconsistency of positions supporting a preferability in ontological terms of abstentionist policies (or their opposite) and demonstrate, instead, the necessity of relating evaluations on the subject to the reality of the institutional and industrial relations contexts existing at a given stage in history.

This must be borne in mind when evaluating the significance attributable to the ASP provisions now embedded in the Treaty, which limit the sphere of "intervention" by the Community legislature to only *one* of the possible manifestations of bargaining by the Community social partners: the "strong" collec-

---

[9] The same author had, however, already made his own position on the matter clear in a previous article (Collins, 1987).

[10] Quotation taken from Lewis, 1979 at p. 218; the passage quoted is, however, also recalled by its author in a later article: cf. Wedderburn, 1983 at p. 46.

tive agreement implemented by way of a Council decision on a proposal from the Commission. It is therefore a matter of verifying whether, beyond this particular hypothesis, the provisions in question enable us to attribute other, different areas of legal relevance to Community collective bargaining. Or whether, as suggested here, collective agreements which are not recognised/implemented by way of a Council decision are, on the contrary, manifestations of bargaining which remain entirely without relevance for the Community legal order and to which it is therefore not possible to apply a scheme of collective laissez-faire, which certainly cannot be equated with the legal irrelevance of manifestations of bargaining not directly regulated by the "law" of the "state".

In this connection, it is the opinion of the present writer (an opinion also shared by others) that any such evaluation must necessarily take into consideration the essential function fulfilled in the evolution of pluralist and "abstentionist" industrial relations systems by the constitutional principle of freedom of association, or by those techniques and instruments which may be considered its functional equivalents in the context of national legal systems which have no constitutional traditions in the formal sense.[11]

The question to which an answer will be attempted can therefore be summed up as follows: within the context of a legal system in which—as is the case in the Community legal order—the spheres of competence of those bargaining phenomena which are intended to have "direct" regulatory relevance[12] are normatively predetermined, what regulatory function is it possible to attribute, *in the absence of a constitutional principle of protection of the freedom of association*, to other bargaining phenomena which diverge, in terms of content and procedure, from the heteronomously predetermined scheme?[13]

It has just been seen that the cognitive scheme of collective laissez-faire does not, on its own, supply the elements needed to resolve the question. To answer it some "excursions" into the field of the general theory of law will therefore be necessary, connected in particular with evaluating the possible conformations to be encountered in the relationship between social systems and the legal system.

State law and the "law" of the industrial relations system

In this field, it is certainly not an overworked description to call the teachings of Norberto Bobbio authoritative, although they have also been mentioned, in

---

[11] The form of wording is, obviously, borrowed from a famous article by Kahn-Freund, 1976 which made a comparative evaluation of the impact of constitutions on labour law; the countries studied included the United Kingdom, described as a country which "has of course a constitution in the substantive sense [but] has no constitution in the formal sense" (at p. 240).

[12] This refers to the "strong" bargaining hypothesis, involving the implementation of agreements "at the joint request of the signatory parties, by a Council decision on a proposal from the Commission".

[13] This refers to the "weak" bargaining hypothesis, involving the implementation of agreements "in accordance with the procedures and practices specific to management and labour and the Member States".

Italy, in other labour law studies devoted to an analysis of the relationship between the industrial relations system and the state legal order (Carabelli, 1986).

In a fundamental work—described by its author, in an excess of modesty, as a "draft outline of the subject"—Bobbio classified the possible relationships between the law of the state system and the law of social systems into three types, a three-way typology which has now become classic. According to the Turinese jurist, when we set about verifying "the validity which a given system attributes to the rules of other systems with which it comes into contact, we encounter three different situations that can be formulated schematically as: a) indifference; b) rejection; c) absorption" (Bobbio, 1960 at pp. 195–196).

In the case of the "indifference" hypothesis, which would appear to be the one closest to the "inconsequentiality" ascribed here to weak European collective agreements, "the state system does not oppose the other system, but nor does it grant it any protection" (Rescigno, 1990 at p. 194). The "indifference" referred to by Bobbio is not, however, the same thing as the "inconsequentiality" which concerns us here. The former merely implies a sphere of total lawfulness, and in particular "a condition of freedom, and hence self-limitation by the state system with respect to the possibility for an organised group . . . of making its own rules for regulating spheres of conduct regarded as lawful by the state system itself" (Carabelli, 1986 at pp. 159–160). However, as was rightly pointed out in this latter study, "that still provides no answer as to the possibility of such social norms [in our case, the industrial relations system's norms, i.e. collective agreements] being able to produce some legally relevant effect in the state system" (Carabelli, 1986 at p. 158). Hence, in a situation of "indifference" in Bobbian terms the question of the legal "relevance" of the norms produced within the non-state system remains open. This is because the two categorisations concern different moments in reality: whereas indifference concerns the moment when a social system is first established and essentially consists in a decision that the system concerned is lawful, legal relevance/irrelevance concerns the norms which then emanate from the system. The mere fact of their lawfulness does not necessarily mean that those norms can be regarded as legally relevant within the state system.

Leaving the field of the general theory of inter-system relationships, it seems true to say that the lawfulness or indifference guaranteed to Community collective bargaining by the provisions originally contained in the ASP is only half-sufficient, and therefore insufficient, to ensure legal relevance for it. The provisions concerned solve only part of the problem, in that they demonstrate a position of indifference (in the sense defined above) on the part of the Community legal order *vis-à-vis* the possible creation of a "Community system of collective labour relations" but still say nothing regarding the legal relevance of the norms produced within the context of that system once it is established in the sphere of lawfulness thereby guaranteed. To say, as these provisions do, that a European collective bargaining system would be "lawful" is not the same as saying that weak European collective agreements would be relevant within the EC legal system.

Solving the problem therefore requires a further order of considerations aimed at clarifying the conditions which would allow Community collective agreements (not implemented by way of a Council decision) to assume such relevance.

Freedom of association and the legal status of collective agreements

It is well known that in the two systems where the pluralist model has found most favour (Italy and the United Kingdom) the mechanisms of the legal effect of collective agreements on the individual employment relationship were initially derived from what may be called a private contract sphere. In both cases the view taken was that acts of collective autonomy acquired effect in the state legal order through the intermediary of the individual contract of employment: in one case through the "machinery" of private law agency (Caruso, 1992 at pp. 332–337) and in the other by way of the "incorporation" mechanisms provided for by the common law of contract.[14]

This type of legal relevance mechanism for collective agreements was subsequently superseded, in Italy at least, by doctrinal constructs which were less tied to private law schemes and sought a basis for the normative value of collective agreements in other arguments more consistent with the pluralist paradigm.

In this latter stage of doctrinal development, certain authors who were particularly susceptible to the attraction of the Luhmannian systems approach embarked on a demanding reconstructional path which, after a "re-reading in functional systems terms" of the theory of *ordinamento intersindacale* (Giugni, 1960: see last chapter, n. 59), arrived at a conceptual systemisation of the relationship between the *ordinamento intersindacale* and the state legal order which extended beyond the sphere of the latter's sheer autonomy and suggested forms of horizontal co-ordination between the two systems as viewed on an equal footing (Vardaro, 1984). Such proposals—which exalted the inherent and pre-statal nature of collective autonomy to the point of regarding earlier theories concerned with defining possible modes of integrating acts of collective autonomy into the state legal order as only "partially" pluralist—were initially greeted with interest on the part of legal scholars both in the field of labour law and elsewhere,[15] although it cannot be said that they succeeded in replacing the models previously regarded as the means of expressing or justifying the normative value of collective bargaining.

---

[14] Normative effect is achieved in this case through the incorporation into the individual contract of the terms and conditions fixed by collective agreement. According to common law mechanisms, such incorporation takes place through a series of bridging terms which may be express, implicit or derive from custom and practice. In general, see Kahn-Freund, 1983 at pp. 166–177; Wedderburn, 1986 at pp. 326–343; Hepple and Fredman, 1992 at pp. 97–101; Deakin and Morris, 1995 at pp. 232–239.

[15] Teubner, 1983; Montanari, 1990.

Leaving aside any judgment as to the overall scientific plausibility of the above-mentioned reconstructions,[16] it is still useful to draw attention to certain profiles which are relevant for the purposes of the arguments being pursued here. The proposals concerned—which, to use the original terminology, may be described as theories of a "social and not merely statal pluralism" (Vardaro, 1984 at p. 107)—find their basis in a twofold presupposition consisting in the existence of a highly developed and mature bargaining system[17] and, above all, optimal status of the *constitutional principle of protection of the freedom of association* (Vardaro, 1984 at pp. 109–110), which is regarded, together with the right to strike, as the justifying element of an autonomy of the industrial relations system which is inherent in the strong sense, unfettered by any need for extension or integration into the state legal system. These latter considerations are enough to exclude the possibility of relating Community collective bargaining to schemes of inherent autonomy and to illustrate, once again, the embryonic stage at which (for more than purely chronological reasons: see Chapter 3, section 3 above) it still stands.

But even if we eschew such a conception in the strong sense of a systems approach to pluralism and remain, instead, in the more reassuring and well-tried sphere of institutionalist conceptions, a critical rethink of the planes through which the presumed collective autonomy of the European social partners acquires (or does not acquire) relevance within the Community legal system is still necessary. This brings us back to the need to find an answer to the question we are confronting here: what—in the absence of private law mechanisms of agency or common law methods of incorporation—is the legal status of collective agreements not directly implemented or "absorbed" by state law (and therefore, in our case, "weak" collective agreements)?

Finding a possible answer can start with a preliminary evaluation of the answers given to the same question in normative and institutional contexts different from the Community one. That can mean, given the nature of the arguments being discussed, systems which recognise a constitutional principle of freedom of association, understood not only (in the negative) as an individual

---

[16] On these reconstructions, and in particular on the associated sociological and general theory presuppositions, see an earlier article by the present writer (Lo Faro, 1993a).

[17] Highly developed and mature to the point of regarding the industrial relations system as a functional social sub-system in Luhmannian terms (Luhmann, 1982 and 1990a). From the point of view of systems orthodoxy this is probably not entirely correct (see the comments made in Lo Faro, 1993a at footnote 6), particularly in the light of the developments which took place in systems theory following the elaboration of Vardaro's proposal (but some doubt was already being expressed by Luhmann in the *Interview* published as an appendix to Vardaro, 1984).

Nevertheless, the more recent literature has featured other proposals directed at using the systems paradigm in the specific area of labour law analysis. One such example is Rogowski, 1991, where the attempt to apply a systems approach to arbitration procedures for industrial dispute resolution is probably impaired by an excessively forced extension of the industrial relations system to the notion of a social system in Luhmannian terms (see, in particular, ch. I). Similar lines of reasoning are again proposed in Rogowski, 1998.

civil liberty and fundamental human right[18] but also and above all (in the positive) as a cardinal principle of a pluralist society, capable of providing, recognising, granting, or delegating a normative function for collective bargaining, depending on the various possible options.[19]

From this viewpoint it is perhaps not committing scientific chauvinism to say that Italian post-constitutional doctrine features a series of contributions which—influenced by very particular historical contingencies and obliged, in a way, to refer to the principle of freedom of association as a key element of a pluralist reconstruction of the collective bargaining system (Mancini, 1963 now 1976)—have all, in their diversity, pointed to the indissoluble connection which links the legal rationalisation of industrial relations systems to constitutional protection of an active or positive principle of freedom of association.

Although it is neither possible nor appropriate to revisit the various stages of this reflection in detail, given our present purposes it seems useful to point out that in institutional contexts characterised by the presence of a principle of freedom of association as understood in the terms outlined above, "bargaining activity is not identifiable with a single unvarying form of collective agreement [and] the constitutional norm cannot be seen as implying some tied form of bargaining" (Giugni, 1979 at p. 281). It is precisely an active and open interpretation of the constitutional principle of freedom of association which attended the advancement, in Italy, of doctrinal proposals aimed at resolving the problem of the normative function attributable to "dynamic" collective bargaining,[20] i.e. bargaining extraneous to the typical model prefigured by the Constitution.

The objection will be raised (and it is undoubtedly true) that in point of fact the interpretations and doctrines just mentioned exclude the plausibility of the thesis being proposed here, to the extent that, far from confirming the legal irrelevance of forms of bargaining which diverge from heteronomously specified models, they actually support their inherent rule-making status irrespective of any formal recognition by the state system: "the fact that the Constitution mentions only the *erga omnes* collective agreement and makes no express reference to a general freedom of collective bargaining does not mean . . . that only the *erga omnes* collective agreement is constitutionally guaranteed (Vardaro, 1984

[18] This is the sense in which it is basically used in international documents mentioning it. On internationalist profiles of recognition of the principle of freedom of association, see Lyon-Caen, G. and Lyon-Caen, A. 1993; Valticos and von Potobsky, 1995; and, with specific reference to collective bargaining, Rodière, 1987.

[19] I use the adjectives "positive" and "negative" not with reference to freedom of association understood as legal protection of the choice either to join or not to join a union (on which, for an analysis centred on the American and UK systems, see Leader, 1992 at pp. 239–266) but in the sense proposed by Vardaro, 1984 at pp. 55–51, in order to distinguish a perception of constitutional protection with resonance on a "liberal" plane from a perception which is more allied to the "overall thrust of industrial relations policies of democratic states in the post-war period". The positive/negative distinction is used in similar terms by Kahn-Freund, 1983 at pp. 202–205. For an exposition on the dual meaning of "constitutional" recognition of a principle of freedom of association in the Community context, see Lo Faro, 1997.

[20] To use the terminology used by Gino Giugni in his famous *Introduction* (Giugni, 1960).

at p. 69). Translating these statements into the Community context would therefore seem to lead to the conclusion that the fact that the provisions originally contained in the ASP expressly provide for the normative value of a typical collective agreement implemented by way of a Council decision by no means implies, by itself, the legal irrelevance of other collective agreements, whether they are called free, dynamic or "weak".

As already mentioned, however, the conclusions reached by the doctrine referred to can be, and even have to be, used *a contrario* in support of the legal irrelevance of weak European collective agreements, precisely because those conclusions *presuppose the presence of a constitutional principle of freedom of association, which is lacking in the Community context*. Furthermore, they presuppose a particular perception of the principle of freedom of association hinging upon and mainly justified on the basis of an overall evaluation of the fundamental principles underlying the economic and social make-up of a given system.[21]

It can therefore be concluded that collective autonomy is not identical with and not restricted to the typical forms of bargaining predetermined by the state legal system, provided that the normative effect of agreements diverging from those typical forms finds support in a constitutionally guaranteed protection of a positive principle of freedom of association.

To sum up, in the European doctrinal tradition of labour law the positive meaning of freedom of association has been coupled with the right to collective bargaining and considered capable of projecting its shadow from the static to the dynamic dimension of trade union activity. In other words, the main consequences deriving from a "positive" perception of freedom of association are to be found in the influence it exerts on the normative status of collective agreements. It is precisely because of their direct connection with constitutional recognition of the freedom of association and right to bargain that private contracts, which collective agreements basically are, have acquired a specific quasi-normative status; it is precisely to the extent that they have been regarded as a dynamic expression of the freedom of association and right to bargain that it has been possible to justify in constitutional terms the collective autonomy of the social actors and the normative relevance of their collective agreements.

However, the European doctrinal tradition embodies another series of evaluations relevant to the approach discussed here. It couples a positive perception

---

[21] On these arguments see—for a perspective specifically referring to the Weimar Constitution, in which "pluralism and collective bargaining had become the very foundations of the social state" (Vardaro, 1982 at p. 86)—the collected articles in Neumann, 1983. More recently, a historical viewpoint on the subject has been expressed by Ritter, 1996 at pp. 111–127. In the context of a recent analysis (openly critical of the postulates of reflexive law, regarded as the normative paradigm of the post-social state), the characterising role assumed by the right of association and the right to strike in the post-war social constitutions is pointed out by Maestro-Buelga, 1996 at pp. 83–89 and 99–100.

of freedom of association capable of justifying the normative function of collective bargaining with another constitutional principle which is likewise absent, and even excluded, from the Community context: the right to strike.[22]

The relevance of the conflictual dimension to the acknowledged normative function of collective bargaining—and, earlier still, to its very historical origin[23]—constitutes, in fact, one of the pivotal elements of the *ordinamento intersindacale* reconstructions which have been referred to several times (see last chapter, n 59), in which it was presented as a sanction mechanism of the industrial relations social system (Giugni, 1960). And we can but agree with an author who pointed out that the evaluation of the conflictual dimension made by those who reconstructed the relationship between collective agreement and strike in mutually exclusive terms led to a literally "halved representation of union self-determination" (Vardaro, 1985a at pp. 186–187). Furthermore, it is simply impossible to imagine a pluralist reconstruction of society and industrial relations which neglected to take account of the "genetic" function assumed by the dimension of conflict as regards the very make-up of the identity of social groups (Grandi, 1982).[24] Lastly, with specific reference to the topics being examined here, it is precisely the absence of the right to strike which one author has identified as the qualitative difference between social dialogue and genuine collective bargaining (Wedderburn, 1994 now 1995a at p. 298).[25]

In the face of such a consensus on the essential function of conflict and recognition of the right to strike in the legal status of bargaining systems, the Community legal order, although endowing collective bargaining with a role which is far from minor,[26] expressly excludes the right to strike from its competences.

A number of comments may perhaps usefully be made on the reasons generally put forward—on the part of the Community and also on the part of doctrine—to justify this exclusion, along with the parallel exclusion of the right of association. Both are normally regarded as choices imposed by the need to safe-

---

[22] On the connection between the two principles, see Wedderburn, 1994 now 1995a at p. 306, who couples them in talking of a "right to freedom of association (with its concomitant right to strike)".

[23] "Collective bargaining exists only because of industrial conflict, whether it be spontaneous or organised" (Romagnoli, 1995a at p. 71).

[24] In a later article specifically devoted to an analysis of the Maastricht Agreement on Social Policy, the same author confirms that it is impossible "not to recognise the functional connection which links bargaining autonomy to the collective power of industrial action, which is its indispensable corollary" (Grandi, 1993 at p. 482).

[25] See the comments made along the same lines by Dølvik, 1997 at p.6, who states that "a central weakness of the current approach has been the preclusion of transnational rights of industrial action. Unless trade unions become capable of countervailing capital exit threats and underpinning their demands by transborder mobilisation, either by seizing the right voluntarily, or by legal reform, their bargaining position will most likely remain inferior to the employers".

[26] See Commission Communication *Adapting and Promoting the Social Dialogue at Community Level* (COM(98) 322 final, 20.05.1998), which points to the "increased opportunities and responsibilities for the social partners at European level in the shaping of social policy".

guard the now mythical "national specificities", if only in the name of the "holy water of subsidiarity" (Wedderburn, 1994 now 1995a at p. 307). The question can, however, be viewed and answered in quite different terms.

Once decided, the intention to draw collective bargaining into the sphere of legal relevance of the *Community* system—which, as the Court of Justice has never tired of repeating for more than thirty years, is an *independent* legal order distinct from those of the Member States[27]—surely implied the need to adjust the principles prevailing in the legal order within which collective bargaining is destined to operate, with the consequent provision of the principles of freedom of association and the right to strike, without which collective autonomy cannot properly be regarded as such.

Invoking national specificities or subsidiarity as a pretext for the exclusion of Community competence in these matters is therefore not sufficient justification to explain the absence of these two principles, which even represents an internal contradiction to the intention—declared in the very same text in which its preconditions were excluded (the ASP)—to guarantee collective agreements a normatively relevant place within the Community legal order. To refrain from harmonising the principles of labour law and the industrial relations systems *of the Member States* is one thing; it is quite a different matter to neglect to adjust the institutional apparatus *of that order itself* to accommodate the very functionality of the choices made. On the contrary by coupling the initial exclusion of freedom of association and the right to strike alongside the present-day attribution of a function of unquestionable political and institutional relevance to collective bargaining[28] the two profiles are improperly overlapped and confused.

The multiplicity of the observations brought together for the purposes of the present section calls for a brief review, in the order in which they have been presented.

Given that an analysis of the provisions originally contained in the ASP allows us to define two different forms of collective agreement, one incorporated in a Council decision ("strong" European collective agreement) and the other implemented in accordance with the practices specific to the social partners and the Member States ("weak" European collective agreement), the question posed at

---

[27] Starting with the judgments in Case 26/62 *Van Gend en Loos v Nederlandse Administratie der Belastingen* [1963] ECR 1 and Case 6/64 *Costa v ENEL* [1964] ECR 585, in which the Court stated that "by contrast with ordinary international treaties, the EEC Treaty has created its own legal system".

[28] "The purpose . . . is to link the work of the social partners more closely to the development and implementation of EU policies" (COM(98) 322, 20.05.1998).

[29] Contrary to the allegation made here of the legal irrelevance of the "weak" form of implementation provided for in Article 4(2) ASP (now Article 139(2) TEC) (see Table I and Section V.1 above), Bercusson argues that in this provision "the reference to management and labour is supplemented by 'and the Member States' ", therefore concluding that "It seems from this formulation that some degree of obligation is imposed directly on Member States by the word 'shall' ". These comments are made by the author in a study recently carried out for the European Parliament (see n. 1 above). See also Bercusson, 1994.

the outset was that of defining the normative status attributable to the latter. Since the ASP itself provides no definite answer,[30] an attempt was first made to verify whether or not this situation of "normative silence" can be related to the schemes of collective laissez-faire and abstention of the law. These schemes were judged to be inapplicable to the particular case in point, and attention was therefore turned to the conclusions reached in the field of general theory, with particular regard to analysis of the legal relevance which norms produced in the context of a non-state system are able to assume in the context of the state system. Lastly, it was demonstrated that in the context of systems characterised by a social Constitution the question of the normative relevance of collective agreements has generally been related to the principles of freedom of association and the right to strike, both of which are explicitly excluded from the sphere of Community competences.

Remembering that the classification of legal relevance progressively developed in this section refers only to "weak" agreements, we may conclude by returning to the question posed at the outset—what is the legal status of collective agreements not directly implemented or "absorbed" by state law? and offering the following answer. Whereas in a system which includes provision for the principle of freedom of association and recognition of the right to strike *all* bargaining phenomena acquire normative relevance, including those which diverge from the model heteronomously stipulated as a precondition for such relevance, in a context where those two principles are absent the legal relevance of bargaining is confined to the form which is expressly defined as "relevant". And in the Community context that means "strong" collective bargaining, which is discussed in the next section.

2 "TIED" COLLECTIVE BARGAINING

If the conclusions stated at the end of the preceding section are correct, or at least plausible, the notion of Community legal relevance for supranational collective bargaining can properly be applied only to "strong" collective agreements implemented "at the joint request of the signatory parties, by a Council decision on a proposal from the Commission" (Article 139(2) TEC). These agreements (or, rather, the mechanisms through which they acquire direct normative relevance within the Community legal order) will therefore be the subject of our scrutiny here.

---

[30] Nor is much attention paid to weak agreements in the three Commission Communications on social dialogue which have been published since 1993 (*Communication Concerning the Application of the Agreement on Social Policy*, COM(93) 600, 14.12.1993; *Communication Concerning the Development of the Social Dialogue at Community Level*, COM(96) 448, 18.09.1996; *Adapting and Promoting the Social Dialogue at Community Level*, COM(98) 322, 20.05.1998).

On first analysis, the above-mentioned provision would appear to represent a somewhat advanced and effective instance of what in other periods of history would have been called "extra-legislative creation of labour law", in that it seems to confirm an inexorable trend towards a further development at Community level of the social partners' collective autonomy. Indeed, it is in just such terms that it has been presented by a far from negligible body of legal scholars (Bercusson, 1992, 1994, 1995; Schnorr, 1993; Blanpain and Engels, 1995; Guarriello, 1992; Guery, 1992; Grandi, 1995; Valdés Dal-Ré, 1997), who have emphasised its function as a "guarantee at European level of a principle of collective autonomy of the social partners . . . destined to take on the special connotations of a fundamental principle of Community law" (Grandi, 1993 at p. 467).

However, it seems possible to conclude that, in reality, the pro-labour nature of the provisions in question is only seemingly so, and that the possibility of classing this form of bargaining activity by the social partners as a manifestation of collective autonomy is countered by limits of two kinds: those relating to the content of the collective agreements concerned (section 2 below) and those relating to the procedure through which such agreements are "implemented" (section 3 below).

2.1 Pre-set limits . . .

The first group of limits imposed on the bargaining activity of the social partners derives from the narrow range of issues within which they are constrained to operate if they intend the agreements they conclude to be lifted out of the area of "inconsequentiality" and acquire the "direct" normative status ensured within the Community legal order by the Council decision mechanism.

Activation of that mechanism cannot be requested for all collective agreements reached by the social partners in the Community context, but only those concluded "in matters covered by Article 137", i.e. only in the matters included in the sphere of Community jurisdiction. Given the restricted range of Community competences in the social field, the inevitable conclusion is that even collective agreements capable of acquiring direct relevance within the Community legal order are confined to rather limited areas of competence.

Not to mention, as well, the innumerable problems of a practical nature which are created by such a limitation of the issues covered by European collective agreements. For example, an agreement covering minimum rates of pay— just to mention a matter which is excluded by the EC Treaty provisions[31] but whose importance is indisputable[32]—could not be implemented by means of the

---

[31] "The provisions of this Article shall not apply to pay" (Article 137(6) TEC).

[32] As acknowledged, among other things, in the Report by the Comité de Sages, chaired by Maria de Lourdes Pintasilgo, *For a Europe of Civil and Social Rights* (Luxembourg: EC Official Publications, 1996) at p. 52.

"legislative" procedure envisaged by Article 139(2) TEC and would therefore, if what has been said above is correct, remain "inconsequential" within the Community legal order. But there is also the hypothesis of a Community collective agreement covering several interrelated matters, some of which are included within Community jurisdiction and others not;[33] or an agreement where all the matters covered are included within Community jurisdiction but whose subsequent adoption by the Council is subject to the unanimity rule for some matters and the qualified majority rule for others.[34] What would have to be done in such cases? A possible answer might be to split the collective agreement, with one part implemented by means of the weak procedure (matters which are excluded from Community jurisdiction) and the other by means of the strong procedure (matters which are included). Or adoption of the agreement by way of two separate Council decisions, one by qualified majority and the other by unanimity. These solutions would, however, clearly contrast with the agreement's much proclaimed "inviolability" by the Commission and Council.

As things stand, the "price" of the normative status of collective agreements within the Community legal order is certainly a very high one. The price paid is the very possibility for the social partners of freely determining themselves the aims and content of their bargaining activities, a freedom which is sacrificed in the name of a reward consisting in implementation of the agreement by way of a Council decision. An exchange, in fact, which seems a hard bargain and almost repressive as regards the social partners' collective autonomy, and confirms the vital need to identify the *cui prodest* of the provisions concerned.

Such a situation of the social partners' "limited sovereignty" in choosing the issues to be negotiated highlights, once again, the question of the lack of recognition of a constitutional principle of freedom of association in the context of the Community legal order and its inevitable repercussions on the status of the bargaining phenomena originally provided for by the ASP. There is certainly no need to dwell further on this other than to recall the major part traditionally reserved in most conceptual reconstructions of freedom of association to "the freedom to decide the content of agreements" (Dell'Olio, 1980 at p. 32) and the evidence that the immediate object of constitutional or international (ILO) recognition of the principle in question is not so much union organisation as union *activity*, which is of course largely identifiable with collective bargaining.

These remarks may perhaps be countered by the objection that the choices originally made by the ASP were merely necessitated by the nature of the implementation mechanisms it envisaged. Once provision had been made for the implementation of collective agreements reached by the social partners to take

---

[33] For example, trade union rights (excluded) of third-country nationals residing in Community territory (included).

[34] For example, social security schemes (unanimity rule) aimed at granting gender equality (qualified majority rule).

place by way of a Council Decision, the limits on the content of the two acts—
a contractual act on the part of the social partners and an institutional act on the
part of the Community—could not but be the same. Certainly, the implementation of an agreement reached by the social partners at Community level cannot
represent for the Community institutions an occasion to overstep the limits of
the jurisdiction reserved to them by the Treaties and the provisions in question.
This objection is undoubtedly well-founded, but for that very reason confirms
rather than negates the basic assumption being advanced here: namely, that the
choices represented by these provisions have little to do with collective autonomy and far more to do with resolving the Community's own regulatory problems. A "collective autonomy" tied to operating within areas of competence
which are heteronomously predetermined and, what is more, reduced in content
cannot properly be called collective autonomy. It has been said that "The possibility of regulating and determining an autonomous level of transnational bargaining relations necessarily involves the capacity and will of the European
social partners to define, in complete autonomy, the boundaries of the collective
interests that can be protected at that level" (Caruso, 1997 at p. 332); certainly
not, it might be added, heteronomous control of the aims of union activity,
something which is by definition incompatible with collective autonomy.

There have, nevertheless, been attempts in the legal literature to deny, on the
basis of a painstaking exegesis of the ASP text, that the content of collective
agreements need necessarily be confined to the matters included within the jurisdiction of the Community institutions (Bercusson, 1994 and 1995). This line of
reasoning holds that it is possible to derive from the ASP a two-pronged and
separated regime of competences in social policy: one relating to the ordinary
decision-making procedures and the other relating to the decision-making procedures in which the social partners are involved. In the context of an overall
redefinition of Community decision-making in the social field, "the detailed limits on competences carefully attached to the old institutions and procedures are
not necessarily to be carried over to the new institutions and procedures". If "the
range of competences in social policy reserved to the social partners is distinct
from that of the Community institutions . . . then it may be that the competences
listed generally in Article 2 are not to limit the potential of the social dialogue
procedure prescribed in Articles 3 and 4" (Bercusson, 1995 at pp. 177–178).

This thesis is not entirely convincing, however, inasmuch as European collective bargaining still cannot be considered an autonomous source of European
social law. To acquire legal effect it still has to lean on the "crutch" of a formal
act of the Community institutions (a Council decision) and so suffers all the limitations as to content which such acts are bound to observe. Besides, the
Commission itself more recently reaffirmed that "the negotiating parties to an
agreement to be implemented through legislation under article 4(2) ASP must
ensure that the subjects for discussion remain within the remit of Article 2 ASP".[35]

[35] Commission Communication, *Adapting and Promoting the Social Dialogue at Community
Level* (COM(98) 322, 20.05.1998).

But the *pre-set* limits as to content set out in Article 2 ASP (now Article 137 TEC) are not the only restrictions imposed on the social partners as the price of the full legal status which is guaranteed to "strong" collective agreements. Another group of limits, *subsequent* to the signing of an agreement, was "invented" by the Commission on the occasion of the first applications of the ASP.

2.2 . . . And subsequent assessments

To the above-mentioned prior delimitation of bargaining issues there has been added the "assessment" of agreements as claimed by the Commission "by virtue of its role as guardian of the Treaties".[36]

This represents a type of monitoring of the outcomes of bargaining of which there is absolutely no mention in the original ASP provisions but to which the Commission has always laid claim since its Communication of December 1993 (cited several times here) and which was tried out for the first time on the occasion of the adoption of Directive 96/34/EC on parental leave and Directive 97/81/EC on part-time work,[37] and subsequently with Directive 99/70/EC on fixed-term work. In the Explanatory Memorandum of each of the relevant directive proposals,[38] the Commission had the opportunity to describe in detail the terms in which it intended and intends in future to safeguard the Treaties against any unlawful "infringements" committed by the social partners in exercising their "collective autonomy". The Commission's "assessment" of the results of European collective bargaining can essentially be broken down in four stages.

Legality

The first of these stages is examination of the legality of the agreement's individual clauses, a process intended to take effect in cases where collective agreements are contrary to provisions or principles of Community law.

---

[36] COM(93) 600, 14.12.1993, para. 39.

[37] Both Directives, adopted on the basis of the ASP, were originally inapplicable to the United Kingdom. However, given the imminent incorporation of the ASP into the Treaty, the Amsterdam European Council decided "that a means had to be found to give legal effect to the wish of the United Kingdom and Northern Ireland to accept the Directives already adopted". That is why the two Directives were extended to the United Kingdom by means of Directive 97/75/EC and Directive 98/23/EC, both adopted under the then Article 100 of the EC Treaty. Another Directive adopted on the basis of the ASP, Directive 97/80/EC on the burden of proof in cases of discrimination based on sex, was extended to the United Kingdom by means of Directive 98/52/EC. On the incorporation of the ASP into the new Treaty, and the UK position towards EC social policy decision-making procedures in the transitional phase before the Amsterdam Treaty came into force, see Betten, 1998.

[38] See, respectively, COM(96) 26, 31.01.1996; COM(97) 392, 23.07.1997 and COM(99) 203, 01.05.1999.

The hypothesis of an outright infringement of Community law committed by the social partners might perhaps seem unrealistically remote, but actually ceases to do so when the differing nature of the planes on which the Community legal order and the social partners each operate is borne in mind. Whereas the general provisions and principles of the former are directed towards the construction of an economic area which is increasingly unitary and structured in accordance with the four freedoms of movement, the latter still embody a summation of national forms of protection and interests, legitimate in themselves but potentially the precursors of multiple clashes with the canons underlying the Community legal order. It is not unrealistic, to name just a few examples, to imagine Community collective agreements in the area of employment policies containing clauses which, with varying degrees of explicitness, establish special forms of employment promotion favouring particular geographical areas or production sectors which in terms of distortions of competition may be interpreted as incompatible with Community law;[39] or which, in anticipation of enlargement, specify favourable conditions for the enterprises and workers of particular Member States and so directly infringe the general principle of non-discrimination set out in Article 12 TEC; or, again, pay systems which are flexible in relation to working time or type of employment relationship, and potentially unlawful principles of indirect discrimination defined by the Court of Justice's now abundant case law.

What is most puzzling, however, is not the possibility of an infringement of Community norms and principles via a collective agreement, nor that the Community institutions should require that there be correlative control, but the fact that it is the Commission which has arrogated to itself the competence to perform a purely *jurisdictional* role which as such more properly lies within the competence of the Court of Justice.

But quite apart from any doubt as to the institutional appropriateness of a control of *legality* entrusted to a non-jurisdictional body like the Commission, this situation provides some indications useful to an overall evaluation of the function which the Community institutions manifestly wish to assign to collective bargaining. To exclude control by the Court of Justice and leave such a function to the Commission is, in my view, a very telling revelation of the Community perception of collective agreements concluded in this context: not acts as a source in the true sense, capable of assuming a Community legal relevance *per se*, but rather mere interlocutory instruments serving the purposes of a more readily effective Community decision-making process.[40]

---

[39] For a review of possible areas of conflict between Community competition policies and social policies, see Meliadò, 1996; Lyon-Caen, A., 1992; Davies, 1995; Deakin and Wilkinson, 1994.

[40] See, along these same lines, Sciarra, 1996a at p. 202, according to whom the ASP marked a transition in the Community conception of the social dialogue "from a non-regulatory institution into a pre-regulatory technique".

Representative status

The second aspect of the assessment claimed and carried out by the Commission (on the occasion of both Directives 96/34/EC and 97/81/EC and the subsequent Directive 99/70/EC) concerns verification of the representativeness of the social partner organisations signatory to the agreement. Here again, there is no mention in the relevant provisions themselves of any Community control over this aspect of the social partners' activity. As in the case of the legality aspect, it originates from the Communication presented by the Commission at the end of 1993 in order to clear up a number of interpretative doubts inevitably arising from the baldness with which the matter was regulated by the original ASP provisions.

Faced with an unavoidable need to be selective, the Commission understandably laid down several filtering criteria so as to restrict the number of organisations eligible to take part in the new procedures. Given that those involved are employers' organisations and trade unions, it enlisted the rule of representativeness, the criterion which is used in most national systems as a means of selecting the actors of consultation and/or collective bargaining. In restating the criteria of the representativeness of collective industrial organisations in terms appropriate to the Community context, the Commission would appear to have resisted, correctly, the "inertial" temptation of an overly mechanical transposition of issues and solutions that have developed in a national context. At the end of a comparative study entrusted to a network of national experts,[41] it stated that "the diversity of practice in the different Member States is such that there is no single model which could be replicated at European level".[42] However, its subsequent choices do not seem wholly consistent with this statement, since the criteria it uses for verifying the existence of representativeness are derived from a debate developed around issues which are of an essentially national nature and can only be partly likened to those applying in a Community context.

The Commission Communication singles out three criteria of Community representativeness which, as already pointed out by some legal scholars, do not appear to capture the special nature of the problems associated with selecting Community bargaining agents. According to the Commission, eligible organisations are ones which:

(a) are cross-industry or relate to specific sectors or categories;
(b) consist of organisations which are themselves an integral and recognised part of Member State social partner structures and possess the capacity to negotiate agreements; and
(c) have adequate structures to ensure their effective participation in the consultation process.

These criteria are then supplemented by a "historical criterion" consisting in

[41] See Annex 3, COM(93) 600, 14.12.1993.
[42] COM(93) 600, 14.12.1993, para. 23.

the express mention of UNICE, CEEP and ETUC by name as organisations whose fulfilment of the previously stated criteria has already been verified.

The extent to which these criteria are capable of reflecting the specific nature of the context in which the organisations concerned have to operate is still somewhat doubtful, as actual developments in the social dialogue have shown in some instances. Even before the issue of representativeness burst clamorously upon the Community scene, with the action for annulment brought against Directive 96/34/EC by an employers' organisation which had been excluded from the negotiations,[43] there had been criticisms of the Commission's approach in the legal literature. Some scholars had predicted that the criteria laid down by the Commission represented short-term solutions which were inappropriate to the specific problems of Community representativeness (Bercusson and van Dijk, 1995 at p. 15). Others pointed out that the lack of clear thinking exhibited by the Commission in laying down a series of "disappointing" criteria was likely to lead to a "comparative muddle" (Wedderburn, 1995b at pp. 400 and 398), owing to the mistaken idea that it was necessary to single out those features of representativeness which are common to the various national systems, when in point of fact Community representativeness should not be conceived as a restatement of criteria already existing at national level but as a unique and specific notion (Sciarra, 1996a at p. 200).

However, not even the 1998 judgment delivered by the Court of First Instance on the occasion of UEAPME's application offers any indication of fresh thinking on this point, since no consideration was given to the question of the true adequacy of the representativeness criteria laid down by the 1993 Commission Communication. The Court expressed no view at all on whether or not those criteria were appropriate to their intended purpose, but confined itself to verifying whether they had been applied correctly.

Apart from the updated lists of representative organisations contained in the Annexes to various Commission Communications, which the Commission promises to review on the basis of an "ongoing representativeness study",[44] it therefore has to be said that, even after the *UEAPME* judgment, the question of the representativeness of collective industrial organisations at Community level is still at square one.

By way of comment on the 1993 Communication, some authors had remarked that the Commission document distinguishes, with "subtle and studied ambiguity" (Bercusson and van Dijk, 1995 at p. 16),[45] the social partners'

---

[43] The reference is to the action for annulment under Article 230 TEC brought by UEAPME (Union Européenne de l'Artisanat et des Petites et Moyennes Entreprises). The action, relating to the Directive on parental leave, ended with the judgment of the Court of First Instance of 17 June 1998 (see n. 47 below).

[44] *Adapting and Promoting the Social Dialogue*, cited at n. 26 above.

[45] These comments are also developed in the *Opinion of the Economic and Social Committee on the Communication concerning the application of the Agreement on Social Policy presented by the Commission to the Council and to the European Parliament* (OJ No C 397/40, 31.12.1994). On the occasion of this Opinion, Jan Jacob van Dijk was the Rapporteur and Brain Bercusson was the Expert consulted.

consultative functions (Article 138(2–3)TEC) from contractual relations proper (Article 138(4) and Article 139) and refers the stated representativeness criteria only to the former. According to the Commission, therefore, those criteria serve purely and simply to identify organisations which are eligible to be consulted by it, not also to verify the social partners' access to actual contractual procedures. This distinction between the consultation and negotiation stages is certainly ingenious and takes no account of the fact that in the original architecture of the ASP itself, as elsewhere, negotiation is a process which is naturally grafted onto consultation,[46] thereby refusing to recognise that the entire procedure, from initial consultation up to the final agreement, should be viewed as constituting a whole.

Nevertheless, in the Arguments submitted by the Council in the *UEAPME* case the distinction between the consultation stage and the actual negotiation stage was vigorously maintained. The Council contended that the relevant provisions establish two separate procedures: one leads to the adoption of a "classic" Directive, even though preceded and supported by an "opinion or, where appropriate, a recommendation" from the social partners (Article 138(3) TEC); and the other leads to the adoption of the Council decision specifically intended to implement the agreement reached by the social partners (Article 139(2)). According to the Council, there is no link between the two procedures as regards the organisations' access to one stage or the other: "there is no provision giving a representative of management or labour the right to negotiate any piece of legislation whatsoever with other such representatives by reason of its right to be consulted by the Commission . . . the fact of having been consulted in the context of the first procedure does not give rise to any right to found on the fact of having been excluded from the second procedure".[47]

The Court, which basically accepted the Council's reconstruction of the provisions concerned, added in its judgment that the list of representative organisations contained in the 1993 Commission Communication "*is drawn up to meet the organisational requirements only of the consultation stage* provided for by Article 3(2) and (3) [Article 138(2) and (3) TEC]"; the negotiation stage, by contrast, is entirely outside the Commission's control and depends exclusively on the initiative of those organisations which "have demonstrated their mutual willingness to initiate the process provided for in Article 4 of the Agreement [Article 139 TEC] and to follow it through to its conclusion".[48]

Two conclusions can be drawn from this new (or confirmed) situation.

First, to maintain (as the Council submitted and the Court confirmed) that the Commission has no control over the social partners' access to the post-consultation negotiation stage is clearly a falsification, part of a strategy

---

[46] Although there is nothing to stop the social partners from voluntarily initiating negotiations and then requesting the Commission to submit a proposal to the Council (see Chaptr 4, Table I above). To date, however, all European collective agreements implemented via a Council decision have been "induced", i.e. have originated from a Community decision-making procedure.

[47] Case T–135/96 *UEAPME v Council* [1998] ECR II–2335 (paras 37 and 36).

[48] *Ibid.*, 77 and 75.

adopted for the purposes of the case and designed to achieve a favourable out-come. There is not the slightest doubt that the examination of representative-ness carried out by the Commission extends beyond the consultation stage and is fully applicable to the negotiation stage. This is in any case perfectly clear from the Explanatory Memorandum of each of the three Directive proposals so far adopted on the basis of Article 139(2), in which the examination of repre-sentativeness is expressly referred to the contracting parties and not to the organisations consulted.[49]

Secondly, if things were really as the Commission, the Council and the Court maintained (i.e. if the representativeness criteria really had nothing to do with the selection of the parties eligible to conclude "strong" collective agreements), the logical and inevitable consequence would be a paradox: the three represen-tativeness criteria laid down in the 1993 Communication would be practically useless as regards their intended purpose. They would be neither sufficient nor necessary in order to verify whether or not a Community collective agreement has been concluded by representative organisations, inasmuch as their one and only purpose would be to identify those parties who are entitled to be consulted by the Commission.

In reality, it is quite obvious that it is the signatory parties whose status is the *primary* concern of the examination of representativeness carried out by the Commission; but it has to be concluded that the three criteria in question repre-sent reference parameters which are neither sufficiently appropriate nor, pre-sumably, definitive for the purposes of that examination. This bears out the statement made above that the question of representativeness in the Community context is still at square one, a fact also acknowledged by the Court itself in stat-ing, at the end of its judgment, that its finding against the admissibility of UEAPME's action for annulment was without prejudice either to UEAPME's status as an organisation effectively representative of small and medium-sized enterprises at European level[50] or to the possibility of the same questions it had raised being subsequently brought before the same Court again in the case of other collective agreements implemented by means of the Council decision mechanism provided for in Article 139(2).[51]

---

[49] COM(96) 26, 31.01.1996 for Directive 96/34/EC; COM(97) 392 for Directive 97/81/EC; and COM(99) 203, 01.05.1999 for Directive 99/70/EC.

[50] It would in any case have been rather hard to say otherwise, given the membership figures pro-duced by UEAPME and essentially undisputed by the Council. These showed that the number of small and medium-sized enterprises affiliated to UEAPME is around 5½ million, increased to over 6½ million following its merger with EUROPMI, another European organisation representing small and medium-sized enterprises. In the circumstances, an express denial of UEAPME's representa-tiveness (for negotiation purposes as well) would have been frankly difficult.

[51] *UEAPME* judgment, n. 47 above, para. 10.

Small and medium-sized enterprises

The Commission's examination on the content of the agreement reached by the social partners and proposed for implementation by way of a Council decision could not fail to include, in addition, the ritual homage to what in Community circles (and elsewhere) constitutes a true obsession: the "protection" of small and medium-sized enterprises. In the Community context these are truly regarded as "angelic creatures"[52] to be preserved and protected from the assaults of labour law provisions considered to be nothing more than "administrative, financial and legal constraints . . . which would hold back [their] creation and development" (Article 137(2) TEC).

This particular aspect of the Community assessment process cannot be accused of suppressing the social partners' collective autonomy, since—in the specific bargaining situation under consideration here—all the collective agreements so far implemented through Directives have shown considerable respect for the need for the development and competitiveness of small and medium-sized enterprises by including a series of clauses expressly designed to guarantee their privileged position.[53]

The objections which can be raised therefore lie on a different plane not directly relevant to the purposes of present analysis, but involving a brief evaluation of the merits of the Community policy of safeguarding small and medium-sized enterprises. Reducing to an absolute minimum what should really be examined in far greater depth, it is impossible not to mention that:

(a) a legitimate and feasible policy to promote small and medium-sized enterprises should not necessarily mean a lowering of the levels of protection guaranteed to the workers employed in them;

(b) it is, in fact, in precisely these areas of economic activity that the most blatant situations of failure to apply labour law standards are found, for reasons including a weaker union presence; and lastly,

(c) there is a danger of the actual effectiveness of policies to promote small and medium-sized enterprises being prejudiced by the total vagueness of the notion concerned, which is identified on the basis of a generic reference to "size" taking no account of a number of trends (technological innovation of production processes, fragmentation of the legal personality of enterprises, delocalisation of certain activities, growing importance of an enterprise's financial situation rather than its workforce size) which mean that it makes no sense to talk of small and medium-sized enterprises without further qualification.

---

[52] To use the well-known expression coined by U. Romagnoli in an article on Italian law on individual dismissals ("Piccole imprese e grandi traumi", *Lavoro e diritto* 1990, No. 3, p. 517).

[53] General Consideration 12 and Clause 2.3(f) of the parental leave agreement; General Consideration 7 of the part-time work agreement; and General Consideration 11 of the fixed-term work agreement.

General approval

Where, however, the Commission's examination would appear to conflict with the full exercise of the social partners' collective autonomy is in the general evaluation of the agreement as a whole which is claimed and presented by the Commission as the fourth element of its assessment of a collective agreement reached by the social partners.

Admittedly, the clash is not expressed in direct terms, or at least not in the case of the assessments made by the Commission concerning the three Directives so far adopted on the basis of prior collective agreements. In the Explanatory Memorandum of the proposal for a Directive on parental leave, for example, the Commission confined itself to backing the choices made by the social partners, declaring that it "wholeheartedly endorses the aims of the social partners' framework agreement and sees it as an important . . . step forward in achieving equal opportunities for men and women [and] likely to increase the number of women in work". According to the Commission, furthermore, the agreement "contributes to realising . . . the introduction of new, flexible ways of organising work [which] meet the needs of enterprises which, faced with international competition, have to increase their competitiveness".[54] And comments of a similar nature are made in the Explanatory Memorandum of the proposal for the Directive on part-time work.[55]

The very fact that these assessments are manifestly rather vague and indefinite assessments makes them all the more irreconcilable with the alleged support of the social partners' collective autonomy at Community level. The Commission's unilateral arrogation to itself of a power of control over the outcomes of Community bargaining, when there is not the slightest mention of any such thing in the provisions originally contained in the ASP, is already questionable *per se*. But it seems totally irrational, or at least out of place, to include in what professes to be an examination of *legality* an appraisal of the political *merits* of the content of the agreement. Although the Commission cannot be denied the right to express assessments of the content of a Community collective agreement destined to be received into a Council decision on the basis of its own proposal, it does not seem feasible for such discretionary assessments to be presented as part of an examination of legality imposed by the Commission itself as a condition which must be satisfied if the agreement is to be implemented. In other words, this represents an out and out "approval clause", whose consistency with the Commission's reiterated wish to guarantee the social partners' autonomy and independence is at least doubtful. One cannot help wondering (even though the hypothesis seems somewhat remote) what the consequences would be if, quite apart from possibly deeming an agreement to

---

[54] COM(96) 26, 31.01.1996, paras 22–26.
[55] COM(97) 392, 23.07.1997, paras 31–35.

be contrary to Community law, the Commission gave a negative assessment of the substantive choices made by the social partners.

The early part of this chapter (sections 1 and 2) was devoted to showing that analysis of the first mode of implementation of Community collective agreements ("weak" implementation in accordance with the practices specific to the social partners and the Member States) makes it possible to depict a form of collective bargaining which is free from any externally imposed restrictions as to content but also lacks any legal relevance. On this basis it has been called "inconsequential" Community collective bargaining.

In the next sections, on the other hand, attention was concentrated on the second mode of implementation ("strong" implementation by way of a Council decision on a proposal from the Commission) and it was concluded that the mechanism concerned ensures the normative status of collective bargaining within the Community legal order but does not guarantee the unfettered self-determination of the areas dealt with.

The section which follows below will also be devoted to the second mode of implementation provided for in Article 139(2) TEC. Here, however, the aspect under consideration will not be the restrictions on content which have so far been demonstrated, but a different group of limits of a *procedural* nature.

3 LESSONS FROM EXPERIENCE: DIRECTIVE 96/34/EC ON PARENTAL LEAVE, DIRECTIVE 97/81/EC ON PART-TIME WORK AND DIRECTIVE 99/70/EC ON FIXED-TERM WORK

The second group of limits which would appear to preclude the possibility of relating Community collective agreements to the collective autonomy category therefore concerns the procedural formalities by means of which they are implemented by a Council decision on a proposal from the Commission.

Doubts as to the effective capacity of such a mechanism to guarantee free exercise of the social partners' bargaining autonomy, already expressed by certain authors (Sciarra, 1992; Aparicio Tovar, 1996b), seem to have been confirmed in the first applications of the provisions concerned, leading to the adoption of Directives 96/34/EC on parental leave, 97/81/EC on part-time work and 99/70/EC on fixed-term work. An analysis of the circumstances involved therefore offers an opportunity to move on from comments based purely on exegetic reconstruction of the original ASP provisions in order to verify whether and to what extent these recent bargaining and institutional events confirm or refute the hypotheses and evaluations advanced up till now.

The three events share something in common which would appear to confirm some of those evaluations: they all represent the eventual outcome of a Community decision-making process initiated and laboriously pursued over a number of years. The start of the procedure that ended with the adoption of

Directive 96/34/EC dates back to 1984[56] and those for Directives 97/81/EC and 99/70/EC date back to 1990.[57] Furthermore, it is extremely and explicitly clear in the Recitals of all three Directives that the Commission's decision to resort to the ASP mechanisms was one of *extrema ratio* with respect to an institutional decision-making procedure that was otherwise destined to remain blocked: "Whereas the Council has not been able to act . . ." and "Whereas the Council has not reached a decision . . .", we therefore (one could perhaps continue on behalf of the Commission) asked the social partners for their assistance in adopting, at last, these long-awaited rules!

It was when the type of Community act to be used to implement the agreement reached by the social partners was decided that the interpretative doubts expressed by early ASP commentators started to take concrete form. As is known, the Commission's choice of instrument, which up till then had remained open, lighted upon the Directive, presented categorically (certainly without overly much effort at explanatory reasoning) as "the proper instrument for implementing this framework agreement" signed by the social partners.[58]

The decision to implement the agreements concerned by way of Directives—with the agreements annexed separately to them—has given rise to a number of perplexities, mainly as regards the resultant difficulty of keeping the entire situation within the sphere of the collective autonomy whose promotion is, nevertheless, asserted by various Community documents to be an objective. The aspects for consideration and comment thrown up by the three cases in point are many and various.

The first problem which arises is that of determining the "fate" of the collective agreement signed by the social partners, which in the case of implementation by means of a Directive cannot be predetermined with any certainty as regards either its content or the identity of those covered by its provisions. No reminder is needed that "A directive shall be binding, as to the result to be achieved, upon each Member State to which it is addressed" (Article 249 TEC) and that it is consequently the Member States which are placed under an obligation by the three Directives concerned *either* to "bring into force the laws, regulations and administrative provisions necessary" *or* to "ensure that . . . the

[56] See the Commission's proposal in OJ C 316, 27.11.1984, p. 7. The proposal was based on Article 100 TEC (now Article 94) and its approval was therefore subject to the unanimity rule.

[57] The Commission's two proposals are in OJ C 224, 8.9.90, pp. 4 and 8. The first, regarding working conditions, was based on Article 100 TEC (now Article 94) and the second, regarding distortions of competition, was based on Article 100a TEC (now Article 95).

[58] Recital 11 of Directive 96/34/EC. Less apodeictic statements backed by more reasoned justification were contained in the Explanatory Memorandum of the Commission's proposal (COM(96) 26, 31.01.1996, para. 33), where the choice of a Directive as instrument was justified on the basis of the particular nature of the agreement in question (a framework agreement). The intimation was therefore, or so it seemed given to understand, that this was not a definitive choice of instrument in favour of the Directive and that the form taken by the implementing instrument was, rather, to be decided on a case-by-case basis, depending on the content of the agreement concerned. However, the identical considerations were then repeated in connection with the adoption of Directives 97/81/EC and 99/70/EC.

social partners have introduced the necessary measures by agreement" (Article 2(1) of the three Directives). It is therefore primarily the Member States which are the addressees of the Directive and consequently, in the situation under discussion, the protectors and guarantors of the effectiveness of the collective agreement reached by the social partners at Community level.

A situation such as that described cannot help but have an impact on the nature of the practical effectiveness of Community collective agreements implemented in accordance with the original ASP mechanisms. In general, it may be said that this form of implementation/incorporation of a collective agreement presupposes what might be termed a "definitive" or "final" act of reception. That is, one which represents not a mere transition leading, in its turn, to other acts or procedures of reception, particularly if the latter imply intervention by sources capable of substantively altering the balance of bargaining power arrived at by the parties. Examples of "definitive" or "final" provisions in this sense are the French ministerial *arrêtés* and Spanish ministerial *decretos* used to effect the extension of collective agreement signed by the most representative unions (Veneziani, 1992a).[59] Directives, however, are neither definitive nor final in the sense indicated. On the contrary, they are by definition interlocutory acts, since they can be regarded as sources creating directly enforceable rights for individuals only in the presence of well-defined conditions. Consequently, the choice of the Directive as the instrument for implementing collective agreements which has so far been followed by the Community institutions does not form the last stage of the implementation procedure but necessarily opens up the way for a subsequent stage: implementation of the Directive by means of the normative instruments particular to each Member State, or by way of national collective agreements in accordance with the mechanism envisaged in Article 137(4) TEC. Hence, European collective agreements have to undergo *double implementation*, first through a Directive and then through national instruments, at the end of which it will presumably be necessary to stop to reconsider the "remains" of the collective autonomy of the social partners signatory to the Community agreement.

A Member State could therefore implement the Community Directives on parental leave, part-time work and fixed-term work by means of a law, a regulation or an administrative act.

It is important not to underestimate the fact, that, in these circumstances, what the Member State has to implement is a Community *Directive* rather than the collective *agreement* annexed to it. This is of some considerable significance as regards the possibility open to the Member State of perhaps making adjustments to the substance of the agreement reached by the social partners. Given the broad discretionary scope allowed by the Directive instrument as regards choosing the form and methods considered most suitable for pursuing "the result to be achieved" (Article 249 TEC), the Member State concerned is, in

[59] Respectively Article 92(2) *Estatuto de los Trabajadores* and Book I, Title III, Chapter III *Code du Travail.*

short, in a position to redefine, unilaterally, a good many aspects of the agreement. Indeed, in its Arguments submitted in the *UEAPME* case the Council itself saw fit to point out that Directive 96/34 "has no application until it has been transposed into domestic law by the Member States, in which they enjoy a very broad discretion".[60] Just how such "broad discretion" for the Member States in implementing the content of the Directive (i.e. of the agreement reached by the social partners) can be reconciled with preserving the original wishes of the parties signatory to the European collective agreement is not altogether clear.

It must not be forgotten that the relative lack of restrictiveness of the Directive instrument which already existed as regards the choice of methods and forms used to achieve the results indicated in it has been backed up, in the provisions originally contained in the ASP, by a series of saving clauses offering Member States the opportunity of partially evading the Directives adopted on its basis. The provisions concerned, as is well known, are those which permit "maintaining or introducing more stringent protective measures compatible with the Treaty" (Article 137(5) TEC) and stipulate that Directives must avoid "imposing administrative, financial and legal constraints in a way which would hold back the creation and development of small and medium-sized undertakings" (Article 137(2) TEC). These discretionary margins left open for a Member State in the implementation of Directives—both those which are general features of the instrument in question and those specifically introduced by the provisions originally contained in the ASP—are, in themselves, justifiable and perhaps to some extent necessary. However, when applied to the slightly "special" Directives which implement Community collective agreements they are likely to prejudice the effectiveness of what may be considered one of the typical functions of the social partners' bargaining autonomy: standardisation of the employment conditions of the employees covered by a collective agreement.[61]

Even assuming that there is no likelihood of the negotiated clauses suffering any gross distortions—introduced by the national laws which implement the Community Directive which implements the social partners' agreement—there are some grounds for fearing that apparently minor adjustments or amendments could upset the balance of the negotiated compromise arrived at by the signatory parties, and therefore prejudice their collective autonomy. For example, it is not altogether fanciful to envisage the possibility of national legislative provi-

---

[60] Case T–135/96 *UEAPME v Council* [1998] ECR II–2335, paragraph 25. The Council's purpose was to show that, since it was primarily addressed to the Member States, the Directive on parental leave was not "of direct and individual concern" to UEAPME, which consequently had no right to bring an application for annulment of the said Directive (Article 230 TEC). The Court essentially concurred with the Council's thesis and dismissed the application as inadmissible.

[61] The correlation between a still uncertain definition of the normative function of Community collective agreements and the absence of the standardisation function is emphasised by Sciarra, 1996a at p. 197. See, along similar lines, the comments of Wedderburn,, 1995b at pp. 399–400, according to whom "an agreement signed at Community level may be 'transposed' to national level with equivalent effect by diverse national agreement, though with obvious risks of national variations, not least on 'normative' effects". However, a potential standardisation function is attributed to Community collective bargaining by Bercusson, 1993 and 1995.

sions transposing the Directive which introduce a substantial redefinition of the agreement's scope in terms of the employers and employees covered, justifying the exclusion of certain categories of employee or sectors of production on the grounds of a presumed (or indeed actual) greater degree of protection provided by national provisions, or a need to safeguard the development of small enterprises. Admittedly, in the case of the Directive on parental leave this latter eventuality was given explicit consideration by the signatories to the agreement themselves, who specified that Member States may "authorise special arrangements to meet the operational and organisational requirements of small undertakings".[62] But that still leaves Member States with the possibility of unilaterally defining the threshold above which a small enterprise ceases to be classed as such, or giving a broad interpretation to the vague notion of "special arrangements" whose introduction is authorised in the interests of small enterprises.

Given that the ability of the contracting parties to define (in both positive and negative terms) the beneficiaries of the agreement they have reached constitutes an integral element of a minimal and generally accepted notion of collective autonomy, it has to be concluded that, from this particular viewpoint as well, the Community provisions mean that European collective bargaining cannot be related to the collective autonomy scheme—at least, and in particular, in the light of their interpretation and application in the instances that have occurred to date. Nor does it hold any real water to argue that reasons of political expediency would presumably dissuade the Member States from actually making excessively intrusive interventions in the sphere reserved to the social partners' autonomy. It is not just the actual occurrence of such a circumstance which jeopardises the social partners' collective autonomy; the mere fact of its possibility conflicts unsustainably with the historically established postulates of collective autonomy.

Furthermore, the social partners signatory to the European framework agreements concerned gave a clear sign themselves that, despite having jointly requested the Commission to initiate the "strong" implementation procedure, they felt some uncertainty as to whether the implementation machinery might relegate them to a marginal position. Even in the case of "legislative" implementation of the agreement by way of normative measures (Directives and national laws), they took care to claim their right not to be "dispossessed" of the agreement they had concluded: "Whereas management and labour are best placed to find solutions that correspond to the needs of both employers and workers and must therefore be given a special role in the implementation and application of this Agreement".[63]

---

[62] Clause 2.3(f) of the Framework Agreement on parental leave. And in similar terms, General Consideration 7 of the Framework Agreement on part-time work and General Consideration 11 of the Framework Agreement on fixed-term work.

[63] General Consideration 8 of the Framework Agreement on part-time work (and, in almost identical terms, General Consideration 13 of the Framework Agreement on parental leave).

Consequently, the Directive instrument does not appear to offer adequate guarantees as regards the social partners' legitimate anxieties concerning the "fate" of the agreement they have concluded. Once it has been received into a Community Directive, a collective agreement "ceases to exist" and is merged into the normative instrument which is its host. A claim by its signatory organisations to "paternity" of the Directive plus Agreement would fall on deaf ears, as happened during the recent *UEAPME* case when the applicant's arguments aimed at demonstrating "the specific nature of Directive 96/34 [. . . whose content] was determined by those organisations themselves" were left largely unanswered in the judgment delivered by the Court, which viewed 96/34/EC as a perfectly ordinary Directive.

To sum up, there is no doubt that, in the transition from agreement to Directive and from there to national implementing legislation, collective autonomy loses something along the way. Even the social partners' claim to their retention of a priority role in the interpretation of the agreement's provisions seems destined to remain frustrated after its "metamorphosis" into a Directive. According to the social partners' expectations, "any matter relating to the interpretation of this agreement at European level should, in the first instance, be referred by the Commission to the signatory parties who will give an opinion".[64] As has already been pointed out, "une telle clause est sans effet sur le mode de règlement des difficultés d'interprétation d'une directive" (Lyon-Caen, A., 1997b at p. 360). Obviously, the social partners are not in a position to change the rules of procedure governing an action seeking interpretation which is brought before the Court of Justice: "the social partners cannot give their advice on their own initiative, but they have to ask the Court to be allowed to intervene in the case. If they are allowed, their advice can only be non-binding" (Franssen, 1998 at p.60). In any event, on the first and only occasion on which a Court has been called upon for a decision relating to a Directive plus Agreement,[65] the social partners' claim to a pre-eminent role in the interpretation of the agreement they concluded has proved a "forlorn hope".

To conclude, it may be said that implementation of a collective agreement by means of a Directive, with the subsequent transposition of that Directive into national legislation, does not guarantee the inviolability of the content of the agreement concerned. This is despite the fact that the Commission has on more than one occasion, with a great show of emphasis, declared its intention to respect that inviolability,[66] even going so far as to "threaten" the Council that it

---

[64] Clause 4.6 of the Framework Agreement on parental leave. A similar provision is implied in the Framework Agreement on part-time work, but—as remarked by Franssen, 1998 at n. 28—in this latter case it is contained (only) in the Preamble and is formulated in slightly different terms, i.e. in the form of a simple "request".

[65] Case T–135/96 *UEAPME v Council* [1998] ECR II–2335.

[66] The Commission has very often repeated, in a series of official documents, its total respect for free manifestations of the social partners' bargaining autonomy: "The Council decision must be limited to making binding the provisions of the agreement concluded between the social partners, so the text of the agreement would not form part of the decision, but would be annexed thereto" (COM(93) 600, 14.12.1993, para. 41). "If the agreement were to be amended, it could no longer be regarded as an agreement freely concluded between the social partners" (*ibid.* at para. 15).

will withdraw its own proposal if the latter fails to exhibit the same degree of reverence towards the agreement concerned.[67] However, the observations made above suggest that these explicit avowals of good intent are likely to remain a dead letter. In other words, there is a danger that the Commission's declared commitment to total observance of the content of the agreement concerned will turn out to be an empty protestation of respect for the social partners if the instrument then chosen to implement the agreement is a Directive, with the scope for adjustments and opportunities for intervention which that instrument reserves to the Member States in the process of the "second implementation" of the collective agreement. The possibility of making changes to the negotiated text, having at first been shown the door (by annexing to the Directive the text of the agreement as concluded) is then allowed to sidle back in through the window (because of the amendments to the text that are admitted in the process of transposing the Directive into national provisions).

In short, without a radical institutional reform bringing the Community legal order into line with its own protestations or intentions, there seems no way out of the impasse of a Community collective bargaining which is *free but inconsequential* ("weak" agreements) or *legally relevant but tied* ("strong" agreements).

---

[67] "If the Council decides . . . not to implement the agreement as concluded by the social partners, the Commission will withdraw its proposal" (COM(93) 600, 14.12.1993, para. 42).

6

Collective Agreements as a Resource of the Community Legal Order

1 "PUBLIC LAW" COLLECTIVE AGREEMENTS AND NEO-CORPORATIST MODELS IN THE COMMUNITY SYSTEM: A STILL UNLIKELY PROSPECT

FROM THE ABOVE analysis of the ASP provisions as embedded in the EC Treaty, it is now possible to begin drawing some conclusions regarding the true function which the Community system reserves to collective bargaining and, consequently, the legal nature attributable to it.

The gradual incorporation of collective industrial organisations and collective bargaining into what may be called a sphere of *public* relevance is not, of course, an exclusive prerogative of the Community system, but a fact of experience common to many national systems. This is something which could appear at first sight to contrast with the terms of a long-standing and now re-emerging debate in which many legal scholars have, in fact, arrived at a quite different conclusion, attributing a wholly *private law* nature to the trade unions and employers' organisations and their bargaining activities.

Without venturing into the territory of dogma or classification—all the more sterile and inconclusive at a time when the public/private distinction between the sources and subjects of law production is becoming ever more blurred and ever less meaningful[1] (Chapter 2, section 1.2)—is nevertheless necessary to examine how the alleged tendency within the Community system for industrial relations to be drawn into the public sphere can be reconciled with the traditional perception of their place in the private sphere. It is well known that in many European systems the doctrinal defence of the private law nature of collective industrial organisations and collective bargaining has generally signified something quite specific: a reaction against earlier historical experiences of a coporatist nature in which incorporation into the public sphere had negated their independence and autonomy.[2]

---

[1] On the ideological function of the public/private distinction in labour law, see Klare, 1982, who observes that keeping labour relations within the private sphere "is a way to explain why the basic principles of democracy do not apply in the [American] workplace".

[2] The debate has been particularly heated in Italy, but elsewhere as well. See, with reference to the Swedish system, the comments by Fahlbeck, 1987 at p. 287: "The *de facto* public statutory character of today's collective agreements is vehemently repudiated by the majority unions, and to some extent, by employers' federations. The main reason, I submit, is the on-going debate in which corporatism has been equated with fascism".

However, that historical fact on its own does not account for the consensus on the matter recorded in the literature. The argument mainly put forward as the basis for this view is a different one, placing the emphasis on the function of employee representation historically assumed by the unions and collective bargaining. The undeniable tendency towards the incorporation of the trade unions into the sphere of public relevance is countered (Fahlbeck, 1987) by the fact of their original function of voluntary and contractual representation of the rights and interests of their members, which is seen as the major factor and sufficient to exclude any type of institutionalised identification of the collective industrial organisations with the public sphere.

Given that it is these two factors which underlie the general perception of the entirely private law nature of trade unions and collective bargaining, what we now have to consider is the extent to which they still hold good in the particular context of the Community system. And the answer has to be in the negative.

The observations presented here, it may be recalled, have sought to demonstrate that, in the Community context, trade unions and collective bargaining as organisations and activities devoted to representing the rights and interests of their member employees in the private law "agency" sense (Chapter 4, section 1) are undergoing re-definition in favour of a view focused more on the relationships established between the social partners and the Community institutions and hence between the former's bargaining activities and the Community legal order. In these circumstances, the importance of collective bargaining as an instrument of confrontation between employers and employee representatives is supplanted by the need to devise a new theoretical reconstruction of collective activity which is geared more to the external relations of collective industrial organisations with public institutions than to their internal relations with their own members.

In short, any attempt at a reconstruction of the Community system must start with a "primordial" and only seemingly obvious question: who are the interlocutors of the trade unions at European level? Given what has already been said earlier about the essential features of the bargaining model specified by the provisions originally contained in the ASP, the answer is obvious: rather than the employers at European level, it is the Community institutions (and in particular the Commission) which must be regarded as the true interlocutors.[3] An analysis of the origins and development of the social dialogue, from Val Duchesse to Maastricht, shows clearly that it is only through the (self-interested) intermediation of the Commission that the European unions have gained a "hearing" from the (reluctant) European employers' associations. In other words—just as

---

[3] Some authors have pointed to a "preponderance, in the legal configuration of the social dialogue, of involvement in the processes of Community rule-making, in a relationship which nowadays seems characterised more by a tripartite dialectic between the Community institutions and the social partners than by a contractual dialectic between the latter" (Scarpelli, 1993b at p. 167).

has been happening in some national systems since the 1970s[4]—it is possible to identify in the Community context a situation in which the legitimacy of the Community-level trade union derives not from the mandate of employees or the associational dimension, which is in fact tending to disappear, but rather from an institutional recognition which is given concrete expression in the conferment on the unions of what are essentially public regulatory functions.

It has to be said that all this evokes a model of union activity which certainly did not begin in the Community context. To talk of a quasi "public" status for the unions and the presence of "statal" authority in the bargaining process is equivalent to talking of neo-corporatist models.[5] It is therefore not by chance that the past few years have witnessed the accumulation of a now abundant literature—of a legal and, even more so, political science nature—on the possibility of presenting the relationship between the Community and the Community social partners in terms of a hypothetical Community neo-corporatist model (Falkner, 1997).[6] That the ASP (and now EC Treaty) provisions do, in fact, contain certain elements which can be related to the neo-corporatist logic in abstract terms is recognised even by those who exclude any possibility of relating the Community bargaining model to it (Obradovic, 1995). As many authors have pointed out, however, these are merely circumstantial elements which on more careful consideration are quickly found to be insufficient to support interpretations seeking to recognise an overall neo-corporatist approach in the Community bargaining system.

According to a doctrinal summing-up which attempts to reconcile some conflicting positions on definition,[7] identification with the neo-corporatist model can be applied to a vast and differentiated range of experiences, characterised by "a tendency towards the monopolisation of representation", in the context of which "the organisations which represent functional interests interact and collaborate *with each other and with the state*[8] in the process of reaching decisions [and] in their implementation; [and in which] involvement and negotiation take

---

[4] For a theoretical reconstruction of these events see, in the case of Italy, Ferraro, 1981. By way of critical comment on the doctrinal positions concerned, this situation has been represented effectively by means of the formula "collective heteronomy" (Scarpelli, 1993a at p. 150) and reference to a "configuration of employees and the collective entity in terms of otherness . . . in the sense of the total irrelevance of the employee's position, from the legal point of view, for the purposes of incorporating collective autonomy" (Scarpelli, 1993a at p. 146).

[5] The literature on neo-corporatism, starting with the now classic paper by Schmitter, 1974, is without exaggeration enormous, and it is possible to mention only a few contributions judged to be among the more important: Pizzorno, 1980; Cawson (ed.), 1985; Schmitter and Lehmbruch (eds), 1979; Streeck and Schmitter (eds), 1985. For a labour law perspective, see the articles collected in Vardaro (ed.), 1988. More recently, a comparative analysis of the "revival of neo-corporatism" has been given by Crouch, 1998.

[6] A more nuanced statement is advanced by Betten, 1998 at p. 28, who talks of a "quasi neo-corporatist model form of social policy law-making".

[7] Numerous different attempts have been made to define neo-corporatism. To compare the two positions on which the definition formulated in the text concerned is based, see Schmitter, 1974 and Lehmbruch, 1977.

[8] Emphasis in the original.

place in a system of institutionalised relations" (Maraffi, 1981 at p. 32).[9] From these brief but highly meaningful comments, formulated with reference to national neo-corporatist models, it is possible to single out a series of characterising elements which preclude application of the neo-corporatist model to the supranational context, even—and this is the point to be stressed here—after the adoption of the Maastricht agreements and the traces of neo-corporatism which they seem at first sight to introduce into the Community system.[10]

First, a feature common to many analyses is the observation that every neo-corporatist system presupposes the presence of a state capable of ensuring the function of exchange which distinguishes democratic neo-corporatist practices from the authoritarian corporatism of the 1920s and 1930s.[11] Even from this preliminary aspect, it seems somewhat doubtful that the institutional characteristics of the Community system are compatible with the neo-corporatist paradigm. For a start, it is widely acknowledged that the very possibility of conceiving of the Community as a state is doubtful (Weiler, 1998). It is true, as was said some time ago, that "the state has become a bit like the weather. Social scientists in recent years have been talking a great deal about it, but haven't been able to do much with it" (Schmitter, 1984 at p. 1). But not even the most relativistic and least definitional of approaches makes it possible to find in the Community the features of an entity of a statal nature, at least not in the sense in which the concept of the state is meant in its capacity as a corporatist actor (Streeck and Schmitter, 1991).[12]

This is because in the latter guise the state participates in bargaining processes as an actor with resources at its disposal—both financial and regulatory—which it is able to use for the purposes of political exchange with the social partners. In the Community context, on the other hand, the public authority has neither at its disposal. It possesses no financial resources in the strict sense, in that—in contrast to what has happened historically within the Member States—Community social policy has never found expression in measures effecting redistribution or direct transfers of resources.[13] Neither does it possess financial resources in the indirect sense, since the main such resource, i.e. the use of taxation as an element of social, industrial or employment policies, is still left in the hands of the Member States. Nor, lastly, does it possess regulatory resources, given that Community jurisdiction in the mat-

---

[9] Essentially similar observations are reiterated by the same author in Maraffi, 1998. For a review of the various doctrinal conceptualisations of neo-corporatism, see Gualmini, 1997 at ch. I.

[10] According to the bold assertion advanced by Rhodes, 1995 at p. 106: "a system of neocorporatist policymaking it is not".

[11] On the state as a corporatist actor which participates in political exchange by making use of the resources at its disposal, see Obradovic, 1995; Rhodes, 1993; Streeck, 1993 and 1994.

[12] Who talks explicitly of the "European Community's quasi-state, or non-state" (p. 142).

[13] The exceptions to this are the common agricultural policy and regional policy; i.e. sectors which are somewhat marginal to the traditional areas of action of national social policies (Pierson and Leibfried, 1995a at p. 33).

ters which normally form the object of neo-corporatist exchange is notoriously limited.[14]

But even when we turn to a second profile which has been singled out as an essential element of a neo-corporatist model—"corporatisation of the processes of representation" (Maraffi, 1981 at p. 23)—we find nothing to corroborate the possibility of describing Community regulatory processes in the social policy field in neo-corporatist terms. Apart from the scant degree of definition and formalisation of one of the necessary premises of neo-corporatist systems, i.e. monopoly of representation (Schmitter, 1974),[15] what is of particular relevance here is the fact that the logic underlying neo-corporatist models presupposes, in the first place, a specific availability of *all* protagonists to be participants in a regulatory mechanism in which they are under no obligation to take part—an availability which is, obviously, identified with the *advantage* they gain (or think they may gain) from such participation, given the overall institutional context within which this participation takes place.

The discourse therefore shifts from a legal plane to an analysis of the political, institutional and economic dynamics which determine the preferences and behaviour of the collective actors; in short, onto an evaluative plane where the instruments and categories of neo-institutionalist analysis operate.[16]

In this area essentially two positions are encountered, envisaging mutually alternative scenarios. According to a first perspective European employers are induced to adopt and cultivate a constructive and co-operative stance in negotiating with the Commission and their union counterparts by reason of a special interest[17] consisting in the joint definition of rules which will guarantee a more efficient functioning of market mechanisms. Grafted onto this viewpoint is another line of argument which derives from economic theories based on the perception of economic rationality as the criterion governing the behaviour of individual and collective actors, and which points out that employers are induced to accept or even promote the adoption of uniform rules on employment conditions, from which they gain benefit, in so far as such rules prove functional in correcting distortions of competition.

---

[14] These conclusions are not shared by those authors who tend to separate the neo-corporatist model from any major policy orientation: "The inclusion of a 'policy dimension' in the definition of corporatism, however, unnecessarily restricts the approach to some regimes only, and to a specific phase of history when Keynesianism was indeed practised. In addition: Only if the notion is divorced from a specific material policy can the economic effects of corporatist systems as such be investigated. There are thus good reasons for perceiving of corporatism as a governance modus rather than as a type of policy" (Falkner, 1997). In the Lehmbruch and Schmitter, 1982 reconstruction, however, the presence of a pro-labour government is deemed to be a condition of the neo-corporatist model.

[15] On these aspects, cf. Obradovic, 1995 at pp. 269–272.

[16] On the revival of the institutionalist paradigm in the 1980s, finding applications in various social disciplines including economics, political science and sociology, see the classic contribution of March and Olsen, 1984. For an analysis involving the neo-institutionalist approach to European integration studies, see Armstrong, 1998b.

[17] Which Streeck, 1995b at p. 408, not concealing his perplexities on the subject, caustically calls "enlightened self-interest".

The above perspective is countered by a second one—less deterministic and more anchored in factual experiences to date—which, unlike the first, rejects the idea that the pursuit of a rational interest can prompt European employers to accept a neo-corporatist system of regulation combined with market-correcting mechanisms. This second branch of doctrine certainly has as one of its advocates a commentator who has devoted tireless efforts over the past few years to illustrating the reasons why an availability of European employers to favour the development of a Community neo-corporatist model is an unlikely prospect (Streeck, 1990, 1992, 1993, 1994, 1995a and 1995b; Streeck and Schmitter, 1991). It counters those who take the view—on the basis of either functionalist arguments or arguments of economic rationality—that it is possible to infer the likelihood of a collaborative and dialogic stance on the part of European employers in the construction of a Community bargaining system inspired by neo-corporatist canons, with the objection that "if rational, self-interested pursuit of economic advantage was enough to bring about a market-correcting social policy, the United States would be the world's leading welfare state" (Streeck, 1995b at p. 411).

The facts show that, at least so far, European employers have not borne out the predictions (neither the neo-institutionalist nor the rational choice ones) which postulated their inevitable receptiveness to a supranational level of regulation and bargaining. On the contrary, there is no doubt that they have always opposed attempts at Community regulation and accept negotiation only as the lesser of two evils and *extrema ratio* compared with legislative intervention. The "change of mind" shown by UNICE in 1998 when, after an initial refusal,[18] it indicated its willingness to return to the negotiating table on national-level information and consultation of employees following the "threat" from the Commission to present a proposal of its own (which was subsequently presented at the end of 1998),[19] would seem to provide concrete evidence of this state of affairs and corroborate the thesis of the above-mentioned commentator, who coined the apt expression "bargaining in the shadow of exit" (Streeck, 1998). Over six years on from the original entry into force of the ASP, an overall assessment of the bargaining processes initiated so far offers little reason for excessive optimism. Of the nine initiatives launched to date, four have been crowned with bargaining success (agreements on parental leave, part-time work, fixed-term work and the organisation of working time of seafarers);[20] five, however, have resulted in substantial failure, i.e. without the conclusion of a collective agreement between the European social partners (European Works

---

[18] See *European Industrial Relations Review* No. 291, April 1998.

[19] COM(98) 612, 11.11.1998. See the information on UNICE's change of mind in *European Industrial Relations Review* No. 295, August 1998.

[20] The first three agreements were implemented by means of Directives, and in the case of the fourth, signed on 30 September 1998, the Commission has presented a proposal for a Directive (COM(98) 662, 23.11.1998).

Councils, burden of proof,[21] prevention of sexual harassment at work,[22] working time in the transport sector[23] and national-level information and consultation).

Besides, even those who maintain that a Community re-emergence of the neo-corporatist model is possible cannot help but admit that "with open economic borders, the political resources of labour (mainly strike) are devaluated as compared to capital's exit option. Only with an even stronger backing from 'the state' than before or under great societal pressure can there nowadays be some sort of equal weight: e.g. if there is a realistic threat of legislation in the case of absence of industry's readiness to bargain with labour; or if a failure of collective negotiations could create social unrest" (Falkner, 1997). Neither of these two conditions appears to be fulfilled at the moment: the "negotiate or we will legislate" formula (Dølvik, 1997) does not seem to represent the ultimate goad in fostering bargaining developments at European level, since it should, more accurately, run "negotiate or we will legislate . . . to the extent that we are able". Here again, the limits of the Community decision-making process turn out to be closely interconnected with the boundaries of European collective bargaining or vice versa.

Consequently, experience to date would appear to support those who take the view that the European employers hold almost absolute sway over the outcomes of Community social policy: "it is hard to see what the Commission or the ETUC could offer to employers as an incentive to become constructive participants in European Community legislation and collective bargaining and refrain from using their newly-won political status under the codecision-making procedure to do even more effectively what they have always done: prevent the replication of the European national welfare at supranational level" (Streeck, 1994 at p. 171). According to this view, in the case of bargaining processes the employers are in a position, simply by being party to the proceedings, to block or delay agreements or empty them of meaningful content; and in the case of legislative intervention they hold similar sway over social policy outcomes because of the singular coincidence of interests between themselves and the Member States, which are anxious to preserve their respective national sovereignty: "the act of defending a country's sovereignty in the councils of Europe and the act of defending the freedom of 'market forces' in the integrated European economy thus came to be one and the same" (Streeck, 1995b at p. 395).

If these conclusions are accepted, it is therefore clear that the scope even for

---

[21] Directive 97/80/EC on the burden of proof in cases of discrimination based on sex (extended to the United Kingdom by Directive 98/52/EC) was adopted in accordance with the ordinary decision-making procedure following the failure of the negotiations between the social partners.

[22] See COM(96) 373, 24.07.1996, *Consultation of Management and Labour on the Prevention of Sexual Harassment at Work*. On the negative outcome of the negotiations, see *European Industrial Relations Review* No. 284, September 1997.

[23] The negotiations, launched in September 1997, were broken off in October 1998.

categorising Community bargaining processes just as neo-corporatist in tendency becomes virtually zero.[24]

However, it is only fair to stress that these views do not represent the entire spectrum of opinion. Another section of sociological and political science doctrine, which has devoted itself just as assiduously to examining the social policy outlook for Community Europe, has maintained that the hyper-scepticism displayed by Streeck with respect to the bargaining stance of the European employers and their tacit alliance with national governments in favour of a "single market without a single state",[25] although not wholly unjustified, cannot be shared in its entirety (Pierson and Leibfried, 1995b). In particular, the authors concerned challenge what Streeck has called the "elective affinity between nationalism and liberalism" (Streeck, 1998), i.e. the presumed coincidence between the interests of the European employers and those of the Member States. These contentions are considered to be arbitrary or overly simplistic, in that they are based on an unjustifiably uniform and undifferentiated assessment of the interests particular to individual Member States. They fail to take account, it is argued, of the reality of a fragmented and non-unitary (multi-tiered)[26] Community policy-making system in which multiple centres and levels of political authority interact in a complex process of reciprocal competition, adjustment and accommodation (Pierson and Leibfried, 1995b at p. 433) and in which it is consequently not possible to attribute to any of the actors involved a predetermined interest which will result in behaviour and strategies which are predictable, let alone immutable.

These objections certainly contain some grains of truth and, from the political science point of view, show up a number of gaps in the hyper-pessimistic interpretation mentioned above. Furthermore, it has to be conceded that from the strictly legal point of view the ASP did not, in fact, grant the European employers any co-decision-making powers over the elaboration of Community legislation on social policy, and that there is therefore probably no justification for assuming that they possess the real power of veto which Streeck's analysis would suggest.

Nevertheless, this does not alter the fact that, from the standpoint of a prospective analysis of Community bargaining dynamics to ascertain whether they are such as to create a system of the neo-corporatist type, the "sceptical" observations in question retain all their validity and are a decisive

---

[24] See, along these same lines, Lange, 1992 at p. 256, according to whom "A social democratic or neocorporatist Europe, redistributing to the 'losers' as markets become freer, is improbable. More likely is a neopluralist social Europe in which temporary coalitions of interests and governments form around proposals for specific European interventions in the social area, while other social issues are left to national or subnational governments or to the results of collective bargaining".

[25] See Streeck, 1995b at p. 414; but similar arguments pointing to the prospect of a "market without a state" were already presented in Streeck, 1990.

[26] For an exposition of the theory concerned, see Pierson and Leibfried, 1995a. References to the *multi-tiered system* in the context of a reconstruction of the legal status of Community collective agreements are made in Sciarra, 1996a.

element in excluding the plausibility of any such hypothesis. Furthermore, if we ignore the divergences of opinion mentioned at the start the actual conclusions reached by the supporters of the multi-tiered system theory also concur in excluding the credibility of the Community neo-corporatist hypothesis.

The corollaries which may be inferred from the theorisation of the Community legal order as a multi-tiered system include some which, in fact, fundamentally undermine the essential presuppositions of any such bargaining system. This applies, in particular, to the *destructuring of the collective interest* of Community employees, an interest which surely constitutes, at least in principle, the very basis and objective of trade union activity at supranational level. It is obvious that, in a context of not only political but especially economic and social fragmentation, defining a uniform collective interest to represent in negotiations with employers represents a difficult exercise in consolidation for the European unions. The combined presence within the context of a single bargaining system of areas which are economically and socially disparate therefore constrains the actors of Community bargaining to bear in mind that the collective interests to be represented may be defined by boundaries which have more to do with Community geo-economics[27] than with a shared identity as workers. Thus, the socio-economic fragmentation of Community Europe lends itself to the formation of unfamiliar "cross-class alliances" structured on a territorial basis (Pierson and Leibfried, 1995b at p. 450), representing an epoch-making break with the century-old traditions of the trade union movement and union activity[28] and something very different from the "borderless solidarity" hoped for by many (Dølvik, 1997). A development of this kind, in my view, inevitably entails consequences for the configuration of the European union entity, in that it is likely to break the potential identification between European workers and the European union constructing and representing their collective interest, on which the chances of success rest for the bargaining system originally outlined by the ASP.[29]

In short, these arguments based on the institutional, economic and social fragmentation of Community Europe offer no certainties whatever—neither negative nor, indeed, positive—but present an open and changeable scenario in the context of which collective bargaining, in the traditional sense of a privileged and potentially single locus of the confrontation between predetermined and opposing subjects and interests, finds more shade than light.

---

[27] For some comments regarding the social and economic geography of Community Europe, see D'Antona, 1992.

[28] But the reality of coalitions of interests formed around territorial rather than class boundaries is not unknown to experiences elsewhere, such as the USA, for example (Pierson and Leibfried, 1995a at p. 28).

[29] For an interesting review of current developments in the Europeanisation of trade union strategy and also of "internal" ETUC dynamics over the 1990s (something not commonly found in the literature), see Dølvik, 1997.

At the beginning of Chapter 4 it was stated that the *pars destruens* of this book would demonstrate what European collective bargaining is not. The sections which followed above were therefore devoted to illustrating that Community collective bargaining is not an activity constituting private law type representation of the rights and interests of Community employees (section 1); it is not a manifestation of pluralism and collective autonomy (section 2 and section 2.1, section 3 and section 3.1); nor, although bearing in mind the tendency towards its incorporation into a sphere of public relevance, is it a first step towards the construction of a Community neo-corporatist model (Chapter 6, section 1).

It is now time to move on to the *pars construens* of my argument, suggesting what European bargaining is or could be.

2 COLLECTIVE BARGAINING AS A RESOURCE OF THE COMMUNITY LEGAL ORDER

Future developments in Community collective bargaining are not readily predictable. Nevertheless, the analysis presented above indicates, I submit, the need to define a new theoretical framework which does not aspire to being prescriptive, but merely descriptive of the terms in which such bargaining seems to have been perceived by those who have done most to plead its cause: the Community institutions.

2.1 European collective bargaining as a regulatory resource

"Consultation of management and labour at Community level provides a firmer foundation for Community social legislation and must therefore be stepped up".[30] In this statement, the "purpose-serving" dimension of European collective bargaining with respect to the functionality of the Community law-making system—asserted more than once in the course of this study—is confirmed *per tabulas* and, so to speak, "authentically" by the Community institutions themselves.[31]

On a number of occasions in the preceding pages emphasis has been placed on the instrumental nature of the support given by the Community to suprana-

[30] Council Resolution of 27 March 1995 on the *Transposition and Application of Community Social Legislation* (95/C 168/01, in OJ C 168/1, 4.7.1995).

[31] The Council is not alone in revealing through its official documents the real perception of collective bargaining held by the Community institutions. In its Social Action Programme 1998–2000 (COM(98) 259, 29.04.1998), the Commission stressed that the legislative progress achieved in the social field "has been facilitated by the use of the more collaborative form of decision-making, involving the social partners, introduced by the Agreement on Social Policy". And in its Resolution on the Commission proposal for a Directive on part-time work (A4–0352/97 of 19 November 1997), the European Parliament stated that "the procedures pursuant to Articles 3 and 4 of the Agreement on Social Policy can in some cases be useful, especially for unblocking an impasse within the Council" (para. 12).

tional collective bargaining, identifying the main motivation for that support as the Community institutions' interest in utilising collective bargaining as a resource to be deployed for the purposes of overcoming the Community regulatory difficulties mentioned earlier (Chapter 2).

And events to date would appear to confirm that view and therefore to confirm the gulf which separates such a genetic code of Community collective bargaining from the notion of collective autonomy traditionally recognised as a fundamental element of national bargaining systems. Even the CES-UNICE-CEEP agreement of 31 October 1991, often cited in the literature as confirming the validity of transnational collective autonomy, was an early indication of the exploitation of this process by the Community institutions for purposes somewhat different from those envisaged by the contracting parties, who certainly did not intend its scope to be confined to only some, albeit most, Member States. However, the collective agreement in question enabled the Community institutions to overcome the British veto regarding the projected (and unsuccessful) reform of the social chapter contained in the EC Treaty, by providing them with a way out which was honourable, albeit by way of a compromise.

But it is the circumstances surrounding the first three Directives to be adopted on the basis of Article 139(2) TEC, as examined in detail above, which provide concrete evidence of the functionality of European collective agreements to the Community's purposes (and the limits of those purposes), with the attendant risk of collective bargaining being turned into an "instrument for the consensual attainment of objectives which have not been selected autonomously but imposed from outside" (Caruso, 1997 at p. 331).

The lack of real autonomy of Community collective bargaining, and its predominantly instrumental role for the purposes of resolving regulatory problems, were further accentuated by what was—prior to the entry into force of the Treaty of Amsterdam—the uncertain institutional framework in which it was embedded: "it only takes the Community to opt for the 'ordinary' decision-making procedure [that laid down in the EC Treaty] for the obligation to consult the social partners to be easily avoided and their supposed bargaining autonomy to be thereby nullified" (Aparicio Tovar, 1996b). And this was an eventuality to which the Commission openly intended to give priority, judging from its declaration on a number of occasions that, whenever possible, preference would be given to the procedure involving the Fifteen, with the consequent exclusion of the social partners.[32]

But there is also a further element which, in conjunction with and perhaps more so than the others, helps to pinpoint the Community system's position with regard to supranational collective bargaining. What the ASP appears to

---

[32] See *Report on the Community Charter of the Fundamental Social Rights of Workers and on the Protocol on Social Policy annexed to the Treaty Establishing the European Union* (COM(95) 184, 24.05.1995), p. 37; *Communication Concerning the Application of the Agreement on Social Policy* (COM(93) 600, 14.12.1993), p. 10.

have been intending to establish is not an autonomous and self-contained collective bargaining *system*, but a very different prospect involving only a highly fragmented and compartmentalised assessment of *individual* collective agreements. This not only excludes even the possibility of talking of a Community collective bargaining system but also, combined with the other elements already examined, unveils the true significance of the Community legislation concerned, which is more concerned with making use of the regulatory support provided by this or that agreement than with promoting the conditions for the full exercise of collective autonomy by the European social partners.

In short, it is the Community's regulatory difficulties which are the real driving force behind Community collective bargaining; and that being so, it is no accident that "the increased institutional support for the social dialogue [has come] just at a time when Community social policy is passing through a phase which certainly cannot be called full of drive" (Aparicio Tovar, 1996b at p. 181). In point of fact, excepting the two equal treatment Directives of 1986 and the 1989 Framework Directive on health and safety at work,[33] the period during which the ASP arrived on the scene coincided with a prolonged black-out in the area of social legislation.[34]

Consequently, presenting a classification of collective bargaining which highlights its function as a *regulatory resource* of the Community legal order basically amounts to stressing that, in the context of a general crisis in Community regulatory mechanisms affecting not only the effectiveness but also, and perhaps in particular, the actual formulation of Community rules,[35] collective bargaining was "conceived"[36] by the Community institutions, and especially the Commission, as a feasible alternative to the traditional method of legislative harmonisation. In this sense it could be said that collective agreements perform for European social law the function which mutual recognition performed for the free movement of goods and services: that of an expedient which can be put to good use in overcoming regulatory uncertainties. However, whereas mutual recognition—leaving aside possible critical evaluations—proved an effective instrument capable of surmounting certain intractable problems in the harmonisation method, Community collective bargaining seems unlikely to achieve the same results: because its phenomenological dimension is still limited; because the Community economic and institutional context by no means guarantees the full co-operation between labour and management which is, however, generally presupposed by Community documents; and because, lastly, the actual rules originally laid down by the ASP do not provide the conditions for fully developed bargaining activity by the social partners.

---

[33] Directives 86/378/EEC (occupational social security schemes) and 86/613/EEC (self-employed women), and Directive 89/391/EEC.

[34] Lasting from Directive 80/987/EEC until Directive 9/533/EEC.

[35] With reference, obviously, to the dual notion of supranationality (respectively normative and decision-related) which has been mentioned on more than one occasion in the course of this study.

[36] In the dual sense of both "procreated" and "perceived".

A patent disproportion is therefore discernible between the scant degree of autonomous legitimacy possessed by the bargaining instrument in the Community context and the Commission's high expectations of it. Given this situation, one of two things is possible: either the Community institutions over-estimated collective bargaining and were the victims of the inertia syndrome consisting in the assumption that Community bargaining is a functional equivalent of national bargaining; or, although aware of its weakness in the Community context they failed to do what was necessary to give the bargaining instrument a more constitutionally adequate status. That being so, and taking the consequences to the extreme, it may be said provocatively that from the viewpoint of the Community institutions' real intention European collective bargaining is—or is quietly left to be—a form of bargaining without effectively representative actors, without any clear validity, without autonomous procedures and rules of administration and without the guarantee of instruments of industrial action. All that matters is that the social partners, through their bargaining activity, should provide the Commission with certain elements which are useful in surmounting the regulatory problems by which it is afflicted.

An accusation of excessive pessimism could be levelled against the above remarks, as indeed against the entire analysis of Community bargaining presented here, on the grounds of their failure to take account of the role which the supranational collective organisations have somehow or other managed to secure for themselves within the Community system. Some authors, certainly not easily moved to euro-optimism,[37] advocate a more moderate or at any rate less immediately dismissive attitude which makes allowance for the "step-by-step approach traditionally adopted for social policies" and the "important implications that any Community source—albeit a very weak one—may have in building up further developments" (Sciarra, 1996a at p. 192).

At first sight, therefore, the "moderate" observations made by such authors would appear to contradict the vigorous conclusions presented here as regards the latter's emphasis on the manifestly instrumental perception of supranational collective bargaining exhibited by the Community institutions. And it is quite true that it would be illusory to have expected anything more than what was actually provided by the ASP, which has to be interpreted and evaluated in clear sight of the fact that it represents the most that the Community was able to offer at the time. In this sense the exhortation to contextualise judgements on the potential effectiveness of the Community collective bargaining system, and the admonition to relate what has already been achieved to what more can be achieved in the future, help to avoid the risk of absolute and definitive conclusions, which are out of place in a Community context where it is never a mistake to view matters in relative and historical terms.

---

[37] Those who may, on the other hand, be classed as incurable optimists include the authors who with regard to the prospects for Community collective bargaining declare, with a confidence whose presuppositions may be sought in vain in the text concerned, that "the path is clear: time to dream" (Blanpain and Engels, 1995 at p. 351). These oneiric sentiments are repeated in Blanpain, 1998b.

On closer examination, however, these observations (and others following a similar line of cautious expectation) may take on a partly different meaning which corroborates or supports the interpretative hypothesis suggested here. Inherent in this "moderate" doctrine there are, in fact, two assertions which are addressed towards different viewpoints, for which they signify potentially contrasting things.

In the first place, a prudently interlocutory approach may be read as a defence thrown up against the pessimistic slant displayed by some authors, the most intransigent of whom would seem, moreover, in no way disposed to retreat from their position, at least judging from the tone of certain statements which represent a kind of "sceptics' manifesto against moderatism": "real Europeanism may be precisely one that does not refuse to consider the weaknesses of present European constructions, and indeed is willing to entertain the possibility that what should and must come about may fail to do so. That this would be a historical tragedy does not mean that it can be avoided by denying its possibility" (Streeck, 1994 at n. 23).

In the second place, however, the "moderate" doctrine's exhortation to caution (Sciarra, 1996a) not only contains an *evaluation* but is subtended by a *factual statement*, difficult to refute, on which even the most radical of sceptics inevitably agree: that the ASP and its collective bargaining arrangements constitute only a semi-finished product (Veneziani, 1992b; Valdés Dal-Ré, 1997) which is by definition perfectible. Those implicitly addressed by this second assertion are necessarily different from those addressed by the first, since the statement that the Community bargaining regime is still incomplete seems likely to take on a very different meaning when directed towards the "optimists", who obviously contest its veracity. And among the optimists on European collective bargaining the foremost are assuredly the Community institutions, which on more than one occasion have displayed their conviction, with the correlative intention to consider that the journey towards full recognition of the Community social partners' collective autonomy is already sufficiently far advanced and hence to regard the ASP as a major work of progress which "confirms the recognition, as already enshrined in Article 118B of the Single Act, of the fundamental role of the social partners . . . The important point . . . is to allow space for natural evolution . . . The creation of heavy structures is not likely to yield the best results".[38] These statements by the Commission, representative of an approach which has been expressed on several occasions, therefore do not exclude the necessity of a settling-in phase for the bargaining mechanisms provided for by the ASP. But there is no precise recognition of the serious shortcomings which threaten their full functionality, and we are even left with the suspicion that the "heavy structures" which are deemed inappro-

---

[38] *Report on the Community Charter of the Fundamental Social Rights of Workers and on the Protocol on Social Policy annexed to the Treaty Establishing the European Union* (COM(95) 184, 24.05.1995), pp. 34 and 40.

priate may be precisely the constitutional bases which were earlier defined as absolutely indispensable to collective autonomy (see Chapter V.1.1 above).[39]

From this point of view, therefore, even the most cautious assertions—postulating that the process which will lead to a fully developed transnational collective autonomy is still at an intermediate stage—concur in unveiling a reality different from the excessively rosy picture painted by the Commission. Relativising judgement as to the structural and functional appropriateness of the ASP regime by stressing that it represents only a first step along the road throws up a defence against the pessimism displayed by some authors, *but also* deprives the optimism displayed by (some) Community institutions of any basis. The present study falls within the second of these perspectives, in that it essentially identifies some fundamental limitations of Community collective bargaining which mean that any show of certainty on the matter has to be a deliberate pretence.

It is therefore not out of a taste for "critical exegeses raising questions to which there is no answer" (Grandi, 1993 at p. 469) that an attempt has been made here to illustrate what seems to be a contradiction internal to the Community legal order itself. To have vested formally relevant regulatory functions in a still weak instrument like Community collective bargaining could perhaps be interpreted as a sign of a wish to promote it,[40] even though some authors argue convincingly that it may also represent a regulatory formality dutifully presented or paraded by the Community institutions as a legal policy option properly observing horizontal subsidiarity.[41] But to exclude *a priori* the possibility of having conditions and instruments needed to consolidate the normative status of collective bargaining, as the Community system does (Article 137(6) TEC, ex Article 2(6) ASP), demonstrates that the promotional attitude which it seems possible to deduce from reading these provisions out of context is not attended by institutional choices and political options consistent with it. Whether this is attributable to a deliberate strategy on the part of the Community institutions or, on the contrary, to a series of constraints which limit their scope and capacity for taking action may be a matter of debate and differing opinions. But the fact that an internal contradiction of this kind is such as to produce mystification regarding the meaning and social function[42] of the

---

[39] The interpretation is perhaps arbitrary, but the documents referred to give no hint of what should be understood by "heavy structures whose creation is unlikely to yield the best results". Although the expression is also repeated in the *Communication Concerning the Application of the Agreement on Social Policy* (COM(93) 600), there too it is used without further elucidation.

[40] As in the view of Grandi, 1993 at p. 471, who imputes to pessimistic commentators a "rather unusual method of argument: it starts out from the observation of a fact to deny the very possibility of experience. That is, the possibility of collective bargaining is denied purely on the strength of the fact that it does not yet exist". What is denied, in reality, is not so much the possibility of European collective bargaining as the likelihood of its being able to take place on the basis of the current provisions.

[41] Sciarra, 1996a; Aparicio Tovar, 1996b; Streeck, 1994.

[42] In the precise sense given to this term in the celebrated work by Renner, 1949 devoted to identifying the social function of the institutions of private law.

provisions originally contained in the ASP is a situation to which legal research must properly draw attention.

2.2 European collective bargaining as a legitimacy resource

Alongside the arguments presented in the preceding section regarding the perception of collective bargaining as a regulatory resource of the Community legal order, there are others which, although of a different type, nevertheless fall within the same line of reasoning in that they support the allegation made here of the instrumental nature of Community collective bargaining.

Some of the more recent and stimulating legal and political science analyses of the Community legal order show that there are two central problematical issues which, more than any others, are likely to prejudice the advancement of European integration: one is the regulatory deficit, which is the main focus of attention in the present study, but the other is the legitimation deficit, on which it is useful at this point to make a few brief observations.

The word "legitimation" can assume a number of different meanings within the Community system. In the context of the familiar debate on the Community democratic deficit it can mainly be understood as a synonym of democracy, and is thus identified with the only modest importance of the role reserved to the European Parliament in Community decision-making processes. Even with specific reference to the decision-making mechanisms outlined by the ASP—which, as is known, exclude the European Parliament—one author has remarked on the total absence of the parliamentary assembly, talking of an "inexplicable silence" (Mancini, 1995 at p. 38). It should be noted, however, that in the interpretation of the ASP provided by the Commission the role of the Parliament in the transposition into law of the agreements concluded by the social partners is spelt out explicitly: "Under the Agreement, the Commission is not legally required to consult the European Parliament . . . However, it does intend to inform the European Parliament and to send the text of the agreement . . . so that the Parliament may, should it consider it advisable, deliver its opinion[43]—an intention which was, in fact, adhered to on the occasion of the adoption of Directives 96/34/EC on parental leave, 97/81/EC on part-time work and 99/70/EC on fixed-term work.[44] Despite these acts of voluntary "homage" by the Commission to the role of the Parliament, however, the Community assembly has called for the specific right to be considered a full part of the new decision-making mechanisms introduced by the ASP; in particular, it "calls for the European Parliament to have the right of codecision under the legislative procedure pursuant to Articles 3 and 4 of the Agreement on social policy [Articles 138

[43] COM(93) 600, 14.12.1993, para. 10 of the *Summary*. See also paras 35 and 40 of the main document.
[44] See Recital 14 of Directive 96/34/EC, Recital 19 of Directive 97/81/EC and Recital 19 of Directive 99/70/EC.

and 139 TEC] analogous to that of the Council, i.e. in the form of overall rejection or assent".[45]

As a growing number of scholars have pointed out, however, the identification of Community legitimacy with parliamentary democracy seems rather reductive and too reliant on previous experiences of national representative democracy.[46] A European "legitimation by parliamentarisation" would not be a viable solution (Jachtenfuchs, 1995 at p. 127). In this scenario, it is precisely the social field which offers some of the most promising prospects for a "genuinely plural and participatory democracy" (Ward, 1996),[47] not least through the social dialogue in its broader and less "ASP-oriented" sense.[48] Furthermore, a renewed idea of Welfare in Europe—as has since been suggested—could help in overcoming the Community "democratic deficit" much more than an increased parliamentarisation of Europe would be able to do (Scharpf, 1997).

Next, there are various interpretations of Community legitimacy which still refer to the connection between the concept in question and the democratic principle, but without going so far as to confine the entire issue to the centrality, or otherwise, of the role fulfilled by the parliamentary assembly. Positions of this kind may be based on the use of a socially widespread consensus in regard to the process of integration[49] or, in accordance with a more theoretically

---

[45] See the *Parliament Resolution on the Commission Proposal for a Council Directive Concerning the Framework Agreement on Part-time Work* (A4–0352/97, 19 November 1997), para. 17.

[46] Although even in the national sphere, legitimation and democracy are not necessarily synonymous. See Weiler, 1993 at p. 19, who takes the cases of the Weimar Republic and the subsequent German National Socialist regime as examples, respectively, of democratic systems without legitimation and vice versa.

[47] This author explicitly denies that the problem of democracy in the Community context can be resolved in a replication of the Westminster model of representative democracy and indicates the need to overcome the "preconception" according to which "a democratic Europe is defined as a representatively democratic Europe" (Ward, 1996 at p. 199).

[48] A similar idea has been expressed by the Court of First Instance in its *UEAPME* judgment (Case T–135/96 *UEAPME v Council* [1998] ECR II–2335): "the principle of democracy on which the Union is founded requires—in the absence of the participation of the European Parliament in the legislative process—that the participation of the people be otherwise assured, in this instance through the parties representative of management and labour who concluded the agreement" (para. 89 of the judgment).

Contrary to this line of reasoning, a strong claim in favour of an increased role for the European Parliament in the shaping of Community social legislation—at worst, even to the detriment of the social partners—is put forward by Betten, 1998, who writes that "the social partners do not represent all or a majority of European citizens, who all have their particular interests in a comprehensive social policy. Right now . . . a handful of organisations are playing a powerful role in the creation of the European social dimension, on dubious foundations of legitimacy. If they [the European unions, *author's note*] were subjected to a democratic election, they would be tiny minority parties" (p. 35).

[49] The arguments concerned are those based on *public support* and the notion of *permissive consensus*, on which see Reif, 1993 at pp. 133–135 and, for a quantitative survey, Anderson and Kaltenthaler, 1996. That such comparisons are really meaningful for the purposes of verifying the degree of legitimation of the integration process is denied by Weiler, 1993 at p. 24 and Jachtenfuchs, 1995 at p. 127.

sophisticated approach, on the formulation of a notion of democratic legitimation constructed from a discursive and procedural validation of political action.[50]

Other positions, on the other hand, enlist the idea of a legitimation of the integration process based on the recognition of a series of fundamental values common to the constitutional traditions of the Member States, in accordance with a model partly used by Article 6(2) (ex F(2)) TEU.[51] In an even more substantialist direction—not expressly referred to the Community system—other authors link the notion of the political legitimacy of a given system with the capacity of that system to universalise ethical norms through the procedures of a pluralistic democracy (Garzòn Valdés, 1998).

Lastly, other authors—after emphasising the almost total absence of debate on the political and ideological options underlying the integration process, at least up till 1992—point out that the necessary presuppositions favouring a greater degree of legitimation of Community integration can ensue only from a confrontation regarding the major basic political choices that will guide the integration process; a legitimation, therefore, which will take root and mature around the definition of a shared Community *ethos* (Weiler, 1993).

To the assertions described in brief above[52] it is now possible to add some more specific considerations aimed at demonstrating the potential relevance of the subject of Community legitimation to the proposal being advanced here that collective bargaining has to be viewed as a resource of the Community legal order.

It is a well-known and generally recognised argument that, between the end of the nineteenth and the beginning of the twentieth centuries, one of the major factors of political legitimation in the process of formation of modern national states was the innovative pre-arrangement of highly developed models of social protection.[53] On what might be called a "public" plane, the early experiences of social policy which evolved during that period proved such as to shape the conceptual and institutional structure of modern democracies, just as—on a

---

[50] This is the approach originally formulated by Habermas, 1973 without considering the supranational dimension but then extended by the author to the processes of European integration (Habermas, 1992). See also the *Governance Progress Report* (CdP(96) 2216, European Commission, Forward Studies Unit, December 1996).

[51] The subject of the potential conflict between national constitutional traditions and the "new" Community order underlies the well-known judgment of the German Federal Constitutional Court (the "Karlsruhe judgment") on the Maastricht Treaty of European Union, in which the national state's insistence on democratic legitimation and the need to safeguard domestic constitutional principles are cited as a basis for limiting supranational competences. On the potential "nationalist" implications of this stance, see the critical comments by Weiler, 1995 and Joerges, 1997.

[52] For further discussions on Community legitimacy, see De Búrca, 1966 and Obradovic, 1996.

[53] According to two of the authors who have studied the subject most closely, "the growth of the modern welfare state may be interpreted as a response to two fundamental processes: the formation of national states and their transformation into mass democracies (Flora and Heidenheimer, 1981 at p. 33). Mention must necessarily be made of the German and English systems, with their respective models of social security traditionally associated with the figures of Bismarck and Beveridge. For a historiographic review of the repercussions of social policies on the form of state, see Gerber, 1995.

"private" plane—the beginning of labour legislation contributed to the anthropological evolution of the subjective identity of *homo oeconomicus* in capitalistic societies.[54] As part of the particular combination of historical, political, legal, social and cultural conditioning factors which determines the form and institutional nature of the state, the pre-arrangement of those social protection models helped, in short, to guarantee the political legitimation of the emerging national state entities and launched a process of progressive establishment of the welfare state.

Various diagnoses are given of the motives which prompted the development of social policies and legislation during the period in question. According to some authors, one factor not entirely unrelated to the promotion of social policies in the early decades of the twentieth century was consideration of the exigencies connected with war, which urged governments into "seeking to increase the identification of the working class with the nation for that purpose" (Crouch, 1993 at p. 175). Another thesis holds that, during the period of the creation of modern welfare states, social legislation to protect labour was accepted by employers in exchange for a promise on the part of states to adopt protectionist policies (Majone, 1992 at p. 14). And in the context of an interesting analysis of the birth and evolution of the American federal system, other authors note that the transition to what is called the "positive state" is attributable to the aim of facilitating free trade and is therefore to be considered functional to liberal ideology (Heller, 1986).

The nature and limits of the present study do not warrant a more searching analysis of the historical processes which led to the formation and establishment of the welfare state;[55] on the contrary, they make it necessary to explain the reasons for mentioning here events which might seem far removed from the arguments under discussion.

The main point which needs to be illustrated, for the limited purposes of this study, is the singular nature of the relationship which has grown up historically between establishment of social rights and policies and consolidation of state entities which are legitimated as such. This relationship could be described as one of reciprocal "paternity" in historical terms in that, in addition to having their own origin in what is recognised as the social state , social policies and rights have, in their turn, helped to mould and identify as "social"—and even earlier as a "state"—the political entity from which they originated. In short, the historical establishment of social rights has fostered and brought about the consolidation of political entities which have ended by constituting—when the

---

[55] On the formation of the employee's identity through his condition of subordination, cf. Supiot, 1994 and the articles by G. Giugni, L. Mengoni and B. Veneziani in *Giornale di diritto del lavoro e di relazioni industriali* No 3, 1995. Lastly, some interesting contributions collected in Brownsword, Howells and Wilhelmsson (eds), 1994 seek to show how the influence of so-called *welfarism* has brought about a change in the general principles governing the law of contract.

[56] The reader is referred to the copious literature which exists on the subject. Cf. Titmuss, 1963 and 1974; Wilensky, 1975; Flora and Heidenheimer (eds), 1981; Flora (ed.), 1986. See also the valuable essay by Ritter, 1991.

process is complete—not just the *origin* but also the actual *outcome* of the concrete establishment and operation of social rights in modern constitutional democracies. In this sense, social policies and rights have undoubtedly been a potent source of political legitimation for modern national states.[56]

It needs to be made clear, however, what significance can be attributed to these statements in the Community context. To say that the development of social legislation, and that of labour law in particular, can be seen as founding elements of the legitimation of political entities of a statal nature is certainly not the same thing as asserting that a similar function can be attributed to them within the Community system. On the contrary, we have to agree with those who observe that the social policies pursued by the Community "will probably not have the tremendous legitimating potential typical of national welfare state-building processes" (Pierson and Leibfried, 1995a at p. 33).[57]

Nevertheless, as properly understood (i.e. without involving false similarities or purely automatic transpositions), consideration of the "legitimating" and stabilising function fulfilled by social policies and rights in the formative phase of national states can contribute to a better understanding of two aspects of the Community social dimension and, within that dimension, collective bargaining. First, it can help in identifying the legal and pre-legal reasons which underlie, or should underlie, Community intervention in the field of social policy and labour law (*i.e. what the Community can give to social policy*); and secondly—and this is the aspect most directly relevant to the purposes of defining the status of collective bargaining within the Community legal order—it can help in identifying the role and significance assumed by such intervention from the different viewpoint of the institutional nature of the supranational entity from which it emanates (*i.e. what social policy can give to the Community*).

These observations are not altogether new. The debate on "welfare state Europe" was launched some time ago between sociologists and political scientists (Leibfried, 1992a, 1992b and 1992c; Leibfried and Pierson, 1993; Ferrera, 1993 and 1993 (ed.); Scharpf, 1997), and is not infrequently directed at the very question of the possible legitimating function which social characterisation of the integration process could produce within the Community system. However, the possible legitimating function of the social dimension for the purposes of stabilising the integration process need not necessarily be viewed in terms of a replication in the supranational context of the policies on redistribution and transfers of resources which are typical of national welfare models. In the debate surrounding welfare state Europe, there is a misunderstanding which must be avoided if the critics of a social characterisation of Europe are not to be handed

---

[56] Flora and Heidenheimer, 1981 at pp. 33–34, point out that the welfare state is much more than the mere product of mass democracy. It implies a fundamental transformation of the state itself, of its structure, its functions and its legitimacy.

[57] On the problematical co-existence of national welfare states with processes of the internationalisation of economies, see the articles by M. Ferrera, R. Gilpin, H. Wilensky, R. Rose, C. Offe and S. Strange in M. Ferrera (ed.), 1993. With specific reference to the evolution of national welfare states in a context of Community integration, see Scharpf, 1997.

an excuse which is difficult to refute: in order to be "social"—and therefore, from the viewpoint being examined here, "legitimated"—Community Europe need not, nor could, reproduce the welfare model as it has been known and theorised over the course of the twentieth century. If the debate surrounding the Community social dimension were confined to a verification of its structural and financial compatibility with a European social state, the result would be an inevitable (negative) outcome for the aspirations concerned.

However, the European social model does not find its identity solely in the redistribution policies which are typical of welfare state action. It also includes other structural elements, no less important to its categorisation, which are more directly relevant to our present purposes.

Even bearing in mind the admonitions of some authors to shun undue simplifications and generalisations (Crouch, 1993 at ch. 1), it can certainly be said that an integral—and, as regards the historically "legitimating" function mentioned above, not secondary—part of a European social model is the primary role reserved to the bargaining source in the regulation of employment relationships and, more generally, in the concerted administration of social policies (Vogel, 1994). The function fulfilled by the bargaining principle in the evolution of the social state and its forms of action and legitimation has been examined in the literature from many viewpoints: general legal theory and legal philosophy (Teubner, 1983 and 1987b, Teubner (ed.), 1986; Habermas, 1984 and 1992), legal sociology (Chazel and Commaille (eds), 1991; Tweedy and Hunt, 1994), sociology (Durkheim, 1930; Luhmann, 1990b; Reynaud, 1989) and industrial relations (Crouch, 1993).

However, in my opinion one of the most effective descriptions of the processes concerned is provided by a doctrine which actually displays an openly and radically critical attitude to the developments described (Barcellona, 1994 at ch. 5). The starting-point of this analysis is a comparison of the waning of formal legal rationality and the correlative strengthening of a Weberian materialisation of law in the social state, which is not without its effects on the institutional configuration of the state and the mechanisms which guarantee its democratic legitimation: "the new functions which the state begins to assume in the experience of the so-called social state call for . . . a fresh approach to the forms through which normative powers are exercised and the whole of state political activity is pursued" (Barcellona, 1994 at p. 206). "The way in which the question of democracy arises in the context of the social state tends to go beyond the traditional aspects of the ways of formation of representation [:] the interpenetration of the social and economic sphere and the political sphere makes it impossible, or at any rate fairly difficult, to maintain a clear separation between the areas in which political democracy and economic democracy are exercised" (Barcellona, 1994 at p. 213).[58] From the perspective adopted by this doctrine,

---

[58] These statements are also echoed in other doctrines, to which the same author does in fact make express, even if partial, reference: "intraparliamentary formation of will represents only a small segment of public life" (Habermas, 1992 at p. 38).

therefore, there emerges clearly the correlation which exists between the changes in the system of sources of law induced by the hypermaterialisation of law in the social state and the search for a renewed democratic legitimation of political and government action: "the answer which in institutional terms gradually began to be given to this problem during the phase of development of the social state essentially consisted in enlarging and broadening the range of subjects who were called on in various ways to become involved in determining juridical control[;] in the face of the crisis in legitimation of the legislative type, the state looks for a way out through a consensual legitimation" (Barcellona, 1994 at p. 215). Consequently, the regulatory deficit of hypermaterialised law and search for a renewed political and democratic legitimation come together, in the mature phase of the social state, in the area of collective bargaining, which is identified as a resource appropriate for overcoming the former and guaranteeing the latter. The political desirability of these developments may well be debated, leading to judgments which are subjective options of an evaluative nature.[59] That they correspond to what has actually happened in the course of the social state's evolution is, however, beyond all doubt.

Within this framework, much of what has been said in the course of the present study can be brought together in a single observation: in national contexts, the regulatory problems that emerged with the materialisation of law, and the institutionalisation of the social partners' collective autonomy as a response to the problems of regulation and democratic legitimation of government and legislative action, have led to collective bargaining being drawn into a sphere of public relevance which has made it a pillar of a widely shared European social model.

Given such a scenario, the question which presents itself to the commentator therefore consists in evaluating whether, at supranational level, collective bargaining is actually able to fulfil the same function of regulatory resource and legitimacy resource which it has assumed at national level.

Any interpretation of the Community institutions' strategy in this respect can only be based on supposition. Certainly, the institutionalisation of collective bargaining for regulatory purposes constitutes an instrument in which legitimation through democratic procedure—with an extended range of subjects called on to "participate in the formation of legislative control" (Barcellona, 1994 at p. 210)—and legitimation through substantive policy—with the consequent incorporation of social justice values in the shaping of Community legislation—could find a potential meeting-point. From this point of view, therefore, it cannot be

---

[59] As already indicated, the same doctrine which describes the changes to legislation and legitimation in the social state is openly critical of their underlying functionalisation with respect to the goal of preservation: "this type of intervention, while apparently motivated by the demands of equity, in reality favours the process of functionalisation in society . . . the device of extension through the participation of diverse subjects in the legislative process represents, in fact, a fictitious way of resolving the problem of consensus . . . allowing participation in institutionalised procedures is essentially utilised to guarantee citizens' disciplined obedience, not effective reference to shared values and interests" (Barcellona, 1994 at pp. 205 and 218).

excluded *a priori* that the "promotion" of collective bargaining also represents a response to the aim of enhancing what is still a low degree of legitimation of Community integration, particularly at a time when the rigid compatibilities imposed by the process of monetary union (Teague, 1998) are in danger of alienating part of the "permissive consensus" so far enjoyed by the Community.

That said, however, it must be added at once that the critical observations developed here are mainly a response to something which is absolutely unavoidable in any study of Community collective bargaining. In other words, they represent an attempt to explain the real significance of a Community stance which is otherwise difficult to grasp, not to say ambiguous: what is revealed by an analysis of the provisions originally contained in the ASP is *an apparent intention to promote which is not, however, backed up by the instruments indispensable to that purpose.* This is internally contradictory stance which leaves room for a number of different interpretative hypotheses, including the one advanced here that it is possible to see in the stance of the Community institutions towards collective bargaining the belief that it offers an expedient solution to their particular regulatory and legitimation problems.[60]

These conclusions may possibly seem ungenerous and hasty. It would perhaps be more prudent not to venture beyond the cautious scepticism displayed by some commentators who have said, with reference to the still fluid and uncertain outlines of Community labour law, that "it is a proper subject only for the chronicler, not yet for the historian" (Romagnoli, 1995a at p. 248). Nevertheless, it is an undoubted fact that, as yet, the existing normative, institutional and industrial relations situation within the Community legal order offers no grounds for refuting those who had occasion some years ago to describe Community collective bargaining as a *parva realidad* (Ojeda Avilés, 1993 at p. 167).

To conclude these observations on the categorisation of collective bargaining as a resource of the Community legal order, it would perhaps be going too far to assert that, in the supranational context, the auxiliary relationship of Kahn-Freundian memory is turned upside-down: it is no longer statute law which supports collective bargaining, but bargaining which helps statute law to resolve the regulatory and legitimation problems described above. Nevertheless, it is still obvious that, for the time being, the form of institutionalisation of collective bargaining as set out by the provisions originally contained in the ASP does not seem such—for the precise reason that it is presented in instrumental terms—as to trigger the launch of bargaining processes which are constitutionally significant, normatively relevant and socially widespread.

---

[60] In a very similar way, Wendon, 1998 depicts the Commission as an "image-venue entrepreneur" in the field of social policy, to the extent that its bureaucracy tends to "exploit" the social dialogue in order to strengthen its own position.

3 REGULATORY TECHNIQUES AND A EUROPEAN SOCIAL CONSTITUTION:
AN INDISSOLUBLE LINK

Within the national systems which until now have been more familiar to labour lawyers, collective autonomy is given a constitutional form of recognition which makes its manifestations legally relevant without entailing any restriction of their freedom of scope. Even in those cases where their incorporation into an area of public or quasi public relevance has been strongest, the "price" paid by the trade unions and employers' organisations for the privilege of acquiring a key role in the state regulatory process (Romagnoli, 1995a at p. 105) has never been translated into a direct limitation of the free exercise of the social partners' autonomy in choosing the issues to be negotiated; at most, it has entailed an opportunistic self-limitation of their respective bargaining strategies.[61]

Community collective bargaining, on the other hand, is neither constitutionally guaranteed nor, it would appear, supported by legitimation "from below" in that—as this study has attempted to demonstrate—it does not constitute an expression of collective autonomy, but rather the product of a normative construction in the form of an Agreement on Social Policy concluded at Maastricht. The fact that it is made primarily functional to the purposes of more effective Community decision-making renders it, in consequence, subject to the same limits as to content within which that decision-making is constrained to operate. It must necessarily conform to the same policy guidelines and observe the same compatibilities which inform and delimit Community regulatory action.

In these circumstances, the limitation of the social partners' bargaining activity ensuing from their incorporation into the sphere of Community public relevance resembles not so much a reasonable price paid for gaining a privilege as a form of blackmail or, if preferred, a harassment clause: for the Community legal order, collective bargaining "exists" only within the limits—as to both content and procedure—which that legal order stipulates in advance when functionalising it to the purposes of a more effective development of its own regulatory process; outside those limits and that functionalisation, bargaining is simply inconsequential (Chapter 5, section 1). In short, Community collective bargaining goes where the Community's (restricted) competences take it or, more accurately, as far as they permit it to go. That being so, it is therefore obvious that—so long as a constitutional principle perceived as the "foundation of the inherent nature of collective autonomy" (Pedrazzoli, 1990b at p. 574) remains absent—any enlargement of the sphere of competence of Community collective bargaining is necessarily dependent on a parallel enlargement of the areas within which the Community's regulatory competence is able to operate.

---

[61] For some critical observations regarding what is described as excessively "costly" trade union institutionalisation in Spain during the period of socialist government, see Baylos Grau, 1985.

Given this objective limitation of collective autonomy, there inevitably emerges the much-discussed question of a "European social constitution";[62] a question which, for the purposes of our line of argument here, can be broken down into two conceptually—but not legally—separate facets. First, on the plane reserved for the political selection of guide values, there is the perspective of defining the social objectives, rights and principles which are to inform the integration process. Secondly, on a plane which is no less political but even more directly "operative", there is the creation of the institutional conditions which take account of the fact that "freedom of association is a good which comes before, not after, the construction of a more just society" (Romagnoli, 1995a at p. 130). Only within an institutional framework of this kind, characterised by the presence of a constitutional dimension of social rights, would collective bargaining cease to be a (mere) regulatory or legitimacy resource of the Community legal order (sections 2 and 3) and become what it probably should be: "both an outcome and a source of social policies" (Sciarra, 1996a at p. 211).

On reaching its conclusion an examination of Community collective bargaining reveals, in short, the latter's inescapable connection with the question of fundamental social rights, coming together in an area in which legal, economic and political science discourses all contribute to defining the co-ordinates of a debate (only seemingly technical, value-free and politically neutral) on the identification of regulatory techniques capable of guaranteeing the effective steering of economic dynamics in the context of a market which extends beyond national confines.

The multidisciplinary debate on issues of the legal regulation of economic dynamics, which has intensified considerably during recent years, is axiomatically of interest to labour lawyers,[63] as specialists in a branch of legislation which is a key example of those capable of affecting the free exercise of the economic rationality of the actors in the market. There can be no doubt, therefore, that this is the area which will witness the mature development in the years to come of the basic policy options destined to influence the economic function of

---

[62] On the agenda of labour law debate for some time now; see Hepple, 1990; Däubler, 1991; Bercusson, 1991; Vogel-Polsky, 1991; Lo Faro, 1992; Lyon-Caen, A. and Simitis, 1993; Rodriguez-Piñero and Casas Baamonde, 1996; Sciarra, 1996b. See also the proposals for a European social constitution formulated by two different networks of European labour lawyers: Blanpain, Hepple, Sciarra and Weiss, 1996; and Kravaritou, Veneziani, Supiot, Koistinen, Bercusson, Deakin and Mückenberger, 1996. Recently, the Community institutions themselves have demonstrated an awareness of these questions by commissioning an expert group to prepare a report on the subject: see the Report of the Expert Group on Fundamental Rights (referred to as the Simitis Commission, after the name of its President), *Affirming Fundamental Rights in the European Union : Time to Act* (European Commission, DGV, Brussels, February 1999).

[63] Indeed, there are signs in the more recent literature of a renewed interest in issues which have perhaps been neglected during the past few decades; see Ichino, A. and Ichino, P., 1994; Ichino P., 1996; Deakin, 1996; Rodriguez-Piñero, 1995; Scarpelli, 1996; Sciarra, 1998; and the contributions in the special issues of *Lavoro e diritto*, Nos 1–2/1996. For an introduction to the debate, see Romagnoli, 1995b. With specific reference to an analysis of the enterprise as an institution, the subject of the relationship between law and the economy is tackled by Jeammaud, Kirat and Villeval, 1996.

labour law norms and, of more immediate interest, the structure of the system of Community labour law sources.

Although the debates mentioned above have been in progress for some time, it was only a few years ago that they began to be directed towards more specific consideration of what happens or ought to happen in the Community context. As regards the literature which is not primarily devoted to analysing the Community system, it is useful to draw attention to certain schools of thought within which theories of legal regulation have been formulated which are strongly influenced by the outcomes of a debate initially developed among economists, I am referring to public choice theories,[64] certainly not marginal in the arena of scientific debate,[65] which are aimed at formulating an economic theory of the formation of political choices inspired by the principle that "non-market political decisions can perfectly well be studied using the same tools as market decisions" (McLean, 1987 at p. 2). It would make little sense here to dwell on the general content and principles of public choice theory, other than to draw attention—if there were any need to do so—to the obvious and marked ideological stance underlying a regulation model based exclusively on the quest for economic efficiency.[66]

It is, however, certainly more relevant to point out that it was not very long before "transnational" and "Community" applications of an approach of this kind to regulation began to appear, not only among economists (Teutemann, 1990; Vaubel and Willet (eds), 1991; Vaubel, 1994 and 1995) but also among jurists (Streit and Mussler, 1995;[67] Petersmann, 1995) and in contributions representing the fruit of collaboration between the two communities (Buchanan, Pöhl, Curzon Price and Vibert, 1990; Pelkmans and Sun, 1994; Schmidtchen and Cooter (eds), 1997; Goerke and Piazolo, 1998). This was, of course, inevitable in the context of a system such as that of the Community, still in its emergent state and therefore potentially suited to providing an ideal hunting-ground for regulation theories openly devoted to repudiating any kind of conditioning of a normative nature likely to disrupt the rational behaviour of subjects (individuals and interest groups, but also political parties, governments and administra-

---

[64] Otherwise indicated by the name of constitutional economics or modern political economy (van Winden, 1988). For an exposition of the main features of public choice theory see Rowley (ed.), 1987; and for an "educational" review expressly addressed to those ignorant of economics, see McLean, 1987.

[65] The award of the 1986 Nobel Prize for economics to James M. Buchanan, one of the foremost theorists of public choice (see Buchanan, 1975) is testimony to the high regard in which these theories are held.

[66] For some critical comments on the economics-driven and "rational" approach to politics and political science advanced by public choice theorists, see Udehn, 1996; Gillroy and Wade (eds), 1992; Green and Shapiro, 1994; and Stretton and Orchard, 1994.

[67] Initially presented at the conference on *European Law in Context: Constitutional Dimensions of European Economic Integration*, EUI Florence, 14–15 April 1994, the paper in question kindled an open debate among jurists. See the reply by C. D. Ehlermann and the counter-reply by Streit and Messler in a subsequent issue (No 2/1995) of the *European Law Journal*. For further comments, see the volume of published conference proceedings (Snyder (ed.), 1996) which includes the replies of the participants L. Hancher and T. Heller.

tions) who base their decisions on the criterion of maximising their respective utility.[68]

It is, in fact, a fairly recent public choice analysis of the ASP (Vaubel, 1995) which offers the opportunity to examine in concrete terms the potential impact of such theories on social regulation within the Community system, particularly when they are intended and presented—as is the case here—in an explicitly "normative" or prescriptive sense.[69] Some passages in the text of this analysis can be regarded as largely self-explanatory and therefore require no further comment. The article begins with the observation that "social regulation is an inefficient instrument for most purposes because it restricts the freedom of contract among individuals" (p.113); it goes on to remark, as regards the disparity in social protection that exists between individual Member States, that "to the extent that differences in social regulations reflect differences in income level and preferences, they do not represent economic distortions at all. On the contrary, the suppression of such differences constitutes a distortion"[70] (p. 115); and it ends by concluding that "social regulation is a case where the freedom of the individual has to be protected against the will of the majority". It takes no great prophetic skills or divinatory gifts to spot the potential implications of such an approach for Community social regulation, as regards its *an*, its *quantum* and its *quomodo*.

Nor can it be said that public choice theorists are alone in seeking to establish a complete dissociation between the quest for economically efficient regulatory techniques and preservation of the *minimum* heritage of historically acquired social rights. It is no accident that labour law is the direct target of some fairly recent manifestations of what is certainly no marginal American legal doctrine (Epstein, 1995) and which, although not explicitly inspired by public choice theory, is testimony to the pervasiveness of a certain cultural climate progressively developing on the other side of the Atlantic.

In this connection, it is not inappropriate to pause to consider the literal tenor of some surprising assertions made by this doctrine, bearing in mind that what we are looking at is not some electoral meeting held in rural small-town America but a work by an esteemed jurist published by the Harvard University Press (Epstein, 1995) to which a special issue of a highly reputed journal has also been devoted.[71] The author in question starts by denying any relevance of contractual disparity in the employment relationship, in order to support a version

---

[68] From the public choice perspective, there is no difference between the motivations which govern the decisions of the subjects mentioned: politicians act like "entrepreneurs" and voters like "consumers".

[69] In the original terminology developed within economic doctrine, the distinction between prescriptive and descriptive purport is indicated by referring to the distinction between "normative" and "positive" public choice (McLean, 1987 at p. 125).

[70] The only possible "rational" justification capable of legitimising Community social regulation is, it is maintained, that demonstrating the fact that some Member States try this as a way of "raising rivals' costs" (p. 119).

[71] *Constitutional Political Economy* Vol 9(2)/1998, special issue on *Richard A. Epstein: Simple Rules for a Complex World*.

of the latter which seems to be drawn directly from the liberal codifications of the nineteenth century: "it does not matter to the law . . . that on one side to the agreement is the employer and on the other side is the employee. These relationships, these categories, are not imposed upon private persons through the operation of the law; these roles are freely chosen by individuals acting within the system" (p. 74). According to this view, the fact that the worker is able to refuse to enter into a contractual employment relationship if the terms do not satisfy him constitutes a guarantee against any form of abuse: "it hardly matters that the wealth of one of the two parties is wildly unequal before the transaction begins . . . The worker's ability to withhold consent stands as a strong bulwark against any form of exploitation" (p. 84). However, the arguments advanced by the author go even further: his aim is not just to demonstrate that the disparity of contractual strength between the parties to the employment relationship does not generate any abuse; what he attempts to refute is that there is any disparity in the first place. If the power relationship were really biased in this way in the employer's favour, he argues, "we should observe people working for employers at zero wage, and we don't" (p. 84). According to Epstein, in short, thinking that the employee is in need of even minimal normative protection amounts to regarding him as incapable of intention or will: "workers who are competent to participate in union politics and union elections, to marry and raise families, to participate in public affairs should not be deemed incompetent to bargain directly with employers if they so choose . . . Indeed, if workers and tenants are so incompetent, why let them vote or participate in political affairs?" (pp. 82–83).[72] But Epstein's final thrust is reserved for the Clayton Anti-Trust Act, the American law of 1914 which, anticipating its adoption by the ILO in 1944 and subsequent incorporation into the ILO constitution, confers normative rank within the American legal system upon the well-known declaration that "the labor of human beings is not a commodity or article of commerce". Even with regard to this hallowed tenet of labour law, our author has an objection to make: "labor becomes a commodity or an article of commerce only if its owner chooses to make it such. People are allowed, not required, to sell their labor, just as they are allowed and not required to sell their homes" (p. 88). Indeed, Epstein enlightens us, the real purpose of the famous phrase contained in the Clayton Act is not to affirm the dignity of the person who labours, but something quite different: "what is desired by invoking this phrase is a very different end: the monopolisation of labour markets through collective bargaining or similar arrangements" (p. 89).[73]

[72] Extolling the individual employee's bargaining capacity in dealings with his employer has a famous precedent in the well-known expression used by Robert Nozick, according to whom "there is no reason to limit capitalist acts between consenting adults" (Nozick, 1974 at p. 163).

[73] A different, although superficially similar, statement is made by O'Higgins, 1997 at p. 229, who points out that "The purpose of this provision was to prevent the Clayton Act being used against trade unions on the grounds of their monopolistic control of labour".

Were it not for the acknowledged authority of the author concerned, one could think of a number of clever challenges. What we have here, however, is a rather striking example of the doctrinal developments in progress on the subject of the relationship between normative regulation and the market; a text which is, in fact, perfectly in tune with the *Zeitgeist*, as is revealed by the zealous respect shown by the author towards the canons of political correctness: in impersonal expressions, Epstein is extremely careful to use "she" and "her" instead of "he" and "his".

The various doctrinal reconstructions to which attention has been drawn here are linked by an obvious nexus[74] and all play a part in defining the overall scenario within which the Community debate on regulation seems destined to unfold.[75] A debate which is not without its relevance to the arguments presented here, in that—as this study has attempted to show—at present European collective bargaining cannot be regarded as anything other than a Community regulatory technique. This is not as inconsequential as it may seem. Given that it is conceived by the Community as a regulatory technique, lacking any constitutional support, European bargaining has to be analysed in the light of an overall debate in which—as has just been demonstrated—labour law and its regulatory sources are often indicated as a field in which a new kind of economic rationality should be tested.

In short, an analysis of Community collective bargaining as a regulatory technique cannot neglect to take account of the fact that, in the field of labour law more than anywhere else, the question of regulatory techniques is first and foremost a question of *rights*; of fundamental social rights on which to base a Community social citizenship. Within the context of the current debates on whether and how to regulate, a call should be made for formal recognition of freedom of association and the right to bargain, on the basic assumption that the shaping of regulatory techniques capable of implementing constitutional values and objectives is as important as the values and objectives themselves.

This reference to collective bargaining as part of a debate on fundamental social rights cannot be left without offering some more precise explanatory comments.

Even over fifty years ago, Georges Gurvitch was already lamenting the fact that a widespread use of the expression "social rights" was not matched by a sufficiently well-defined or shared interpretation of the concept concerned (Gurvitch, 1946 at p. 63). Nor does the situation seem to have improved that much over the intervening half-century if it is true, as one author writes, that "few objects of analysis are as difficult to master, without abandoning certain

---

[74] In some passages of Epstein's text there are hints, although no express mention, of the fundamental assumptions of what could be called the "anthropology" of public choice theory: "it is true that all individuals differ in natural endowments, in personal ambitions, in social roles, and in institutional expectations. But there is one thing that each of them wants . . .: *more*" (Epstein, 1995 at pp. 73–75). The emphasis is in the original.

[75] The influence that public choice theory is beginning to show in the context of some legal reconstructions of Community Europe is pointed out by De Búrca, 1996 at p. 354.

prejudices and ideas entrenched by tradition, as the vast field which we identify with the elliptic expression 'social rights' " (Luciani, 1995 at p. 546).

It is not possible here to give the question the attention it merits, still less to resolve it. Nonetheless, what needs to be demonstrated is the fact that relating collective bargaining back to the sphere of fundamental social rights (by virtue of the connection between Community regulatory techniques and the Community social constitution) should not be regarded as conceptually arbitrary.

In a more directly and intuitively relevant sense, the notion of social rights can refer to a series of predominantly, but not exclusively, financial benefits bestowed by the public machinery within the context of social policies of the redistributive type.

From one point of view, the relationship of co-essentiality in which fundamental social rights stand with respect to the idea of democracy is recognised in some reconstructions which identify "the subject who is the holder of fundamental social rights not with an abstract individual, but with a concrete 'social person' [;] if it is true that the great novelty of contemporary constitutional experiences is the link between social state and emancipating democracy, it becomes difficult to assert that only rights to freedom, and not also social rights, form part of the 'basic structures' which support the very idea of a 'person'" (Luciani, 1995 at p. 562). However, these convincing observations, with which we have to agree, are mainly referred to the sphere of social rights that may be called "substantive", for the purpose of asserting their equal constitutional ranking with the traditional fundamental rights to freedom which are civil and political.

The interpretation of social rights as rights whose satisfaction requires "public intervention and specific institutions which replace the natural rules of the market with public law rules" (Luciani, 1995 at p. 563) explains why doubts are frequently expressed as to the possibility of identifying, in such circumstances, subjective situations which can be classed as rights in the true sense (Bobbio, 1990 at p. 8; Barbalet, 1988); and also why many authors talk of social rights as imperfect or conditional rights "because their realisation depends on political decisions and economic policy" (Barcellona, 1988 at p. 60).

But an interpretation of fundamental social rights as rights to benefits guaranteeing social security and assistance, which in the final analysis therefore means identifying social rights purely in terms of "costs" to the public purse, is not the only one possible. It is well known that this configuration of social rights has been accused (by a far from conservative number of scholars) as embodying the excess of bureaucratisation, juridification and "colonisation of life's worlds" found in the context of welfare systems (Habermas, 1984).[76] On the basis of these observations, a branch of philosophical and legal doctrine of Germanic

---

[76] For a useful analysis of the positions adopted by Habermas towards social rights and the welfare state, see Tweedy and Hunt, 1994.

origin has therefore suggested a new interpretation of fundamental social rights, essentially viewed as procedural rights (Ladeur, 1995b) to discursive participation (Habermas, 1992) in the relational determination (Willke, 1986) of social policies.

A *procedural* interpretation of fundamental social rights—or, better, the possibility of identifying certain fundamental social rights which are of a procedural nature—has the merit of distancing the concept from the constraints of financial compatibility which are often invoked in order to exclude them and makes it possible, on the contrary, to indicate a further aspect which makes the idea of social rights co-essential with democracy.

It is therefore on a different plane that we confront the question of the possibility or advisability of constitutionalising a series of social rights (or principles),[77] procedural in nature, through which the thing to be guaranteed is not a service or benefit bestowed by the public structures of security and assistance, but the possibility of a "procedural foundation in law [which] can enable an impartial process for the foundation and critical comparison of different principles" (Habermas, 1992 at pp. 15–30). It is certainly undeniable, following this line of reasoning, that constitutionalisation of the social partners' collective autonomy through the recognition of freedom of association and the right to bargain has been decisive in providing social pluralism with a definite and concrete juridical dimension. A procedural interpretation of fundamental social rights can therefore be regarded as co-essential with the idea of democracy, particularly in so far as they represent collective social rights capable of guaranteeing "rights of participation by groups and individuals in the autonomous and self-governing wholes in which they are integrated, rights guaranteeing the democratic character of these latter" (Gurvitch, 1946 at p. 70).

An attempt can be made at this point to contextualise the discourse with specific reference to the profiles which feature here. In the context of the legal regulation of employment, procedural social rights consist, in essence, in the right of association and the right to bargain[78] together with, as their indispensable corollary, the right to strike. Only their express constitutional recognition within the Community system can prevent European collective bargaining from being reduced to the status of a mere regulatory technique which, as such, is conditioned by Community competences and objectives as well as subject to the "rationalisation" tendencies that have been mentioned. Thus, in place of the enfeebled Community collective bargaining that we know, new constitutional provisions on the matter could give rise to a reinvigorated conception of the social dialogue as the principle informing a consensus-based administration of social and labour policies.

Given such a shape, manifestations of the social partners' autonomy would constitute not a paltry regulatory technique squeezed into the narrow mould

---

[77] See, on this distinction, the comments by B. Hepple in Snyder (ed.), 1996.

[78] For an examination of the right to bargain as a fundamental principle of economic democracy see, with specific reference to the French system, Morin, 1994.

described here, but the *object* and *expression* of collective social rights which are positively constitutionalised and match the duality of functions already emphasised by Otto Kahn-Freund: "Freedom of organisation has the dual aspect of being an individual human right and a condition of social organisation" (Kahn-Freund, 1972 at p. 138). Even to consider a Community social constitution which fails to include the procedural aspect of social rights as outlined here would be to neglect, from the outset, the objective which underlies any constitutionalisation of social rights: "A true bill of social rights must be a weapon in the struggle for democracy and can be nothing less than that" (Gurvitch, 1946 at p.34).

Concluding Remarks

I F WE TAKE the "conclusions" of a research study to mean the interpretative proposals in which the observations made throughout the work are drawn together, Chapter 6, section 2 essentially represents the conclusion of the present study. In that sense, any further concluding remarks therefore serve no purpose. However, the study of Community collective bargaining presented above has been pursued by way of a multi-faceted and necessarily heterogeneous logic path which it seems useful to retrace in as succinct and schematic a form as possible.

(A)

Numerous attempts have been made to qualify the Community experience conceptually. None, however, can be regarded as truly definitive, when even today policy experts charged with the task of solving the enigma describe it as "*exploring the nature of the beast*" (Risse-Kappen, 1996). Other scientific communities, and jurists in particular, can only acknowledge the truth of this: "We simply do not know of any grand theory that would enable us to fully understand the present course of European integration" (Joerges, 1994 at p. 30).

In such a context of enduring uncertainty, legal integration has undoubtedly been one of the tracks along which the Community integration process has advanced most speedily. The success of the Community project—whatever its meaning—therefore owes a great deal to law. Under the escort of what has been called normative supranationalism (Weiler, 1985), in the first three decades of its existence the Community succeeded in overcoming the numerous political and identity crises which on more than one occasion threatened to block its path. Built on the jurisprudential principles of direct effect and supremacy, Community legal integration fostered institutional developments which parallel political and decision-making advances would certainly not have made possible.

On the regulatory plane, Community integration has essentially been pursued by way of a model of legislative harmonisation by Directive, which, at least up to the first half of the 1980s, was given absolute primacy. The 1985 White Paper on *Completing the Internal Market* and the 1987 Single European Act signify a radical turning-point in this situation. These two events are generally recognised as marking the start of the problems of the Community regulatory system's functionality which are nowadays referred to as its *regulatory deficit*.

(B)

The emergence of regulatory problems linked to the complexity of the social systems to be regulated is not, on the other hand, an exclusive prerogative of the Community legal order.

These are issues which have confronted general legal theory, legal philosophy and legal sociology before they ever arose in the Community context, as evidence of a crisis in state normative regulation due to the hypermaterialisation of law and the consequent loss of what is called the epistemic authority of law (Teubner, 1989). In other words, what is evidenced is the difficulty for any legal system of including provision for the overall social reality in order to be able to regulate it. On the basis of these presuppositions, the theoretical debate of the past few years has been strongly oriented towards identifying and evaluating a series of "alternatives to legislation", giving rise to all kinds of proposed options.

The developments in this debate are inevitably of relevance to the course of Community regulation, in that they help to explain some of its underlying reasons and, in addition, point to the prospect of a multiplication of the centres of law production—relatable to the pluralist paradigm, even if in a "revisited" sense—which certainly has many resonances in the Community context.

(C)

This is the framework—institutional (A) and theoretical (B)—within which an analysis of Community collective bargaining has to be sited.

The particular forms in which bargaining has been institutionalised within the Community legal order, and the first examples of their application, reveal that it is the Community's own regulatory difficulties, and not the emergence of a presumed supranational collective autonomy of which only the dawning can be glimpsed, which lie behind the incorporation of collective bargaining into the sphere of Community decision-making processes. This is something which it is essential to take into account for the purposes of qualifying Community bargaining conceptually and identifying its true function within the Community legal order.

(D)

Before presenting a new proposal for qualifying supranational collective bargaining, however, it is first necessary to examine the hermeneutic categories traditionally used for rationalising national bargaining phenomena.

From this point of view, an analysis of the notion of collective autonomy, the pluralist model of industrial relations and certain features of neo-corporatist regimes reveals that any similarity between the "two forms of bargaining" is little more than one of name alone. Indeed, they are divided by an absence of comparability—phenomenological, structural and functional—which is neither explained nor cancelled out by the different stages reached in their respective development.

The impossibility of viewing Community bargaining as a phenomenon of socially widespread and typified normative autonomy, the reversal of the sequence that has traditionally existed between the initial formation of collective autonomy and the subsequent intervention of normative rationalisation, the uncertain representative legitimacy of the bargaining agents and the difficulty even of identifying any relationship of representation between Community employees and Community trade union are all elements which, in conjunction with others, preclude any attempt at qualifying Community bargaining which "automatically" applies the same conceptual categories as those used in analysing the bargaining phenomena that have become historically established at national level.

(E)

"Although many things can be achieved with the legislative instrument, it is difficult to create practices not rooted in the social dynamic" (Mariucci, 1985 at p. 149).

By contrast, Community collective bargaining primarily represents an "invention" of the Community legal order, which proved itself more than adept at this maieutic role, in creating the Community bargaining system in its own image and likeness and—behind the "honeyed words" (Wedderburn, 1997 at p. 33) often lavished upon such bargaining—in reality making the system functional to its own regulatory objectives and strategies.

From an exegetic analysis of the provisions originally contained in the ASP it is possible to deduce two possible types of Community bargaining, essentially distinguishable according to their genesis and the means by which the resultant agreements acquire effect (see Chapter 4, Table I above).

Neither of these types corresponds to the canons of collective bargaining as a manifestation of collective autonomy and expression of social and normative pluralism. What the ASP provisions reveal is a somewhat unhappy alternative: the choice between one form of collective bargaining which is free but inconsequential (weak agreements), and another which is legally relevant but tied (strong agreements).

That is not to say that the ASP restricts the social partners in freely selecting issues on which they wish to negotiate. European trade unions and employers may also decide to bargain on matters which are excluded from Community jurisdiction, but any agreements they conclude on such matters cannot be implemented through a Council decision and therefore, if what this study has attempted to demonstrate is correct, remain entirely without relevance to the Community legal order. Consequently, the Community legal relevance of European-level collective agreements is conditional on the observance, on the

bargaining side, of predefined limits as to content which are imposed from outside by the Community institutions themselves.

In addition, predefining the margins of relevance of supranational collective
autonomy by identifying them with the Community's restricted competences in
the social field denies the European collective organisations, from the outset,
any opportunity of giving a free interpretation to instances of protection originating from areas where social exclusion is greatest and the need for solidarity
which has always been the basis of union activity and legitimacy is strongest.
Quite apart from the denial of the social partners' autonomy which such prede-
finition of bargaining scope embodies, compartmentalising employment-related
social issues in this way is clearly at odds with what is happening in the context
of the most recent and highly developed bargaining experiences, which show
that it is not possible to specify the outlines of an effective labour and employment policy without taking account of other factors such as training, research,
fiscal, environmental and infrastructure policies.

The unhappy choice between bargaining which is free and inconsequential or
relevant but tied is the inevitable outcome of a contradiction internal to the
Community legislature which reveals the latter's true intentions: a contradiction
which consists in having assigned a regulatory function to collective bargaining
while "forgetting" to provide the conditions that would have enabled it to
become independent of the protection benignly prepared for it by the
Community institutions. I am referring here to the absence of Community
recognition of the constitutional presumptions which any bargaining system
needs in order to establish its status and guarantee the normative relevance of its
bargaining phenomena: freedom of association and the right to strike. Both are
expressly excluded—on the basis of questionable arguments derived from a
questionable interpretation of the principle of subsidiarity—from the sphere of
Community competences.

(F)

Already lacking the constitutional presumptions necessary to its full recognition
within the Community legal order, the potentiality of supranational collective
autonomy (or of what is generally called the European industrial relations system) would also appear to be seriously prejudiced by the multi-tiered political
institution configuration of Community Europe, the overall political ideology
options underlying the integration process and the foreseeable strategies of the
bargaining agents on the employers' side.

Viewed from this different aspect, the effectiveness of the Community bargaining system is threatened by the circumstance of operating in a political, economic and institutional environment which is quite uncommon and somewhat
removed from the reassuring "unitary" certainties offered by national systems.
As the most astute of political science doctrine emphasises, the strategic choices
of the actors of bargaining and the normative choices of the Community insti-

tutions are by no means impervious to the Community's institutional configuration: "the design of political institutions has crucial effects on policymaking" (Pierson and Leibfried, 1995b at p. 457).

The political and institutional fragmentation of the economic context within which Community collective bargaining has to operate is therefore a far from secondary factor in the assessment of possible developments in a supranational collective autonomy. The Community's institutional arrangements constitute a factor capable of conditioning the substance of the political and normative choices by which Community bargaining, owing to the lack of inherent legitimacy, is in its turn conditioned.

(G)

Therefore, given that the Community legal order does not provide the instruments of a constitutional nature which would give grounds for regarding the ASP as promotional legislation (E), and that in addition—at least according to some authors whose view I share—the overall economic, political and institutional Community panorama does not provide the conditions which make it feasible to imagine a replication of concertation models tried and tested at national level (see above), we are left with the question of identifying the reasons why the Community institutions saw fit to recognise the (limited) regulatory competences granted to the social partners by the ASP.

The hypothesis given priority in the present study links the normative strategy adopted at the time by the Community institutions to the situation of regulatory crisis mentioned at the start of these concluding remarks. The institutionalisation of collective bargaining—with a contextual limitation of the competences concerned to the Community's own restricted jurisdiction in the social field and with the continued exclusion of freedom of association and the right to strike—corresponds to a specific intention on the part of the Community institutions: that of exploiting collective bargaining as a regulatory resource to go some way towards surmounting the problems afflicting the Community in this field. European collective agreements cannot be regarded as the dynamic dimension of a constitutionally recognised fundamental right to freedom of association, but merely as regulatory techniques potentially useful in overcoming the regulatory problems affecting the Community decision-making and implementation processes.

Secondly, and on a different but complementary plane of assessment, the Community institutions' "halfway" promotional legislation can be ascribed to the "minor vice—typical of states which have lost authority and credibility—of making a parade of regulatory schemes which involve an immoderate amount of creative contribution from autonomous sources, despite the absence of clear criteria governing the interaction between law and agreement" (Romagnoli, 1995a at p. 174). In other words, the hypothesis advanced here suggests that the "lame" normative support for collective bargaining supplied by the Community can be interpreted as an attempt to increase the democratic legitimacy of the integration process by utilising the bargaining principle which has played so large a part in the historical formation of what is called the European social model.

In the sense described, therefore, collective bargaining constitutes a regulatory and legitimacy resource of the Community legal order. Or at least, these are the terms in which it seems to have been viewed by those who have done most to plead its cause: the Community institutions, with the Commission foremost among them.

(H)

Perceiving collective bargaining as a regulatory and legitimacy resource of the Community legal order implies postulating its essentially instrumental or functionalised nature, for use in pursuing externally imposed strategies and objectives.

This leads us to conclude the line of reasoning followed up until now by pointing to the connection which it establishes between the analysis of Community collective bargaining, the overall characterisation of the integration process, the prospects for regulating the economic dynamics of the market and the much-discussed question of the Community social constitution.

As a legitimacy resource of the Community legal order, collective bargaining is in danger of becoming, as has been said provocatively, "the transmission belt of transnational competition" (Mahnkopf and Altvater, 1995). This means to say that, in the final analysis, the compression of the room left for an autonomy which would be guaranteed only by recognition of the constitutional principles still non-existent in the Community system, and the functionalisation of collective bargaining to the purpose of stabilising the integration process, represent a legitimation of a political project which is still essentially based on the creation and functioning of a single market.

And as a regulatory resource, Community collective bargaining is a candidate for falling within the scope of the debate currently in progress between economists and jurists on the definition of economically "efficient" regulatory techniques—a debate which, in some more recent manifestations, seems not to leave much scope for retaining heteronomous interventions to redress the balance between the contractual positions of those who take part in the (labour) market, ignoring the fact that "Pareto efficiency does not seem to constitute a valid criterion for regulation" (Hepple, 1995 at p. 44).

In short, we again find the eternal basic problem: to establish politically what are the values and principles that steer the Community integration process, by first providing the institutional conditions which allow not an implausible Community projection of national welfare states but a way of managing the internationalisation of economies which is informed by the dialogic and procedural ethic of participation and consensus. In this context, the constitutionalisation of collective social rights reveals its not only symbolic but also directly operative relevance, far beyond the mere "comparative labour law exercise" (Streeck, 1995b at p. 428) which the 1989 Community Social Charter represented.

It has been written, as a paraphrase of Groucho Marx's famous saying, that the Community would not accept as one of its Member States a state whose constitution was similar to its own (Vogel, 1994 at p. 205). The sentence captures perfectly the inherent asymmetry which exists to this day between the social constitutional traditions of the national systems and the shortcomings which in this sense characterise the Community system. In the absence of constitutional recognition of freedom of association and the right to strike, the promotion of collective bargaining seemingly ensured by the ASP is a *fiction* which does nothing to hide the real *function* attributed to the social partners' involvement in the Community decision-making process: a function which is no more than one of providing support for Community regulation and legitimacy. Beyond that, Community collective bargaining remains what its own continuing weaknesses and a still incomplete Community legal order permit it to be.

References

ADINOLFI, A. (1988), "The Implementation of Social Policy Directives Through Collective Agreements?", *Common Market Law Review*, no. 25, p. 291.

ALIPRANTIS, N. (1980), *La place de la convention collective dans la hiérarchie des normes*, Paris: L.G.D.J.

ALTER, K. and MEUNIER-AITSAHALIA, S. (1994), "Judicial Politics in the European Community. European Integration and the Pathbreaking Cassis de Dijon Decision", *Comparative Political Studies*, Vol. 26, no. 4, p. 535.

ALTER, K. (1996), "The European Court's Political Power", *West European Politics*, Vol. 19, p. 458.

ANDERSON, C.J. and KALTENTHALER, K.C. (1996), "The Dynamics of Public Opinion toward European Integration. 1973–93", *European Journal of International Relations*, Vol. 2, no. 2, p. 175.

APARICIO TOVAR, J. (1996a), "Salute e sicurezza", in BAYLOS GRAU, A., CARUSO, B., D'ANTONA, M. and SCIARRA, S. (eds).

APARICIO TOVAR, J. (1996b), "Contrattazione collettiva e fonti comunitarie", in BAYLOS GRAU, A., CARUSO, B., D'ANTONA, M. and SCIARRA, S. (eds).

ARBOS, X. (1991), "Notes sur la crise de la régulation étatique", *Revue interdisciplinaire d'études juridiques*, no. 26, p. 123.

ARMSTRONG, K.A. (1998a), "Legal Integration: Theorizing the Legal Dimension of European Integration", *Journal of Common Market Studies*, Vol. 36, no. 2, p. 155.

ARMSTRONG, K.A. (1998b), "New Institutionalism and European Union Legal Studies", in CRAIG, P. AND HARLOW, C. (eds).

ARNAUD, A.J. (1991), *Pour une pensée juridique européenne*, Paris: Presses Universitaires de France.

ARNAUD, A.J. (1995), "Legal Pluralism and the Building of Europe", in PETERSEN, A. and ZAHLE, H. (eds).

ARNULL, A. (1996), "The European Court and Judicial Objectivity: a Reply to Professor Hartley", *The Law Quarterly Review*, Vol. 112, p. 411.

ARRIGO, G. and VARDARO, G. (eds) (1981), *Laboratorio Weimar. Conflitti e diritto del lavoro nella Germania prenazista*, Rome: Edizioni Lavoro.

ARRIGO, G. (1996), "Politiche sociali comunitarie", in BAYLOS GRAU, A., CARUSO, B., D'ANTONA, M. and SCIARRA, S. (eds).

ARTHURS, H. (1998), "Landscape and Memory: Labour Law, Legal Pluralism and Globalization", in WILTHAGEN, T. (ed.).

BALANDI, G.G. and SCIARRA, S. (eds) (1982), *Il Pluralismo e il diritto del lavoro. Studi su Otto Kahn-Freund*, Rome: Edizioni Lavoro.

BALDWIN, R. and MCCRUDDEN, C. (eds) (1987), *Regulation and Public Law*, London: Weidenfeld & Nicolson.

BALDWIN, R. (1990), "Why Rules Don't Work", *The Modern Law Review*, Vol. 53, no. 3, p. 321.

BALDWIN, R. (1992), "The Limits of Legislative Harmonization", in BALDWIN R. and DAINTITH T. (eds), *Harmonization and Hazard. Regulating Health and Safety in the European Workplace*, London: Graham & Trotman.

BALLESTRERO, M.V. (1982), "Otto Kahn-Freund e il pluralismo degli italiani", in BALANDI G.G. and SCIARRA, S. (eds).

BALLESTRERO, M.V. (1998), "Corte costituzionale e Corte di giustizia. Supponiamo che . . .", *Lavoro e diritto*, no. 3, p. 485.

BANKS, K. (1993), "L'art. 118A, élément dynamique de la politique sociale communautaire", *Cahiers de droit européen*, no. 5–6, p. 537.

BARAV, A. (1997), "State Liability in Damages for Breach of Community Law in National Courts", *Yearbook of European Law*, Vol. 16, p. 87, Oxford: Clarendon Press.

BARBALET, J.M. (1988), *Citizenship*, Milton Keynes: Open University Press.

BARCELLONA, P. (1988), *L'egoismo maturo e la follia del capitale*, Turin: Bollati Boringhieri.

BARCELLONA, P. (1994), *Dallo Stato sociale allo Stato immaginario. Critica della "ragione funzionalista"*, Turin: Bollati Boringhieri.

BARNARD, C. (1996), *EC Employment Law*, Chichester: Wiley.

BAYLOS GRAU, A., CARUSO, B., D'ANTONA, M. and SCIARRA, S. (eds) (1996), *Dizionario di diritto del lavoro comunitario*, Bologna: Monduzzi.

BAYLOS GRAU, A. (1985), "I rapporti sindacali dopo il 'cambio' socialista", *Politica del diritto*, no. 2, p. 291.

BELARDINELLI, S. (1993), *Una sociologia senza qualità*, Milan: Franco Angeli.

BENGOETXEA, J. (1991), "Institutions, Legal Theory and EC Law", *Archiv für Rechts- und Sozialphilosophie*, Vol. LXXVII, p. 195.

BENGOETXEA, J. (1994), "An Institutional Theory for European Community Law?", in *European Yearbook in the Sociology of Law 1993*, (eds Febbrajo, A. and Nelken, D.), Milan: Giuffrè.

BERCUSSON, B. and VAN DIJK, J.J. (1995), "The Implementation of the Protocol and Agreement on Social Policy of the Treaty on European Union", *International Journal of Comparative Labour Law and Industrial Relations*, Vol. 11, no. 1, p. 3.

BERCUSSON, B. (1991), "Fundamental Social and Economic Rights in the European Community", in CASSESE, A. and CLAPHAM, A. (eds), *Human Rights and the European Community*, Vol. II: *Methods of Protection*, Baden-Baden: Nomos Verlagsgesellschaft.

BERCUSSON, B. (1992), "Maastricht: a fundamental change in European labour law", *Industrial Law Journal*, Vol. 21, p. 177.

BERCUSSON, B. (1993), "European Labour Law and Sectorial Bargaining", *Industrial Relations Journal*, Vol. 24, no. 4, p. 257.

BERCUSSON, B. (1994), "Social Policy at the Crossroads: European Labour Law after Maastricht", in DEHOUSSE, R. (ed.).

BERCUSSON, B. (1995), "The Collective Labour Law of the European Union", *European Law Journal*, Vol. 1, no. 2, p. 157.

BERCUSSON, B. (1996), *European Labour Law*, London: Butterworths.

BERLIN, D. (1992), "Interactions between the Lawmaker and the Judiciary within the EC", *Legal Issues of European Integration*, no. 2, p. 17.

BETTEN, L. (1998), "The Democratic Deficit of Participatory Democracy in Community Social Policy", *European Law Review*, Vol. 23, no. 1, p. 20.

BIEBER, R., DEHOUSSE, R., PINDER J. and WEILER, J.H.H. (1988), "Back to the Future:

Policy, Strategy and Tactics of the White Paper on the Creation of a Single European Market", in BIEBER, R., DEHOUSSE, R., PINDER J. and WEILER, J.H.H. (eds).

BIEBER, R., DEHOUSSE, R., PINDER J. and WEILER, J.H.H. (eds) (1988), *1992: One European Market?*, Baden-Baden: Nomos Verlagsgesellschaft.

BIEBER, R. and SALOMÉ, I. (1996), "Hierarchy of Norms in European law", *Common Market Law Review*, Vol. 33, p. 907.

BIRNBAUM, P. (1990), "Individual Action, Collective Action and Workers' Strategy", in BIRNBAUM, P. and LECA, J. (eds), *Individualism. Theories and Methods*, Oxford: Clarendon Press.

BLACK, J. (1996), "Constitutionalising Self-Regulation", *Modern Law Review*, Vol. 59, no. 1, p. 24.

BLANPAIN, R. and ENGELS, C. (1995), *European Labour Law*, III edn, Deventer: Kluwer.

BLANPAIN, R., HEPPLE, S., SCIARRA, S. and WEISS, M. (1996), *Fundamental Social Rights: Proposals for the European Union*, Leuven: Peeters.

BLANPAIN, R. and WINDEY, P. (1994), *European Works Councils: Information and Consultation of Employees in Multinational Enterprises in Europe: the European Directive (94/45) of September 22, 1994*, Leuven: Peeters.

BLANPAIN, R. (1998a), "European Works Councils: A Comparative Overview", *Bulletin of Comparative Labour Relations*, Vol. 32, p. 2.

BLANPAIN, R. (1998b), "Europe: Employment and Labour Policies", in *Scritti in onore di Giuseppe Federico Mancini*, Vol. I, Milan: Giuffrè.

BOBBIO, N. (1960), *Teoria dell'ordinamento giuridico*, Turin: Giappichelli.

BOBBIO, N. (1990), *L'età dei diritti*, Turin: Einaudi.

BORENFREUND, G. (1988), "Propos sur la représentativité syndical", *Droit social*, p. 476.

BORENFREUND, G. (1991), "La représentation des salariés et l'idée de représentation, *Droit social*, p. 685.

BORENFREUND, G. (1997), "Pouvoir de représentation et négociation collective", *Droit social*, p. 1006.

BROWNSWORD, R., HOWELLS, G. and WILHELMSSON, T. (eds) (1994), *Welfarism in Contract Law*, Aldershot: Dartmouth.

BUCHANAN, J. (1975), *The Limits of Liberty: between Anarchy and Leviathan*, Chicago: Chicago University Press.

BUCHANAN, J.M., PÖHL, K.O., CURZON PRICE, V. and VIBERT, F. (1990), *Europe's Constitutional Future*, London: Institute of Economic Affairs.

BURLEY, A.M. and MATTLI W. (1993), "Europe before the Court: a Political Theory of Legal Integration", *International Organization*, Vol. 47, p. 41.

BURNS, T. (1998), "Better Lawmaking? An Evaluation of Lawmaking in the European Community", in CRAIG, P. and HARLOW, C. (eds).

CAPPELLETTI, M., SECCOMBE, M. and WEILER J. (1986), "A General Introduction", in CAPPELLETTI, M., SECCOMBE, M. and WEILER, J. (eds), Vol. 1: *Methods, Tools and Institutions*, Book 1: *A Political, Legal and Economic Overview*.

CAPPELLETTI, M., SECCOMBE, M. and WEILER J. (eds) (1986), *Integration Through Law: Europe and the American Federal Experience*, Berlin: Walter de Gruyter.

CARABELLI, U. (1986), *Libertà e immunità del sindacato. Ordinamento statuale, organizzazione sindacale e teoria della pluralità degli ordinamenti*, Naples: Jovene.

CARLIN, F. (1995), "The European Works Council Directive", *European Law Review*, Vol. 20, no. 1, p. 96.

CARTABIA, M. (1995), *Principi inviolabili e integrazione europea*, Milan: Giuffrè.

CARUSO, B. (1989), "Rappresentanza negoziale del sindacato e consenso. Un profilo storico del dibattito", *Rivista critica del diritto privato*, no. 1, p. 81.

CARUSO, B. (1990a), "Per una regolazione riflessiva della rappresentanza sindacale", *Lavoro e diritto*, p. 593.

CARUSO, B. (1990b), "Rappresentanza e rappresentatività sindacale", in D'ANTONA, M. (ed.).

CARUSO, B. (1992), *Rappresentanza sindacale e consenso*, Milan: Franco Angeli.

CARUSO, B. (1994), "Processi reali e processi mentali nella costruzione dell'Europa sociale: il caso della contrattazione collettiva", in ATTINÀ, F. and VELO, D. (eds), *Dalla Comunità all'Unione*, Bari: Caucci.

CARUSO, B. (1997), "Il contratto collettivo europeo", in RIZZO, V. (ed.), *Diritto privato comunitario*, Vol. II: *Lavoro, impresa e società*, Naples: Edizioni Scientifiche Italiane.

CASAS BAAMONDE, M.E. (1990), "Sulla rappresentatività sindacale ovvero alla ricerca della legittimazione perduta", *Lavoro e diritto*, p. 449.

CAWSON, A. (ed.) (1985), *Organized Interests and the State: Studies in Meso-Corporatism*, London: Sage Publications.

CHAZEL F. and COMMAILLE J. (eds) (1991), *Normes juridiques et régulation sociale*, Paris: L.G.D.J.

CLARK, J. and HALL, M. (1992), "The Cinderella Directive? Employee Rights to Information about Conditions Applicable to their Contract or Employment Relationship", *Industrial Law Journal*, Vol. 21, no. 2, p. 106.

CLARK, J. and WEDDERBURN, LORD (1987), "Juridification: a Universal Trend? The British Experience in Labour Law", in TEUBNER, G. (ed.), *Juridification of Social Spheres*, Berlin: de Gruyter.

CLARK, J. (1985), "The Juridification of Industrial Relations: a Review Article", *Industrial Law Journal*, Vol. 14, no. 1, p. 69.

CLEGG, H.A. (1975), "Pluralism in Industrial Relations", *British Journal of Industrial Relations*, Vol. 13, no. 3, p. 309.

CLEGG, H.A., (1983), "Otto Kahn-Freund and British Industrial Relations", in WEDDERBURN, LORD, LEWIS, R. and CLARK, J. (eds).

COHEN-TANUGI, L. (1985), *Le droit sans l'Etat*, Paris: Presses Universitaires de France.

COLAIANNI, T. (1996), *European Works Councils: a Legal and Practical Guide: information and consultation of employees in multinational companies: what management needs to know before starting negotiations with the workforce*, London: Sweet & Maxwell.

COLLINS, H. (1987), "Against Abstensionism in Labour Law", in BELL, J. and EEKELAAR, J. (eds), *Oxford Essays in Jurisprudence*, Oxford University Press.

COLLINS, H. (1997), "The Productive Disintegration of Labour Law", *Industrial Law Journal*, Vol. 26, no. 4, p. 295.

COMMONS, J. (1923, now 1968), *Legal Foundations of Capitalism*, Macmillan Company, now Madison: University of Wisconsin Press.

CORSALE, M. (1993), "La codificazione vista dall'età della decodificazione", *Materiali per una storia della cultura giuridica*, no. 2, p. 423.

CRAIG, P. and HARLOW, C. (eds) (1998), *Lawmaking in the European Union*, London: Kluwer Law International in collaboration with the Institute of Advanced Legal Studies.

CRAIG, P. (1997), "Directives: Direct Effect, Indirect Effect and the Construction of National Legislation", *European Law Review*, Vol. 22, p. 519.

CROUCH, C. and MARQUAND, D. (1995), "Re-inventing Collective Action", in *idem* (eds), *Reinventing Collective Action. From the Global to the Local*, Oxford: Blackwell.

CROUCH, C. (1982), *Trade Unions: the Logic of Collective Action*, Glasgow: Fontana.

CROUCH, C. (1993), *Industrial Relations and European State Traditions*, Oxford: Clarendon Press.

CROUCH, C. (1998), "Non amato ma inevitabile il ritorno al neocorporatismo"; *Giornale di diritto del lavoro e di relazioni industriali*, p. 55.

CROZIER, M. (1991), "Le problème de la régulation dans les sociétés complexes modernes", in CHAZEL, F. and COMMAILLE, J. (eds), *Normes juridiques et régulation sociale*, Paris: L.G.D.J.

CRUZ VILLALON, J. (1996), "Comitati aziendali europei", in BAYLOS GRAU, A., CARUSO, B., D'ANTONA, M. and SCIARRA, S. (eds).

CURTIN, D. (1993), "The Constitutional Structure of the Union: a Europe of Bits and Pieces", *Common Market Law Review*, Vol. 30, p. 17.

CURTIN, D. (1997), *Postnational Democracy: European Union in Search of a Political Philosophy*, The Hague: Kluwer Law International.

D'ANTONA, M. (1987), "Pubblici poteri nel mercato del lavoro. Amministrazioni e contrattazione collettiva nella legislazione recente", *Rivista italiana di diritto del lavoro*, I, p. 226.

D'ANTONA, M. (1990), "L'anomalia post positivista nel diritto del lavoro e la questione del metodo", *Rivista critica di diritto privato*, no. 1–2, p. 207.

D'ANTONA, M. (1992), "Mercato unico europeo ed aree regionali deboli: le conseguenze giuridiche", *Lavoro e diritto*, p. 49.

D'ANTONA, M. (1994), "Armonizzazione del diritto del lavoro e federalismo nell'Unione Europea", *Rivista trimestrale di diritto e procedura civile*, no. 3, p. 695.

D'ANTONA, M. (1996), "Sistema giuridico comunitario", in BAYLOS GRAU, A., CARUSO, B., D'ANTONA, M. and SCIARRA, S. (eds).

D'ANTONA, M. (ed.) (1990), *Letture di diritto sindacale. Le basi teoriche del diritto sindacale*, Naples: Jovene.

DAHL, R. (1956), *A Preface to Democratic Theory*, Chicago: University of Chicago Press.

DAHL, R. (1989), *Democracy and its Critics*, Yale University Press.

DAINTITH, T. (1995), "European Community Law and the Distribution of Regulatory Power in the United Kingdom", *European Law Journal*, Vol. 1, no. 2, p. 134.

DASHWOOD, A. (1981), "The Harmonisation Process", in TWITCHETT, C. (ed.), *Harmonisation in the EEC*, London: Macmillan Press.

DÄUBLER, W. (1991), "Market and Social Justice in the EC. The rationale and Substance of a European Fundamental Rights Act", in *idem* (ed.), *Market and Social Justice: the Other Side of the Internal Market*, Gütersloh: Bertelsmann Foundation.

DÄUBLER, W. (1998), "Verso un diritto del lavoro europeo?", in *Scritti in onore di Giuseppe Federico Mancini*, Vol. I, Milan: Giuffrè.

DAVIES, P. and FREEDLAND, M. (1983), "Editors' Introduction", in *Kahn-Freund's Labour and the Law*, 3rd edn, London: Stevens & Sons.

DAVIES, P. and FREEDLAND, M. (1993), *Labour Legislation and Public Policy. A Contemporary History*, Oxford: Clarendon Press.

DAVIES, P., LYON-CAEN, A., SCIARRA, S. and SIMITIS, S. (eds) (1996), *European Labour Law: Principles and Perspectives. Liber Amicorum Lord Wedderburn of Charlton*, Oxford: Clarendon Press.

DAVIES, P. (1992), "The Emergence of European Labour Law", in MCCARTHY, W. (ed.), *Legal Intervention in Industrial Relations. Gains and Losses*, Oxford: Blackwell.

DAVIES, P. (1995), "Market Integration and Social Policy in the Court of Justice", *Industrial Law Journal*, Vol. 24, no. 1, p. 49.

DAVIES, P. (1996), "The European Court of Justice, National Courts and the Member States", in DAVIES, P., LYON-CAEN, A., SCIARRA, S. and SIMITIS, S. (eds).

DE BURCA, G. (1992), "Giving Effect to European Community Directives", *Modern Law Review*, Vol. 55, p. 215.

DE BURCA, G. (1996), "The Quest for Legitimacy in the European Union", *The Modern Law Review*, Vol. 59, no. 3, p. 349.

DE SOUSA SANTOS, B. (1987), "Law: A Map of Misreading. Towards a Postmodern Conception of Law", *Journal of Law and Society*, Vol. 14, no. 3, p. 279.

DE SOUSA SANTOS, B. (1990), "Stato e diritto nella transizione post-moderna. Per un nuovo senso comune giuridico", *Sociologia del diritto*, no. 3, p. 5.

DEAKIN, S. and MORRIS, G. (1995), *Labour Law*, London: Butterworths.

DEAKIN, S. and WILKINSON, F. (1994), "Rights vs Efficiency? The Economic Case for Transnational Standards", *Industrial Law Journal*, Vol. 23, no. 4, p. 289.

DEAKIN, S. (1996), "Labour Law as Market Regulation", in DAVIES, P., LYON-CAEN, A., SCIARRA, S. and SIMITIS, S. (eds).

DEHOUSSE, R., JOERGES, C., MAJONE, G. and SNYDER, F. (1992), *Europe After 1992. New Regulatory Strategies*, Florence: EUI Working Paper, LAW, No. 92/31.

DEHOUSSE, R. and WEILER, J.H.H. (1990), "The Legal Dimension", in WALLACE, W. (ed.), *The Dynamics of European Integration*, London: Pinter Publishers.

DEHOUSSE, R. (1989), "1992 and Beyond: the Institutional Dimension of the Internal Market Programme", *Legal Issues of European Integration*, no. 1, p. 109.

DEHOUSSE, R. (1994), "Some Reflections on the Crisis of the Harmonization Model", in SNYDER F. (ed.), *A Regulatory Framework for Foodstuff in the Internal Market*, Florence: EUI Working Paper, LAW, No. 94/4.

DEHOUSSE, R. (1997), "Regulation by networks in the European Community: the role of the European agencies", *Journal of European Public Policy*, Vol. 4, no. 2, p. 246.

DEHOUSSE, R. (ed.) (1994), *Europe after Maastricht. An Ever Closer Union?*, Münich: Law Books in Europe.

DELL'OLIO, M. (1980), *L'organizzazione e l'azione sindacale in generale*, in DELL'OLIO, M. and BRANCA, G., *L'organizzazione e l'azione sindacale*, Padua: Cedam.

DESPAX, M. (1989), *Négociations, conventions et accords collectifs de travail*, II edn, in *Traité de droit du travail*, (ed.) G.H. CAMERLYNCK, Tome 7, Paris: Dalloz.

DØLVIK, J.E. (1997), *Redrawing Boundaries of Solidarity? ETUC, Social Dialogue and the Europeanisation of Trade Unions in the 1990s*, Paper presented to the Fifth IIRA European Regional Industrial Relations Congress, Dublin, 26–29 August 1997.

DUGUIT, L. (1928), *Traité de droit constitutionnel*, Vol. 2, *La théorie générale de l'Etat*, Paris: Fontemoing.

DUNLOP, J. (1958), *Industrial Relations System*, New York: Henry Holt & Co.

DURAND, P. (1939), "Le dualisme de la convention collective de travail", *Revue trimestrielle de droit civil*, p. 353.

DURKHEIM, E. (1930), *Le suicide. Etude de sociologie*, Paris: Presse Universitaires de France.

EASSON, A. (1989), "Legal Approaches to European Integration: the Role of the Court and

Legislator in the Completion of the European Common Market", *Journal of European Integration*, Vol. XII, no. 2–3, p. 101.

EHLERMANN, C.D. (1995), "Compétition entre systèmes réglementaires", *Revue du Marché commun et de l'Union Européenne*, no. 387, p. 220.

EHRLICH, E. (1913), *Grundlegung der Soziologies des Rechts*, Münich-Leipzig: Duncker & Humblot (Engl. transl., *Fundamental Principles of the Sociology of Law*, New York, 1962).

EICHENER, V. (1997), "Effective European Problem-Solving: Lessons from the Regulation of Occupational Safety and Environmental Protection", *Journal of European Public Policy*, Vol. 4, no. 4, p. 1350.

EIDE, A., KRAUSE, C. and ROSAS, A. (eds) (1995), *Economic, Social and Cultural Rights*, Dordrecht: Martinus Nijhoff Publishers.

ELEFTHERIADIS, P. (1997), "The Direct Effect of Community Law: Conceptual Issues", in *Yearbook of European Law*, Vol. 16, Oxford: Clarendon Press.

EMMERT, F. and PEREIRA DE AZEVEDO, M. (1995), "Les jeux sont faits: rien ne va plus ou une nouvelle occasion perdue par la CJCE", *Revue Trimestrielle de droit Européen*, no. 1, p. 11.

EPSTEIN, R. (1995), *Simple Rules for a Complex World*, Cambridge, Mass: Harvard University Press.

ESCUDERO RODRIGUEZ, R. (1990), *La representatividad de los sindicatos en el modelo laboral español*, Madrid: Tecnos.

EVERSON, M. (1995), "Independent Agencies: Hierarchy Beaters?", *European Law Journal*, Vol. 1, no. 2, p. 180.

EVERSON, M. (1998), "Administering Europe?", *Journal of Common Market Studies*, Vol. 36, no. 2, p. 195.

FAHLBECK, R. (1987), "Collective agreements: A Crossroad between Public Law and Private Law", *Comparative Labor Law Journal*, Vol. 8, p. 268.

FALKNER, G. (1996), "European Works Councils and the Maastricht Social Agreements: Towards a New Policy Style?", *Journal of European Public Policy*, Vol. 3, no. 2, p. 192.

FALKNER, G. (1997), "Corporatist Governance and Europeanisation: No Future in the Multi-level Game?", *European Integration Online Papers*, Vol. 1, no. 11; http://eiop.or.at/eiop/texte/1997–011a.htm

FEBBRAJO, A. (1986), "Regolazione giuridica e autoregolazione sociale", *Sociologia del diritto*, no. 2–3, p. 145.

FERRARI, V. (1993), "Note sull'alternativa del diritto contemporaneo", *Sociologia del diritto*, no. 1, p. 19.

FERRARO, G. (1981), *Ordinamento, ruolo del sindacato, dinamica contrattuale di tutela*, Padua: Cedam.

FERRERA, M. (1993), "Nuovi modelli per il welfare europeo", *Il Mulino*, no. 2, p. 347.

FERRERA, M. (ed.) (1993), *Stato sociale e mercato. Il welfare state europeo sopravviverà alla globalizzazione dell'economia?*, Turin: Fondazione Agnelli.

FITZPATRICK, B. (1992), "Community Social Law after Maastricht", *Industrial Law Journal*, Vol. 21, no. 3, p. 199.

FLANDERS, A. and CLEGG. H.A. (eds) (1954), *The System of Industrial Relations in Great Britain*, Oxford: Blackwell.

FLANDERS, A. (1968), "Collective Bargaining: A Theoretical Analysis", *British Journal of Industrial Relations*, Vol. 6, no. 1, p. 1.

FLORA, P. and HEIDENHEIMER, A.J. (1981), "Il nucleo storico e il cambiamento dei confini del "Welfare State", in *idem* (eds).

FLORA, P. and HEIDENHEIMER, A.J. (eds) (1981), *The Development of Welfare States in Europe and America*, New York: Transaction Books.

FLORA, P. (ed.) (1986), *Growth to Limits: the Western European Welfare States Since World War* II, Berlin: De Gruyter.

FOSTER, N. (1994), "The German Constitution and E.C. Membership", *Public Law*, p. 392.

FOUCAULT, M. (1969), *L'archéologie du savoir*, Paris: Gallimard.

FOX, A. and FLANDERS, A. (1969), "The Reform of Collective Baragining: From Donovan to Durkheim", *British Journal of Industrial Relations*, Vol. 7, no. 2, p. 151.

FOX, A. (1973), "Industrial Relations: a Social Critique of Pluralist Ideology", in CHILD, J. (ed.), *Man and Organization: the Search for Explanation and Relevance*, London: Allen & Unwin.

FOX, A. (1974), *Beyond Contract: Work, Power and Trust Relations*, London: Faber & Faber.

FRANSSEN, E. (1998), "Implementation of European Collective Agreements: Some Troublesome Issues", *Maastricht Journal of European and Comparative Law*, Vol. 5, no. 1, p. 53.

FRIEDMAN, L.M. (1993), "Verso una sociologia del diritto transnazionale", *Sociologia del diritto*, no. 1, p. 39.

GARAPON, A. (1995), "French Legal Culture and the Shock of Globalization", *Social & Legal Studies*, Vol. 4, no. 4, p. 493.

GARZON VALDÉS, E. (1998), "On the Concept of Legitimacy of a Political System", *Associations*, Vol. 2, no. 1, p. 55.

GENSCHEL, P. and PLÜMPER, T. (1997), "Regulatory Competition and International Co-operation", *Journal of European Public Policy*, Vol. 4, no. 4, p. 626.

GERBER, L. (1995), "Corporatism and State Theory", *Social Science History*, Vol. 19, no. 3, p. 313.

GIDDENS, A. (1982), *Profiles and Critiques in Social Theory*, London: Macmillan.

GILLROY, J.M. and WADE, M. (eds) (1992), *The Moral Dimension of Public Choice: Beyond the Market Paradigm*, Pittsburgh: Pittsburgh University Press.

GIUGNI, G. (1960), *Introduzione allo studio della autonomia collettiva*, Milan: Giuffrè.

GIUGNI, G. (1970, now 1989), "Il diritto sindacale e i suoi interlocutori", *Rivista trimestrale di diritto e procedura civile*, p. 369, now in *idem*, 1989.

GIUGNI, G. (1979), "Art. 39", in *Commentario della Costituzione*, ed. Giuseppe Branca, *Rapporti economici, Tomo I, Art. 35–40*, Bologna/Rome: Zanichelli/Soc. Ed. del Foro Italiano.

GIUGNI, G. (1982, now 1989), "Il diritto del lavoro negli anni '80", *Giornale di diritto del lavoro e di relazioni industriali*, p. 373, now in *idem*, 1989.

GIUGNI, G. (1987), "Juridification: Labour Relations in Italy", in TEUBNER, G. (ed.), *Juridification of Social Spheres*, Berlin: de Gruyter.

GIUGNI, G. (1989), *Lavoro, leggi, contratti*, Bologna: Il Mulino.

GOERKE, L. and HOLLER, M. (1998), "Strategic Standardization in Europe: A Public Choice Perspective", *European Journal of Law and Economics*, Vol. 6, p. 95.

GOERKE, L. and PIAZOLO, K. (1998), "Decision Making under the EU's Social Chapter", *International Review of Law and Economics*, Vol. 18, p. 217.

GOFFIN, L. (1997), "A propos des principes régissant la responsabilité non contractuelle des États membres en cas de violation du droit communautaire", *Cahiers de droit européen*, no. 5–6, p. 531.

GOLDTHORPE, J.H. (1974), "Industrial Relations in Great Britain: a Critique of Reformism", *Politics & Society*, no. 4, p. 419.

GOLUB, J. (1996), "The Politics of Judicial Discretion: Rethinking the Interactions between National Courts and the European Court of Justice", *West European Politics*, Vol. 19, p. 360.

GORMLEY, L. and DE HAAN, J. (1996), "The Democratic Deficit of the European Central Bank", *European Law Review*, Vol. 21, no. 2, p. 95.

GRANDI, M. (1982), "Otto Kahn-Freund: un "pluralista" atipico?", in BALANDI, G.G. and SCIARRA, S. (eds).

GRANDI, M. (1993), "Le parti sociali e l'autonomia contrattuale di fronte all'Unione economica e monetaria", *Lavoro e diritto*, p. 463.

GRANDI, M. (1995), "Diritto del lavoro e Comunità Europea", *Rivista italiana di diritto del lavoro*, no. 2, I, p. 133.

GREEN, D.P. and SHAPIRO, I. (1994), *Pathologies of Rational Choice Theories: a Critique of Applications in Political Science*, New Haven: Yale University Press.

GUALMINI, E. (1997), *Le rendite del neo-corporativismo*, Catanzaro: Rubbettino Editore.

GUARRIELLO, F. (1992), "L'Europa sociale dopo Maastricht", *Lavoro e diritto*, p. 223.

GUERY, G. (1992), "European Collective Bargaining and the Maastricht Treaty", *International Labour Review*, Vol. 131, no. 6, p. 581.

GURVITCH, G. (1946), *The Bill of Social Rights*, New York: International Universities Press.

HABERMAS, J. (1973), *Legitimationsprobleme im Spätkapitalismus*, Frankfurt am Main: Suhrkamp, (Engl. transl., *Legitimation crisis*, Cambridge: Polity Press, 1986).

HABERMAS, J. (1984), *The Theory of Communicative Action*, Vol. II, Cambridge: Polity Press.

HABERMAS, J. (1988), "Excursus on Luhmann's Appropriation of the Philosophy of the Subject through Systems Theory", in *idem*, *The Philosophical Discourse of Modernity*, Cambridge: Polity Press.

HABERMAS, J. (1992), *Morale, diritto, politica*, Turin: Einaudi.

HÄGG, P.G. (1997), "Theories on the Economics of Regulation: A Survey of the Literature from a European Perspective", *European Journal of Law and Economics*, Vol. 4, p. 337.

HAIBACH, G. (1997), "Comitology: A Comparative Analysis of the Separation and Delegation of Legislative Powers, *Maastricht Journal of European and Comparative Law*, Vol. 4, p. 373.

HALL, M. (1994), "Industrial Relations and the Social Dimension of European Integration: Before and After Maastricht", in HYMAN, R. and FERNER, A. (eds), *New Frontiers in European Industrial Relations*, Oxford: Blackwell.

HARDING, C. (1997), "Member State Enforcement of European Community Measures: the Chimera of Effective Enforcement", *Maastricht Journal of European and Comparative Law*, Vol. 4, no. 1, p. 5.

HARLOW, C. (1997), "Francovich and the Problem of the Disobedient State", *European Law Journal*, Vol. 2, no. 3, p. 199.

HARTLEY, T.C. (1996), "The European Court, Judicial Objectivity and the Constitution of European Union", *The Law Quarterly Review*, Vol. 112, p. 94.

HAURIOU, M. (1925), "La théorie de l'institution et de la fondation", *Cahiers de la nouvelle journée*, 1925.

HAYWARD, J. (1995), "Europe's Endangered Industrial Champions", in *idem* (ed.), *Industrial Enterprise and European Integration. From National to International Champions in Western Europe*, Oxford University Press.

HEERMA VAN VOOS, G. (1995), "The Directive on European Works Councils in Community-Scale Undertakings. The Introduction of Double Subsidiarity in European Labour Law", *Maastricht Journal of European and Comparative Law*, Vol. 2, no. 4, p. 339.

HELLER, T. (1986), "Legal Theory and the Political Economy of American Federalism" in CAPPELLETTI, M., SECCOMBE, M. and WEILER J. (eds), Vol. 1: *Methods, Tools and Institutions*, Book 1: *A Political, Legal and Economic Overview*.

HEPPLE, B. - FREDMAN, S. (1992), *Labour Law and Industrial Relations in Great Britain*, II edn, Deventer: Kluwer.

HEPPLE, B. (1990), "The Implementation of the Community Charter of Fundamental Social Rights", *Modern Law Review*, Vol. 53, p. 643.

HEPPLE, B. (1995), "Social Values and European Law", *Current Legal Problems*, Vol. 48, Part 2: Collected Papers, p. 39.

HIRST, P. (ed.) (1989), *The Pluralist Theory of the State. Selected Writings of G.D.H. Cole, J.D. Figgis, H. Laski*, London: Routledge.

HOWARTH, D. (1988), "The Autonomy of Labour Law: A Response to Professor Wedderburn", *Industrial Law Journal*, Vol. 17, no. 1, p. 11.

HUISKAMP, R. (1995), "Collective bargaining in transition", in VAN RUYSSEVELDT, J., HUISKAMP, R. and VAN HOOF, J. (eds), *Comparative Industrial & Employment Relations*, London: Sage Publications.

HYMAN, R. (1978), "Pluralism, Procedural Consensus and Collective Bargaining", *British Journal of Industrial Relations*, Vol. 16, no. 1, p. 16.

HYMAN, R. (1994), "Theory and Industrial Relations", *British Journal of Industrial Relations*, Vol. 32, no. 2, p. 165.

HYMAN, R. (1996), "Union Identities and Ideologies in Europe", in PASTURE, P., VERBERCKMOES, J. and DE WITTE, H. (eds), *The Lost Perspective? Trade Unions Between Ideology and Social Action in the New Europe*, Aldershot: Avebury.

ICHINO, A. and ICHINO, P. (1994), "A chi serve il diritto del lavoro. Riflessioni interdisciplinari sulla funzione economica e la giustificazione costituzionale dell'inderogabilità delle norme giuslavoristiche", *Rivista italiana di diritto del lavoro*, I, p. 459.

ICHINO, P. (1996), *Il lavoro e il mercato. Per un diritto del lavoro maggiorenne*, Milan: Mondadori.

IN'T VELD, R. and SCHAAP, L. (eds) (1991), *Autopoiesis and Configuration Theory: New Approaches to Societal Steering*, Dordrecht: Kluwer.

JACHTENFUCHS, M. (1995), "Theoretical Perspective on European Governance", *European Law Journal*, Vol. 1, no. 2, p. 115.

JEAMMAUD, A., KIRAT, T. and VILLEVAL, M.C. (1996), "Les règles juridiques, l'entreprise et son institutionnalisation: au croisement de l'économie et du droit", *Revue Internationale de Droit Economique*, p. 99.

JEAMMAUD, A. (1991), "Le droit constitutionnel dans les relations du travail", *Actualité juridique—Droit administratif*, p. 612.

JEAMMAUD, A. (1994). "La place du salarié individu dans le droit français du travail", in ALIPRANTIS, N. and KESSLER, F. (eds), *Le droit collectif du Travail. Questions fonda-*

mentales, évolutions récentes. Études en hommage à Madame le Professeur Hélène Sinay, Frankfurt am Main: Peter Lang GmbH.

JEAMMAUD, A. (1998), "Per una discussione sulla contrattazione collettiva europea dal punto di vista degli ordinamenti nazionali", in LETTIERI, A. and ROMAGNOLI, U. (eds).

JOERGES, C., LADEUR, K.H. and VOS, E. (eds) (1997), *Integrating Scientific Expertise into Regulatory Decision-Making: National Traditions and European Innovations*, Baden-Baden: Nomos Verlagsgesellschaft.

JOERGES, C. and TRUBECK, D.M. (eds), (1989) *Critical Legal Thought. An American-German Debate*, Baden-Baden: Nomos Verlagsgesellschaft.

JOERGES, C. (1990), "Paradoxes of Deregulatory Strategies at Community Level: the Example of Product Safety Policy", in MAJONE, G. (ed.).

JOERGES, C. (1994), "European Economic Law, the Nation-State and the Maastricht Treaty", in DEHOUSSE R. (ed.).

JOERGES, C. (1996), *Integrating Scientific Expertise into Regulatory Decision-Making. Scientific Expertise in Social Regulation and the European Court of Justice: Legal Frameworks for Denationalized Governance Structures*, Florence: EUI Working Paper, RSC, No. 96/10.

JOERGES, C. (1997), *States Without a Market? Comments on the German Constitutional Court's Maastricht-Judgment and a Plea for Interdisciplinary Discourses*, European Integration Online Papers (EIoP) Vol. 1 No. 20; http://eiopag.or./at./eiop/texte/ 1997-01920htm

JOERGES, C. (ed.) (1991), *European Product Safety, Internal Market Policy and the New Approach to Technical Harmonisation and Standards*, Florence: EUI Working Paper, LAW, No. 91/10–14.

KAHN-FREUND, O. (1954a), "Legal Framework", in FLANDERS, A. and CLEGG. H.A. (eds).

KAHN-FREUND, O. (1954b), "Intergroup Conflicts and their Settlement", in *The British Journal of Sociology*, p. 193.

KAHN-FREUND, O. (1959), "Labour Law", in GINSBERG, M. (ed.), *Law and Opinion in England in the Twentieth Century*, Berkeley: University of California Press (reprint Westport: Greenwood Press, 1974).

KAHN-FREUND, O. (1972), "Labour Relations and International Standards. Some Reflections on the European Social Charter", in *Miscellanea W.J. Ganshof Van der Meersch*, Vol. I, Brussels: Bruylant/Paris: LGDJ.

KAHN-FREUND, O. (1976), "The Impact of Constitutions on Labour Law", *Cambridge Law Journal*, Vol. 35, no. 2, p. 240.

KAHN-FREUND, O. (1977), *Labour and the Law*, II ed., London: Stevens.

KAHN-FREUND, O. (1979), *Labour Relations: Heritage and Adjustment*, Oxford: University Press.

KAHN-FREUND, O. (1983), *Kahn-Freund's Labour and the Law*, III edn, edited by Davies and Freedland, London: Stevens & Sons

KEARNS DAVIS, W. (1996), "Sigurjonsson v. Iceland: The European Court of Human Rights Expands the Negative Right of Association", *The Irish Journal of European Law*, Vol. 5, no. 1, p. 45.

KENNEDY, D. (1982), "The Stages of the Decline of the Public/Private Distinction", *University of Pennsylvania Law Review*, Vol. 130.

KENNER, J. (1995), EC Labour Law: the Softly Softly Approach"; *The International Journal of Comparative Labour Law and Industrial Relations*, Vol. 11, no. 4, p. 307.

KETTLER, D. (1987), "Legal Reconstitution of the Welfare State: a Latent Social Democratic Legacy", *Law and Society Review*, Vol. 21, no. 1, p. 278.

KLARE, K. (1982), "The Public/Private Distinction in Labor Law", *University of Pennsylvania Law Review*, Vol. 130, p. 1358.

KNILL, C. (1998), "European Policies: The Impact of National Administrative Traditions", *Journal of Public Policy*, Vol. 18, no. 1, p. 1.

KNUTSEN, P. (1997), "Corporatist Tendencies in the Euro-polity: The EU Directive of 22 September 1994 on European Works Councils", *Economic and Industrial Democracy*, Vol. 18, no. 2, p. 289.

KOOPMANS, T. (1986), "The Role of Law in the Next Stage of European Integration", *The International and Comparative Law Quarterly*, Vol. 35, p. 925.

KOVAR, R. (1987a), "Osservazioni alla sentenza CGCE 294/83 del 23 aprile 1986 ('Les Verts')", *Cahiers de droit européen*, Vol. 23, p. 314.

KOVAR, R. (1987b), "Observations sur l'intensité normative des directives", in CAPOTORTI, F., EHLERMANN, C.D., FROWEIN, J., JACOBS, F., JOLIET, R., KOOPMANS, T. and KOVAR, R. (eds), *Du droit international au droit de l'integration. Liber Amicorum Pierre Pescatore*, Baden-Baden: Nomos Verlagsgesellschaft.

KRAVARITOU, Y., VENEZIANI, B., SUPIOT. A., KOISTINEN, P., BERCUSSON, B., DEAKIN, S. and MÜCKENBERGER, U. (1996), *A Manifesto for Social Europe*, Brussels: European Trade Union Institute.

KREHER, A. (1997), "Agencies in the European Community. A Step Towards Administrative Integration in Europe", *Journal of European Public Policy*, Vol. 4, no. 2, p. 225.

LA TORRE, M. (1994), "Formalism and Anti-Formalism in Modern Law. State Law and Beyond", in KRAWIETZ, W., MACCORMICK, N. and VON WRIGHT, G.H. (eds), *Prescriptive Formality and Normative Rationality in Modern Legal Systems. Festschrift for Robert S. Summers*, Berlin: Duncker & Humblot.

LADEUR K.H. (1995a), *Social Risks, Welfare Rights and the Paradigm of Proceduralisation. The Combining of the Institutions on the Liberal Constitutional State and the Social State*, Florence: EUI Working Paper, LAW, No. 95/2.

LADEUR K.H. (1995b), *Post-Modern Constitutional Theory. A Prospect for the Self-Organizing Society*, Florence: EUI Working Paper, LAW, No. 95/6.

LADEUR, K.H. (1997), "Towards a Legal Theory of Supranationality. The Viability of the Network Concept", *European Law Journal*, Vol. 3, no. 1, p. 33.

LANGE, P. (1992), "The Politics of Social Dimension", in SBRAGIA, A. (ed.), *Euro-Politics: Institutions and Policymaking in the "New" European Community*, Washington D.C: The Brookings Institution.

LANGLOIS, P. (1975), "Contrat individuel de travail et convention collective: un nouveau cas de représentation", *Droit social*, p. 283.

LANGLOIS, P. (1988), "Droit civil et contrat collectif de travail", *Droit social*, no. 5, p. 395.

LASKI, H. (1919, now 1968), *Authority in the Modern State*, New Haven: Yale University Press, now Hamden: Archon Books.

LASKI, H. (1921), *The Foundations of Sovereignty*, London: Allen & Unwin.

LAULOM, S. (1995), "La Direttiva sui comitati aziendali europei. L'importanza di una transizione, *Giornale di diritto del lavoro e di relazioni industriali*, p. 603.

LEADER, S. (1992), *Freedom of Association. A Study in Labor Law and Political Theory*, New Haven-London: Yale University Press..

LEHMBRUCH, G. and SCHMITTER, P. (1982), *Patterns of Corporatist Policy Making*, London: Sage.

LEHMBRUCH, G. (1977), "Liberal Corporatism and Party Government", *Comparative Political Studies*, Vol. X, p. 91.

LEIBFRIED, S. and PIERSON, P. (1993), "Le prospettive dell'Europa sociale", *Stato e mercato*, no. l, p. 42.

LEIBFRIED, S. and PIERSON, P. (eds) (1995), *European Social Policy. Between Fragmentation and Integration*, Washington D.C: The Brookings Institution.

LEIBFRIED, S. (1992a), "Towards a European Welfare State?" in FERGE, Z. and KOLBERG, J.E. (eds), *Social Policy in a Changing Europe*, Boulder: Westview Press.

LEIBFRIED, S. (1992b), "Welfare State Europe?", in HEINZ, W.R. (ed.), *Status Passages and the Life Course*, Vol. III: *Institutions and Gatekeping in the Life Course*, Weinheim: Deutscher Studien Verlag.

LEIBFRIED, S. (1992c), "Europe's Could-Be Social State: Social Policy in European Integration after 1992", in ADAMS, W.J. (ed.), *Singular Europe. Economy and Polity of the European Community after 1992*, Ann Arbor: The University of Michigan Press.

LENAERTS, K. (1993), "Regulating the Regulatory Process: Delegation of Powers in the European Community", *European Law Review*, Vol. 18, no. 1, p. 23.

LENOBLE, J. (1994), *Droit et communication. La transformation du droit contemporain*, Paris: Les Editions du Cerf.

LETTIERI, A. and ROMAGNOLI, U. (eds) (1998), *La contrattazione collettiva in Europa*, Centre for International Social Studies with the contribution of the European Comission, Rome: Ediesse.

LEWIS, R. and CLARK, J. (eds) (1981), *Labour Law and Politics in the Weimar Republic*,Oxford: Blackwell.

LEWIS, R. (1979), "Kahn-Freund and Labour Law: An Outline Critique", *Industrial Law Journal*, VIII, pp. 202–221.

LIEBMAN, S. (1990), "Autonomia collettiva e legge", in D'ANTONA, M. (ed.).

LO FARO, A. (1992), "EC Social Policy and 1993: the Dark Side of European Integration?", *Comparative Labor Law Journal*, Vol. 14, no. 1, p. 1.

LO FARO, A. (1993a), "Teorie autopoietiche e diritto sindacale", *Lavoro e diritto*, p. 129.

LO FARO, A. (1993b) "Maastricht ed oltre. Le prospettive sociali dell'Europa comunitaria tra resistenze politiche, limiti giuridici ed incertezze istituzionali", *Diritto delle relazioni industriali*, no. 1, p. 125.

LO FARO, A. (1997), "The Social Manifesto: Demystifying the Spectre Haunting Europe", *European Law Journal*, 1997, Vol. 3, no. 3, p. 300.

LO FARO, A. (1998), "La Corte di Giustizia e i suoi interlocutori giudiziari nell'ordinamento giuslavoristico italiano", *Lavoro e diritto*, no. 3, p. 583.

LORBER, P. (1997), "The Renault Case: The European Works Councils Put to the Test", *International Journal of Comparative Labour Law and Industrial Relations*, Vol. 13, no. 2, p. 135.

LOTMAR, P. (1900, now 1984), "I contratti di tariffa tra datori di lavoro e prestatori di lavoro", *Giornale di diritto del lavoro e di relazioni industriali*, p. 313.

LUCIANI, M. (1995), "Sui diritti sociali", *Democrazia e diritto*, no. 4/94–1/95, p. 545.

LUHMANN, N. and DE GIORGI, R. (1992), *Teoria della società*, Milano Franco Angeli.

LUHMANN, N. (1982), *The Differentiation of Society*, Columbia University Press.

LUHMANN, N. (1990a), *Sistemi sociali. Fondamenti di una teoria generale*, Bologna: Il Mulino.

LUHMANN, N. (1990b), *Political Theory in the Welfare State*, Berlin: de Gruyter.

Lyon-Caen, A. and Simitis, S. (1993) "L'Europe sociale à la recherche de ses références", *Revue du Marché Unique Européen*, no. 4, p. 109.

Lyon-Caen, A. and Verdier, J.M. (1995), "Sur le lock-out et l'Accord européen relatif à la politique sociale du 7 février 1992", *Droit social*, p. 49.

Lyon-Caen, A. (1992), "Droit social et droit de la concurrence: observations sur une rencontre", in *Ecrits en l'honneur du Pr. Jean Savatier*, Paris: Presses Universitaires de France.

Lyon-Caen, A. (1997a), "Le rôle des partenaires sociaux dans la mise en œuvre du droit communautaire", *Droit social*, p.68

Lyon-Caen, A. (1997b), "La négociation collective dans ses dimensions internationales", *Droit social*, p. 352

Lyon-Caen, G. and Lyon-Caen, A. (1993), *Droit social international et européen*, Paris: Dalloz.

Lyon-Caen, G., Pélissier, J. and Supiot, A. (1994), *Droit du travail*, 17th edn, Paris: Dalloz.

Lyon-Caen, G. (1973–74), "Négociation et convention collective au niveau européen", *Revue trimestrielle de droit européen*, no. 4/1973, p. 583 (Part I) and no. 1/1974, p. 1 (Part II).

Lyon-Caen, G. (1990), "Propos d'un nouveau docteur: réflexions à l'usage des jeunes juristes", *Lavoro e diritto*, p. 509.

Lyon-Caen, G. (1992), "L'infiltration du Droit du travail par le Droit de la concurrence", *Droit Ouvrier*, no. 525, p. 313.

Lyon-Caen, G. (1997), "Un droit sans papiers d'identité", *Archives de philosophie du droit*, Tome 41: *Le privé et le public*, p. 181.

MacCormick, N. and Weinberger, O. (1990), *Il diritto come istituzione*, Milan: Giuffrè.

MacCormick, N. (1993), "Beyond the Sovereign State", *The Modern Law Review*, Vol. 56, no. 1, p. 1.

Maestro Buelga, G. (1996), "Reforma del mercado de trabajo y estado social", *Sociologia del diritto*, no. 1, p. 73.

Mahnkopf, B. and Altvater, E. (1995), "Transmission Belts of Transnational Competition? Trade Unions and Collective Bargaining in the Context of European Integration", *European Journal of Industrial Relations*, Vol. 1, no. 1, p. 101.

Majone, G. (1992), *The European Community Between Social Policy and Social Regulation*, EUI Working Paper, SPS, No. 92/27.

Majone, G. (1993), *Mutual Recognition in Federal Type Systems*, Florence: EUI Working Paper, SPS, No. 93/1.

Majone, G. (1995), "The development of Social Regulation in the European Community: Policy Externalities, Transaction Costs, Motivational Factors", *Aussenwirtschaft*, Vol. 50, p. 79.

Majone, G. (1996), *La Communauté européenne: un Etat régulateur*, Paris: Montchrestien.

Majone, G. (1998), "Europe's Democratic Deficit: The Question of Standards", *European Law Journal*, Vol. 4, no. 1, p. 5.

Majone, G. (ed.) (1990), *Deregulation or Re-regulation?*, *Regulatory Reform in Europe and the United States*, London: Pinter.

Mancini, G.F. and Keeling, D.T. (1994), "Democracy and the European Court of Justice", *Modern Law Review*. Vol. 57, no. 2 , p. 175.

MANCINI, G.F. (1963, now 1976), "Libertà sindacale e contratti collettivi *erga omnes*", *Rivista trimestrale di diritto e procedura civile*, p. 570, now in *idem*, *Costituzione e movimento operaio*, Bologna: Il Mulino.

MANCINI, G.F. (1989), "The Making of a Constitution for Europe", *Common Market Law Review*, Vol. 26, p. 595.

MANCINI, G.F. (1990), "Attivismo e autocontrollo nella giurisprudenza della Corte di Giustizia", *Rivista di diritto europeo*, Vol. 30, p. 229.

MANCINI, G.F. (1995), "Regole giuridiche e relazioni sindacali nell'Unione Europea", in *Protocollo sociale di Maastricht: realtà e prospettive*, Supplement to *Notiziario di giurisprudenza del lavoro*, Rome.

MANCINI, G.F. (1998), "Europe: The Case for Statehood", *European Law Journal*, Vol. 4, no. 1, p. 29.

MARAFFI, M. (1981), "Introduzione", in *idem* (ed.).

MARAFFI, M. (1988), "Dal corporativismo autoritario al corporativismo liberale in Europa", in VARDARO, G. (ed.).

MARAFFI, M. (ed.) (1981), *La società neo-corporativa*, Bologna: Il Mulino.

MARCH, J. and OLSEN, J. (1984), "The New Institutionalism: Organizational Factors in Political Life", *American Political Science Review*, Vol. 78, p. 734.

MARIUCCI, L. (1985), *La contrattazione collettiva*, Bologna: Il Mulino.

MARSHALL, T.H. (1950), "Citizenship and Social Class", in *Citizenship and Social Class and Other Essays*, Cambridge: Cambridge University Press.

MARSHALL, T.H. (1964), *Class, Citizenship and Social Development*, New York: Doubleday & Co.

McCARTHY, W. (1992), "The Rise and Fall of Collective Laissez Faire", in *idem* (ed.), *Legal Intervention in Industrial Relations. Gains and Losses*, Oxford: Blackwell.

McGLYNN, C. (1995), "European Works Councils: Towards Industrial Democracy?", *Industrial Law Journal*, Vol. 24, no. 1, p. 78.

McLEAN, I. (1987), *Public Choice. An Introduction*, Oxford: Basil Blackwell.

MELIADO, G. (1996), "Concorrenza e politiche sociali", in BAYLOS GRAU, A., CARUSO, B., D'ANTONA, M. and SCIARRA, S. (eds).

MENGONI, L. (1975, now 1985), "Il contratto collettivo nell'ordinamento giuridico italiano", *Jus*, p. 167, now in *idem*, *Diritto e valori*, Bologna: Il Mulino.

MENGONI, L. (1988), "La questione del diritto giusto nella società post-liberale", *Relazioni industriali*, no. 13, p. 3.

MENGONI, L. (1990), "L'influenza del diritto del lavoro sul diritto civile", *Giornale di diritto del lavoro e di relazioni industriali*, p. 5.

MESSINA, G. (1907, now 1986), "Per un regolamento legislativo dei concordati di tariffa", *Giornale di diritto del lavoro e di relazioni industriali*, p. 113.

MILWARD, A., SØRENSEN, V. (1993), "Interdependence or Integration? A National Choice", in MILWARD, A., LYNCH, F., RANIERI, R., ROMERO, F. and SØRENSEN, V. (eds), *The Frontier of National Sovereignty. History and Theory 1945–1992*, London: Routledge.

MOMMSEN, W.J. (ed.) (1981), *The Emergence of Welfare State in Britain and Germany*, London: Croom Helm.

MONTANARI, B. (1990), *Effettività e giuridificazione*, Milan: Franco Angeli.

MONTANARI, B. (1994), "Soggetto e pluralità delle culture giuridiche", *Sociologia del diritto*, no. 1, p. 85.

MORAVCSIK, A. (1993), "Preferences and Power in the European Community: a Liberal Intergovernmentalist Approach", *Journal of Common Market Studies*, Vol. 31, no. 4, p. 473.

MORIN, M.L. (1994), *Le droit des salariés à la négociation collective. Principe général du droit*, Paris: L.G.D.J.

NEGRELLI, S. and TREU, T. (1994), "L'integrazione europea come fattore di stabilità delle relazioni industriali italiane", *Rivista italiana di diritto del lavoro*, no. 1, I, p. 29.

NEUMANN, F. (1983), *Il diritto del lavoro fra democrazia e dittatura*, Bologna: Il Mulino.

NIELSEN, R. and SZYSZCZAK, E. (1997), *Social Dimension of the European Union*, Copenhagen: Handelshøjskolens Forlag.

NORTHRUP, H.R. and ROWAN, R.L. (eds) (1979), *Multinational Collective Bargaining Attempts. The Records, the Cases, and the Prospects*, Philadelphia: The Wharton School, University of Pennsylvania.

NOZICK, R. (1974), *Anarchy, State and Utopia*, New York: Basic Books.

O'HIGGINS, P. (1997), "Labour is Not a Commodity. An Irish Contribution to International Labour Law", *Industrial Law Journal*, Vol. 26, no. 3, p. 225.

O'KEEFFE, D. and TWOMEY, P. (eds) (1994), *Legal Issues of the Maastricht Treaty*, Chichester: Chancery.

OBRADOVIC, D. (1995), "Prospects for Corporatist Decision-Making in the European Union: the Social Policy Agreement", *Journal of European Public Policy*, Vol.2, no. 2, p. 261.

OBRADOVIC, D. (1996), "Policy Legitimacy and the European Union", *Journal of Common Market Studies*, Vol. 34, no. 2, p. 191.

OGUS, A. (1994), *Regulation. Legal Form and Economic Theory*, Oxford: Clarendon Press.

OGUS, A. (1995), "Rethinking Self-Regulation", *Oxford Journal of Legal Studies*, Vol. 15, no. 1, p. 97.

OJEDA AVILÉS, A. (1993), "La negociación colectiva europea", *Relaciones Laborales*, no. 15, p. 67.

OLSON, M (1965), *The Logic of Collective Action. Public Goods and the Theory of Group*, Cambridge, Mass.: Harvard University Press.

PAPAEFTHYMIOU, S. (1990), "Constructivist Epistemology of Law", Florence: EUI Working Paper, LAW, No. 90/3.

PARSONS, T. (1951), *The Social System*, London: Routledge & Kegan.

PARSONS, T. (1971), *The System of Modern Societies*, Englewood Cliffs: Prentice-Hall.

PEDRAZZOLI, M. (1985), *Democrazia industriale e subordinazione. Poteri e fattispecie nel sistema giuridico del lavoro*, Milan: Giuffrè.

PEDRAZZOLI, M. (1990a), "Qualificazioni della autonomia collettiva e procedimento applicativo del giudice (Parte I)", *Lavoro e diritto*, p. 355.

PEDRAZZOLI, M. (1990b), "Qualificazioni della autonomia collettiva e procedimento applicativo del giudice (Parte II)", *Lavoro e diritto*, p. 549.

PELKMANS, J. and SUN, J.M. (1994), "Towards a European Community Regulatory Strategy: Lessons from 'Learning-by-Doing' ", in *Regulatory Co-operation for an Interdependent World*, Paris: OECD.

PELKMANS, J. (1987), "The New Approach to Technical Harmonization and Standardization", *Journal of Common Market Studies*, Vol. XXV, no. 3, p. 249.

PERLMAN, S. (1928, repr. 1970), *A Theory of the Labor Movement*, New York: The Macmillan Company; repr., New York: Kelley Publishers.

PESCATORE P. (1983a), "La carence du législateur communautaire et le devoir du juge", in LÜKE G., RESS G. and WILL M.R. (eds), *Rechtsvergleichung, Europarecht und Staatenintegration. Gedächtnisschrift für Léontin-Jean Constantinesco*, Cologne: Carl Heymann Verlag KG.

PESCATORE, P. (1983b), "The Doctrine of "Direct Effect": An Infant Disease of Community Law", *European Law Review*, Vol. 8, p. 155.

PETERSEN, A. and ZAHLE, H. (eds) (1995), *Legal Polycentricity. Consequences of Pluralism in Law*, Aldershot: Dartmouth.

PETERSMANN, E.H. (1995), "Proposals for a New Constitution for European Union: Building-blocks for a Constitutional Theory and Constitutional Law of the EU", *Common Market Law Review*, Vol. 32, p. 1123.

PIERSON, P. and LEIBFRIED, S. (1995a), "Multitiered Institutions and the Making of Social Policy", in LEIBFRIED, S. and PIERSON, P. (eds).

PIERSON, P. and LEIBFRIED, S. (1995b), "The Dynamics of Social Policy Integration", in LEIBFRIED, S. and PIERSON, P. (eds).

PIPKORN, J. (1990), "Le rapprochement des législations à la lumière de l'Acte unique européen", *Collected courses of the Academy of European Law 1993*, Vol. I, The Hague: M. Nijhoff Publishers.

PIZZORNO, A. (1980), *I soggetti del pluralismo*, Bologna: Il Mulino

POIARES MADURO, M. (1998), *We the Court: the European Court of Justice and the European Economic Constitution: a critical reading of article 30 of the EC Treaty*, Oxford: Hart Publishing.

PRECHAL, S. (1995), *Directives in European Community Law. A Study of Directives and their Enforcement in National Courts*, Oxford: Clarendon Press.

RADAELLI, C. (1998), *Governing European Regulation: The Challenges Ahead*, Florence: EUI, RSC Policy Paper No. 98/3.

RAWORTH, P. (1994), "A Timid Step Forwards: Maastricht and the Democratisation of the European Community", *European Law Review*, no. 2, p. 16.

REICH, N. (1983), *The Regulatory Crisis. Does it Exist and Can it be Solved?*, Bremen: Zentrum für europäische Rechtspolitik (ZERP), Diskussions-Papier no. 8/83.

REIF, K. (1993), "Cultural Convergence and Cultural Diversity as Factors in European Identity", in GARCÍA S. (ed.), *European Identity and the Search for Legitimacy*, London: Pinter Publishers.

RENNER, K. (1949), *The Institutions of Private Law and their Social Functions*, London: Routledge & Kegan, 1976.

RESCIGNO, G.U. (1990), *Corso di diritto pubblico*, III edn, Bologna: Zanichelli.

REYNAUD, J.D. (1989), *Les règles du jeu. L'action collective et la régulation sociale*, Paris: Armand Colin.

RHODES, M. (1993), "The Social Dimension after Maastricht: Setting a New Agenda for the Labour Market", *International Journal of Comparative Labour Law and Industrial Relations*, Vol. 9, no. 4, p. 297.

RHODES, M. (1995), "A Regulatory Conundrum: Industrial Relations and the Social Dimension", in LEIBRIED and PIERSON (eds).

RICHARD, D. (1995), "Le comité d'entreprise européen", *Rivista di diritto europeo*, no. 2, p. 257.

RISSE-KAPPEN, T. (1996), "Exploring the Nature of the Beast: International Relations Theory and Comparative Policy Analysis Meet the European Union", *Journal of Common Market Studies*, Vol. 34, no. 1.

RITTER, G.A. (1991), *Der Sozialstaat. Entstehung und Entwicklung im internationalen Vergleich*, Münich: R. Oldenburg Verlag GmbH.

ROCCELLA, M. (1997), *La Corte di giustizia e il diritto del lavoro*, Turin: Giappichelli.

RODIERE, P. (1987), *La convention collective de travail en droit international: contribution a l'étude des normes juridiques de source professionnelle*, Paris: Litec.

RODIERE, P. (1995), "Le comité d'entreprise à l'heure européenne", *Droit ouvrier*, February 1995, p. 61.

RODOTÀ, S. (1994), "Cittadinanza: una postfazione", in ZOLO D. (ed.), *Cittadinanza. Appartenenza, identità, diritti*, Rome-Bari: Laterza.

RODRIGUEZ-PIÑERO, M. and CASAS BAAMONDE, M.E. (1996), "In Support of a European Social Constitution", in DAVIES, P., LYON-CAEN, A., SCIARRA, S. and SIMITIS, S. (eds).

RODRIGUEZ-PIÑERO, M. (1995), "Diritto del lavoro e mercato", *Lavoro e diritto*, p. 39.

ROGOWSKI, R. and WILTHAGEN, T. (eds) (1994), *Reflexive Labour Law. Studies in Industrial Relations and Employment Regulation*, Deventer: Kluwer.

ROGOWSKI, R. (1991), *The Resolution of Labour Conflicts: an International Comparison*, Florence: Ph.D Thesis, European University Institute.

ROGOWSKI, R. (1998), "Autopoietic Industrial Relations and Reflexive Labour Law in the World Society", in WILTHAGEN, T. (ed.).

ROMAGNOLI, U. (1974), *Lavoratori e sindacati tra vecchio e nuovo diritto*, Bologna: Il Mulino.

ROMAGNOLI, U. (1990), "La déréglementation et les sources du droit du travail", *Revue Internationale de Droit Comparé*, no. 1, p. 9.

ROMAGNOLI, U. (1995a), *Il lavoro in Italia. Un giurista racconta*, Bologna: Il Mulino.

ROMAGNOLI, U. (1995b), "Lavoro e non lavoro", *Lavoro e diritto*, p. 3.

ROMAGNOLI, U. (1996), "L'inutile necessità di una disputa", *Giornale di diritto del lavoro e di relazioni industriali*, p. 1.

ROMEI, R. (1996), "Rapporti di lavoro atipici", in BAYLOS GRAU, A., CARUSO, B., D'ANTONA, M. and SCIARRA, S. (eds).

ROSANVALLON, P. (1988), *La question syndicale. Histoire et avenir d'une forme sociale*, Paris: Calmann-Lévy.

ROTTLEUTHNER, H. (1988), "Three Legal Sociologies: Eugen Ehrlich, Hugo Sinzheimer, Max Weber", in *New Paradigms in Legal Theory and Sociology of Law*, *European Yearbook of Sociology of Law 1988*, Milan: Giuffrè.

ROTTLEUTHNER, H. (1989), "The Limits of Law. The Myth of a Regulatory Crisis", *International Journal of the Sociology of Law*, Vol. 17, p. 273.

ROWLEY, C.K. (ed.) (1987), *Democracy and Public Choice: Essays in Honour of Gordon Tullock*, Oxford: Blackwell.

RUSCIANO, M. (1984), *Contratto collettivo e autonomia sindacale*, Turin: EGES (and in *Trattato di diritto privato*, (ed.) by Pietro Rescigno, Turin: UTET).

SAND, I.J. (1995), "From the Distinction between Public Law and Private Law to Legal Categories of Social and Institutional Differentiation, in a Pluralistic Context", in PETERSEN, A. and ZAHLE, H. (eds).

SANTORO PASSARELLI, F. (1949, now 1961), "Autonomia collettiva, giurisdizione, diritto di sciopero", *Rivista italiana per le scienze giuridiche*, p. 138, now in *idem*, *Saggi di diritto civile*, I, Naples: Jovene.

SANTORO PASSARELLI, F. (1959), "Autonomia collettiva", in *Enciclopedia del diritto*, IV, p. 369, Milan: Giuffrè.

SANTORO PASSARELLI, F. (1969), "Specialità del diritto del lavoro", in *Studi in memoria di Tullio Ascarelli*, Vol. IV, Milan: Giuffrè.

SCARPELLI, F. (1993a), *Lavoratore subordinato e autotutela collettiva*, Milan: Giuffrè.

SCARPELLI, F. (1993b), "Diritto comunitario, diritto sindacale italiano e sistema di relazioni industriali: principi e compatibilità", *Diritto delle relazioni industriali*, no. 1, p. 151.

SCARPELLI, F. (1996), "Iniziativa economica, autonomia collettiva, sindacato giudiziario: dall'art. 41 della Costituizone alla recente legislazione sulle trasformazioni dell'impresa", *Lavoro e diritto*, p. 15.

SCHARPF, F. (1997), "Economic Integration, Democracy and the Welfare State", *Journal of European Public Policy*, Vol. 4, no. 1, p. 18.

SCHMIDTCHEN, D. and COOTER, R. (eds) (1997), *Constitutional Law and Economics of the European Union*, Cheltenham: Edward Elgar.

SCHMITT VON SYDOW, H. (1988), "The Basic Strategies of the Commission's White Paper", in BIEBER, R., DEHOUSSE, R., PINDER J. and WEILER, J.H.H. (eds).

SCHMITTER, P. and LEHMBRUCH, G. (eds) (1979), *Trends towards Corporatist Intermediation*, London: Sage Publications.

SCHMITTER, P. (1974), "Still the Century of Corporatism?", *The Review of Politics*, Vol. XXXVI, p. 85.

SCHMITTER, P. (1984), *Neo-Corporatism and the State*, EUI Working Paper, no. 106.

SCHNORR, G. (1993), "I contratti collettivi in un'Europa integrata", *Rivista italiana di diritto del lavoro*, I, p. 319.

SCHULTEN, T. (1996), "European Works Councils: Prospects for a New System of European Industrial Relations", *European Journal of Industrial Relations*, Vol. 2, no. 3, p. 303.

SCHWARZE, J., BECKER, U. and POLLAK, C. (1994), *The Implementation of Community Law*, Baden-Baden: Nomos Verlagsgesellschaft.

SCIARRA, S. (1987), "Plant Bargaining: the Impact of Juridification on Current Deregulative Trends in Italy", *Comparative Labour Law Journal*, p. 123.

SCIARRA, S. (1990), "La libertà sindacale nell'Europa sociale", *Giornale di diritto del lavoro e di relazioni industriali*, p. 653.

SCIARRA, S. (1992), "Il dialogo tra ordinamento comunitario e nazionale del lavoro: la contrattazione collettiva", *Giornale di diritto del lavoro e di relazioni industriali*, p. 715.

SCIARRA, S. (1995a), "Social Values and the Multiple Sources of European Social Law", *European Law Journal*, Vol. 1, no. 1, p. 60.

SCIARRA, S. (1995b) "European Social Policy and Labour Law. Challenges and Perspectives", in *Collected Courses of the Academy of European Law 1993*, Vol. IV, Book 1, The Hague: M. Nijhoff Publishers.

SCIARRA, S. (1996a), "Collective Agreements in the Hierarchy of European Community Sources", in DAVIES, P., LYON-CAEN, A., SCIARRA, S. and SIMITIS, S. (eds).

SCIARRA, S. (1996b), "Diritti sociali fondamentali", in BAYLOS GRAU, A., CARUSO, B., D'ANTONA, M. and SCIARRA, S. (eds).

SCIARRA, S. (1998), "How Global is Labour Law?The Perspective of Social Rights in the European Union", in WILTHAGEN, T. (ed.).

SELZNICK, P. (1969), *Law, Society and Industrial Justice*, New Brunswick-London: Transaction Books.

SHAPIRO, M. (1997), "The Problems of Independent Agencies in the United States and the European Union", *Journal of European Public Policy*, Vol. 4, no. 2, p. 276.

SHAW, J. (1994), "Twin-Track Social Europe. The Inside Track", in O'KEEFFE, D. and TWOMEY, P. (eds).

SIEBERT, H. (1990), "The Harmonisation Issue in Europe", in *idem* (ed.), *The Completion of the Internal Market*, Tübingen: Mohr.

SIMITIS S. and LYON-CAEN, A., (1996), "Community Labour Law: A Critical Introduction to its History", in DAVIES, P., LYON-CAEN, A., SCIARRA, S. and SIMITIS, S. (eds).

SIMITIS, S. (1987), "Juridification of Labour Relations", in TEUBNER, G. (ed.), *Juridification of Social Spheres*, Berlin: de Gruyter.

SIMITIS, S. (1996), "Dismantling or Strengthening Labour Law: The Case of the European Court of Justice", *European Law Journal*, Vol. 2, no. 2, p. 156.

SNYDER, F. (1993a), "The Effectiveness of European Community Law: Institutions, Processes, Tools and Techniques", *The Modern Law Review*, Vol. 56, no. 1, p. 19.

SNYDER, F. (1993b), " 'Soft law' e prassi istituzionale nella Comunità europea", *Sociologia del diritto*, p. 79.

SNYDER, F. (ed.) (1996), *Constitutional Dimensions of European Integration*, The Hague: Kluwer Law International.

STEINER, J. (1998), "The Limits of State Liability for Breach of European Community Law", *European Public Law*, Vol. 4, no. 1, p. 69.

STONE SWEET, A. and BRUNELL, T.L. (1998), "The European Court and the National Courts: A Statistical Analysis of Preliminary References, 1961–95, *Journal of European Public Policy*, Vol. 5, no. 1, p. 66.

STREECK, W. and SCHMITTER, P. (1991), "From National Corporatism to Transnational Pluralism: Organized Interests in the Single European Market", *Politics and Society*, Vol. 19, p. 133.

STREECK, W. and SCHMITTER, P. (eds) (1985), *Private Interest Government. Beyond Market and State*, London: Sage.

STREECK, W. (1990), "La dimensione sociale del mercato unico europeo: verso un'economia non regolata?", *Stato e Mercato*, p. 29.

STREECK, W. (1992), "National Diversity, Regime Competition and Institutional Deadlock: Problems in Forming a European Industrial Relations System", *Journal of Public Policy*, Vol. 12, no. 4, p. 301.

STREECK, W. (1993), *The Rise and Decline of Neocorporatism*, in ULMAN, L., EICHENGREEN, B. and DICKENS, W.T. (eds), *Labor and an Integrated Europe*, Washington D.C: The Brookings Institution.

STREECK, W. (1994), "European Social Policy after Maastricht: the 'Social Dialogue' and 'Subsidiarity' ", *Economic and Industrial Democracy*, Vol. 15, p. 151.

STREECK, W. (1995a), "Neo-voluntarism: A New European Social Policy Regime?", *European Law Journal*, Vol. 1, no. 1, p. 31.

STREECK, W. (1995b), "From Market Making to State-Building? Reflections on the Political Economy of European Social Policy", in LEIBFRIED, S. and PIERSON, P. (eds).

STREECK, W. (1997a), "Industrial Citizenship under Regime Competition: the Case of the European Works Councils", *Journal of European Public Policy*, Vol. 4, no. 4, p. 643.

STREECK, W. (1997b), "Neither European nor Works Councils: a Reply to Paul Knutsen", *Economic and Industrial Democracy*, Vol. 18, no. 2, p. 325.

STREECK, W. (1998), *The Internationalization of Industrial Relations in Europe: Prospects and Problems*, Politics & Society, Vol. 26, no. 4, p. 429.

STREIT, M. and MUSSLER, W. (1995), "The Economic Constitution European Community: from Rome to Maastricht", *European Law Journal*, Vol. 1, p. 5.

STRETTON, H. and ORCHARD, L. (1994), *Public Goods, Public Enterprise and Public Choice: Theoretical Foundations of the Contemporary Attack on Government*, New York: St. Martin's Press.

SUN, J.M. and PELKMANS, J. (1995), "Regulatory Competition in the Single Market", *Journal of Common Market Studies*, Vol. 33, no. 1, p. 67.

SUNSTEIN, C.R. (1988), "Protectionism, the American Supreme Court, and Integrated Markets", in BIEBER, R., DEHOUSSE, R., PINDER J. and WEILER, J.H.H. (eds).

SUNSTEIN, C.R. (1990), *After the Rights Revolution. Reconceiving the Regulatory State*, Cambridge (Mass.)/London: Harvard University Press.

SUPIOT, A. (1994), *Critique du droit du travail*, Presses Universitaires de France.

SUPIOT, A. (1996), "Malaise dans le social", *Droit Social*, no. 2, p. 115.

SZYSZCZAK, E. (1995), "Future Directions in European Union Social Law", *Industrial Law Journal*, Vol. 24, no. 1, p. 19.

TARELLO, G. (1972), *Teorie e idelogie nel diritto sindacale. L'esperienza italiana dopo la Costituzione*, Milan: Ed. Comunità.

TEAGUE, P. (1998), "Monetary Union and Social Europe", *Journal of European Social Policy*, Vol. 8, no. 2, p. 117.

TEMPLE LANG, J. (1998), "The Duties of National Authorities Under Community Constitutional Law", *European Law Review*, Vol. 23, p. 109.

TEUBNER, G. and FEBBRAJO, A. (eds) (1992), *State, Law and Economy as Autopoietic Systems. Regulation and Autonomy in a New Perspective*, Milan: Giuffrè.

TEUBNER, G. (1983), "Substantive and Reflexive Elements in Modern Law", *Law and Society Review*, p. 239.

TEUBNER, G. (1986), "After Legal Instrumentalism? Strategic Models of Post-Regulatory Law", in *idem* (ed.).

TEUBNER, G. (1987a), "L'ordre social par le bruit législative? La fermeture autopoietique comme un problème de régulation juridique", *Archives de philosphie du droit*, p. 249.

TEUBNER, G. (1987b), "Juridification. Concepts, Aspects, Limits, Solutions", in TEUBNER, G. (ed.), *Juridification of Social Spheres*, Berlin: de Gruyter.

TEUBNER, G. (1989), "How the Law thinks: Toward a Constructivist Epistemology of Law", *Law and Society Review*, Vol. 23, no. 5, p. 727.

TEUBNER, G. (1991), "Regulatorisches Recht: Cronik eines angekündigten Todes", in KOLLER, P. and WEINBERGER, O. (eds), *Grundlagen der Rechtspolitik*, Wiesbaden: Steiner (now translated into French in TEUBNER, G. (1994)).

TEUBNER, G. (1992), "The Two Faces of Janus: Rethinking Legal Pluralism", *Cardozo Law Review*, p. 1443.

TEUBNER, G. (1993a), *Law as an Autopoietic System*, Oxford: Blackwell.

TEUBNER, G. (1993b), "The "State" of Private Networks: the Emerging Legal Regime of Polycorporatism in Germany", *Brigham Young University Law Review*, no. 2, p. 553.

TEUBNER, G. (1994), *Droit et réflexivité. L'auto-référence en droit et dans l'organisation*, Diegem-Paris: Story-Scientia - L.G.D.J.

TEUBNER, G. (1996), *Le jeu infini du renvoi: la collision du droit avec d'autres prétentions à l'universalité*, mimeo (translated from German by Nathalie Boucquey).

TEUBNER, G. (ed.), (1986), *Dilemmas of Law in the Welfare State*, Berlin: de Gruyter.

Teutemann, M. (1990), *Completion of the Internal Market: an Application of Public Choice Theory*, Economic Papers, no. 83, Commission of the European Communities, Directorate General for Economic and Financial Affairs.

Teyssie, B. (1995), *Les accords portant creation anticipée d'instances européennes de réprésentation du personnel: directive no. 94/45/CE du 22 septembre 1994, article 13*, Paris: Litec.

Timmermans, C. (1997), "How Can One Improve the Quality of Community Legislation?", *Common Market Law Review*, Vol. 34, p. 1229.

Titmuss, R.M. (1963), *Essays on the "Welfare State"*, II edn, London: Unwin University Books.

Titmuss, R.M. (1974), *Commitment to Welfare*, IV edn, London: Allen & Unwin.

Treu, T. (1979), "Comparazione e circolazione dei modelli nel diritto del lavoro italiano", *Giornale di diritto del lavoro e di relazioni industriali*, p. 167.

Turner, L. (1996), "The "Europeanization" of Labour: Structure before Action", *European Journal of Industrial Relations*, Vol. 2, no. 3, p. 325.

Tweedy, J. and Hunt, A. (1994), "The Future of the Welfare State and Social Rights: Reflections on Habermas", *Journal of Law and Society*, Vol. 21, no. 3, p. 288.

Udehn, L. (1996), *The Limits of Public Choice: a Sociological Critique of the Economic Theory of Politics*, London: Routledge.

Valdés Dal-Ré, F. (1997), "La contratación colectiva europea: más que un proyecto y menos que una realidad consolidada", *Relaciones laborales*, no. 21, p. 1

Valticos, N. and von Potobsky, G. (1995), *International Labour Law*, Deventer: Kluwer.

Van Empel, M. (1992), "The 1992 Programme: Interaction Between Legislator and Judiciary", *Legal Issues of European integration*, no. 2, p. 1

Van Gerven, W. (1994a) "Non-Contractual Liability of Member States, Community Institutions and Individuals for Breaches of Community Law with a View to a Common Law for Europe", *Maastricht Journal of European and Comparative Law*, Vol. 1, no. 1, p. 6.

Van Gerven, W. (1994b), "The Legal Dimension: the Constitutional Incentives for and Constraints on Bargained Administration", Paper presented to the conference on *European Law in Context: Constitutional Dimension of European Integration*, Florence: European University Institute, 14–15 April 1994 (DOC IUE 74/94), now in F. Snyder (ed.), 1996.

Van Winden, F. (1988), "The Economic Theory of Political Decision-Making", in Van den Broeck, J. (ed.), *Public Choice*, Dordrecht: Kluwer and Association of Post-Keynesian Studies.

Vardaro, G. (1982), "Otto Kahn-Freund e l'emigrazione dei giuslavoristi weimariani", in Balandi, G.G. and Sciarra, S. (eds).

Vardaro, G. (1984), *Contrattazione collettiva e sistema giuridico*, Naples: Jovene.

Vardaro, G. (1985a), *Contratti collettivi e rapporto individuale di lavoro*, Milan: Franco Angeli.

Vardaro, G. (1985b), "Verso un nuovo rapporto tra legge e contratto", *Politica del diritto*, no. 3, 1985.

Vardaro, G. (1987), "Giuridificazione, colonizzazione e autoreferenza nel diritto del lavoro", *Politica del diritto*, no. 4, p. 601.

Vardaro, G. (ed.) (1988), *Diritto del lavoro e corporativismi in Europa: ieri e oggi*, Milan: Franco Angeli.

VAUBEL, R. and WILLET, T. (eds) (1991), *The Political Economy of International Organisation: a Public Choice Approach*, Boulder: Westview Press.

VAUBEL, R. (1994), "The Public Choice Analysis of European Integration. A Survey", *European Journal of Political Economy*, Vol. 10, p. 227.

VAUBEL, R. (1995), "Social Regulation and Market Integration: a Critique and Public-Choice Analysis of the Social Chapter", *Aussenwirtschaft*, Vol. 50, p. 111.

VENEZIANI, B. (1992a), *Stato e autonomia collettiva. Diritto sindacale italiano e comparato*, Bari: Cacucci.

VENEZIANI, B. (1992b), "La politica sociale comunitaria dopo Maastricht", *Lavoro Informazione*, no. 2, p. 3.

VERDIER, J.M. (1991), "Sur la relation entre représentation et représentativité syndicales", *Droit social*, p. 5.

VOGEL, J. (1994), "Déclin du modèle social européen?", in TELO, M. and GOBIN, C. (eds), *Quelle union social européenne? Acquis institutionnel, acteurs et défis*, Brussels: Institut d'Etudes Européennes.

VOGEL-POLSKY, E. (1991), "Quale futuro per una politica sociale europea?", *Lavoro e diritto*, p. 331.

VOS, E. (1998), *Institutional Frameworks of Community Health and Safety Regulation*, Oxford: Hart Publishing.

WAELBROECK, M. (ed.) (1976), *Les instruments du rapprochement des législations dans la Communauté économique européenne*, Brussels: Editions de l'Université de Bruxelles.

WALZER, M. (1983), *Spheres of Justice. A Defence of Pluralism and Equality*, New York: Basic Books.

WARD, I. (1993), "Making Sense of Integration: a Philosophy of Law for the European Community", *Journal of European Integration*, Vol. XVII, no. 1, p. 101.

WARD, I. (1996), "(Pre)conceptions in European Law", *Journal of Law and Society*, Vol. 23, no. 2, p. 198.

WATHELET, M. and VAN RAEPENBUSCH, S. (1997), "La responsabilité des Etats membres en cas de violation du droit communautaire. Vers un alignement de la responsabilité de l'Etat sur celle de la Communauté ou l'inverse?", *Cahiers de droit européen*, no. 1–2, p. 13.

WATSON, P. (1994), "The Role of the European Court of Justice in the Development of Community Labour Law", in EWING, K.D., GEARTY, C.A. and HEPPLE, B.A. (eds), *Human Rights and Labour Law. Essays for Paul O'Higgins*, London: Mansell Publishing.

WEDDERBURN, LORD, LEWIS, R. and CLARK, J. (eds.) (1983), *Labour Law and Industrial Relations: Building on Kahn-Freund*, Oxford: Clarendon Press.

WEDDERBURN, LORD (1972a), "Labour Law and Labour Relations in Britain", *British Journal of Industrial Relations*, Vol. 10, no. 2, p. 270.

WEDDERBURN, LORD (1972b), "Multi-national Enterprise and National Labour Law", *Industrial Law Journal*, Vol. 1, p. 12.

WEDDERBURN, LORD (1983), "Otto Kahn-Freund and British Labour Law", in WEDDERBURN, LORD, LEWIS, R. and CLARK, J. (eds). *¿*

WEDDERBURN, LORD (1986), *The Worker and the Law*, III edn, London: Sweet & Maxwell.

WEDDERBURN, LORD (1987, now 1991), "Labour Law: From Here to Autonomy?", *Industrial Law Journal*, Vol. 16, no. 1, p. 1., now in *idem* (1991).

WEDDERBURN, LORD (1991), *Employment Rights in Britain and Europe*, London: Lawrence & Wishart.

WEDDERBURN, LORD (1994, now 1995a), "Labour Law and the Individual in the Post-Industrial Societies", in WEDDERBURN, LORD, ROOD, M., LYON-CAEN, G., DAÜBLER, W. and VAN DER HEIJDEN, P., *Labour Law in the Post-Industrial Era*, Aldershot: Dartmouth, now in *idem* (1995a).

WEDDERBURN, LORD (1995a), *Labour Law and Freedom: Further Essays in Labour Law*, London: Lawrence & Wishart.

WEDDERBURN, LORD (1995b), "Freedom and Frontiers of Labour Law", in *idem* (1995a).

WEDDERBURN, LORD (1996), "Laski's Law Behind the Law. Laski e il diritto dietro la legge: dal 1906 al diritto del lavoro europeo", *Lavoro e diritto*, p. 511.

WEDDERBURN, Lord (1997), "Consultation and Collective Bargaining in Europe: Success or Ideology?", *Industrial Law Journal*, Vol. 26, no. 1, p. 1.

WEILER, J.H.H. (1981), "The Community System: the Dual Character of Supranationalism", *Yearbook of European Law*, Vol. 1, p. 267.

WEILER, J.H.H. (1982), "*Supranational Law and the Supranational System: Legal Structure and Political Process in the European Community*, Florence: Ph.D Thesis, European University Institute.

WEILER, J.H.H. (1985), *Il sistema comunitario europeo*, Bologna: Il Mulino

WEILER, J.H.H. (1991), "The Transformation of Europe", *The Yale Law Journal*, Vol. 100, p. 2403.

WEILER, J.H.H. (1993), "After Maastricht: Community Legitimacy in Post-1992 Europe", in ADAMS, W.J. (ed.), *Singular Europe. Economy and Polity of the European Community after 1992*, Ann Arbor: University of Michigan Press.

WEILER, J.H.H. (1995), "Does Europe Need a Constitution? Reflections on Demos, Telos, and the German Maastricht Decision", *European Law Journal*, Vol. 1, no. 3, p. 219.

WEILER, J.H.H. (1998), Europe: The Case Against the Case for Statehood, *European Law Journal*, Vol. 4, no. 1, p. 43.

WENDON, B. (1998), "The Commission as Image-Venue Entrepreneur in EU Social Policy", *Journal of European Public Policy*, Vol. 5, no. 2, p. 339.

WESSELS, W. (1998), "Comitology: Fusion in Action. Politico-Administrative Trends in the EU system", *Journal of European Public Policy*, Vol. 5, no. 2, p. 209.

WHEELER, S. (1997), "Works Councils: Towards Stakeholding?", *Journal of Law and Society*, Vol. 24, no. 1, p. 44.

WHITEFORD, E. (1995), "Whiter Social Policy"?, in SHAW, J. and MORE, G. (eds), *New Legal Dynamics of European Union*, Oxford: Clarendon Press.

WIETHÖLTER, R. (1986), "Materialization and Proceduralization in Modern Law", in TEUBNER, G. (ed.).

WIETHÖLTER, R. (1989), "Proceduralization of the Category of Law", in JOERGES, C. and TRUBECK, D.M. (eds).

WILENSKY, H.L. (1975), *The Welfare State and Equality*, Berkeley: University of California Press.

WILHELMSSON, T. (1995a), *Social Contract Law and European Integration*, Aldershot: Dartmouth.

WILHELMSSON, T. (1995b), "Legal Integration as Disintegration of National Law", in PETERSEN, A. and ZAHLE, H. (eds).

WILLKE, H. (1986), "Three Types of Legal Structure: the Conditional, the Purposive and the Relational Program", in TEUBNER (ed.).

WILLKE, H. (1992), "Social Guidance through Law?", in TEUBNER, G. and FEBBRAJO, A. (eds).

WILTHAGEN, T. (ed.) (1998), *Advancing Theory in Labour Law and Industrial Relations in a Global Context*, Amsterdam: North-Holland.

WINCOTT, D. (1995), "The Role of Law or the Rule of the Court of Justice? An Institutional Account of Judicial Politics in the European Community", *Journal of European Public Policy*, Vol. 2, no. 4, p. 583.

YANNAKOUROU, S. (1995), *L'Etat, l'autonomie collective et le travailleur. Étude comparée du droit italien et du droit français de la représentativité syndicale*, Paris: L.G.D.J.

ZOLO, D. (1994), "La strategia della cittadinanza", in *idem* (ed.), *Cittadinanza. Appartenenza, identità, diritti*, Rome-Bari: Laterza.

Index